Cases on Database Technologies and Applications

Mehdi Khosrow-Pour, D.B.A.
Editor-in-Chief, Journal of Cases on Information Technology

IDEA GROUP PUBLISHING
Hershey • London • Melbourne • Singapore

Acquisitions Editor: Michelle Potter
Development Editor: Kristin Roth
Senior Managing Editor: Amanda Appicello
Managing Editor: Jennifer Neidig
Typesetter: Sharon Berger
Cover Design: Lisa Tosheff
Printed at: Integrated Book Technology

Published in the United States of America by
Idea Group Publishing (an imprint of Idea Group Inc.)
701 E. Chocolate Avenue, Suite 200
Hershey PA 17033
Tel: 717-533-8845
Fax: 717-533-8661
E-mail: cust@idea-group.com
Web site: http://www.idea-group.com

and in the United Kingdom by
Idea Group Publishing (an imprint of Idea Group Inc.)
3 Henrietta Street
Covent Garden
London WC2E 8LU
Tel: 44 20 7240 0856
Fax: 44 20 7379 0609
Web site: http://www.eurospanonline.com

Library of Congress Cataloging-in-Publication Data

Cases on database technologies and applications / Mehdi Khosrow-Pour, editor.
p. cm.
Summary: "This case book presents many real-life examples and experiences of those involved in database research and database technology applications and management"--Provided by publisher.
Includes bibliographical references and index.
ISBN 1-59904-399-8 (hardcover) -- ISBN 1-59904-400-5 (softcover) -- ISBN 1-59904-401-3 (ebook)
1. Information technology--Management--Case studies. 2. Database management--Case studies. I. Khosrowpour, Mehdi, 1951-
HD30.2.C3787 2006
005.74068--dc22

2006003564

British Cataloguing in Publication Data
A Cataloguing in Publication record for this book is available from the British Library.

Cases on Information Technology Series

ISSN: 1537-9337

Series Editor
Mehdi Khosrow-Pour, D.B.A.
Editor-in-Chief, *Journal of Cases on Information Technology*

- Cases on Database Technologies and Applications
  Mehdi Khosrow-Pour, Information Resources Management Association, USA
- Cases on Electronic Commerce Technologies and Applications
  Mehdi Khosrow-Pour, Information Resources Management Association, USA
- Cases on Global IT Applications and Management: Success and Pitfalls
  Felix B. Tan, University of Auckland, New Zealand
- Cases on Information Technology and Business Process Reengineering
  Mehdi Khosrow-Pour, Information Resources Management Association, USA
- Cases on Information Technology and Organizational Politics and Culture
  Mehdi Khosrow-Pour, Information Resources Management Association, USA
- Cases on Information Technology Management In Modern Organizations
  Mehdi Khosrow-Pour, Information Resources Management Association, USA & Jay Liebowitz, George Washington University, USA
- Cases on Information Technology Planning, Design and Implementation
  Mehdi Khosrow-Pour, Information Resources Management Association, USA
- Cases on Information Technology, Volume 7
  Mehdi Khosrow-Pour, Information Resources Management Association, USA
- Cases on Strategic Information Systems
  Mehdi Khosrow-Pour, Information Resources Management Association, USA
- Cases on Telecommunications and Networking
  Mehdi Khosrow-Pour, Information Resources Management Association, USA
- Cases on the Human Side of Information Technology
  Mehdi Khosrow-Pour, Information Resources Management Association, USA
- Cases on Worldwide E-Commerce: Theory in Action
  Mahesh S. Raisinghani, Texas Woman's University, USA
- Case Studies in Knowledge Management
  Murray E. Jennex, San Diego State University, USA
- Case Studies on Information Technology in Higher Education: Implications for Policy and Practice
  Lisa Ann Petrides, Columbia University, USA (?)
- Success and Pitfalls of IT Management (Annals of Cases in Information Technology, Volume 1)
  Mehdi Khosrow-Pour, Information Resources Management Association, USA
- Organizational Achievement and Failure in Information Technology Management (Annals of Cases in Information Technology, Volume 2)
  Mehdi Khosrow-Pour, Information Resources Management Association, USA
- Pitfalls and Triumphs of Information Technology Management (Annals of Cases in Information Technology, Volume 3)
  Mehdi Khosrow-Pour, Information Resources Management Association, USA
- Annals of Cases in Information Technology, Volume 4 - 6
  Mehdi Khosrow-Pour, Information Resources Management Association, USA

IDEA GROUP INC.

Cases on Database Technologies and Applications

Detailed Table of Contents

Chapter I
LIBNET: A Case Study in Information Ownership and Tariff Incentives in a Collaborative Library Database 1
A. S. C. Hooper, Victoria University of Wellington, New Zealand

A South African library network company (LIBNET) provided a networked service to participating libraries. This case study explores some of the issues influencing tariff determination in a cooperative database. Questions of data ownership and the provision of incentives for the uploading of data also raise legal and ethical issues. The case study provides a basis for exploring business strategy in collaborative database management.

Chapter II
Evolution of an Executive Information System: The Replenishment Data Warehouse at JeansWear 26
Hamid Nemati, University of North Carolina, USA
Keith Smith, VF Corporation, USA

This case is a description of how a successful executive information system evolved into a data warehouse at VF Corporation, the largest publicly held apparel manufacturer in the world (www.vfc.com). The case discusses the forces that necessitated the development of this data warehouse and the challenges that the development team faced in achieving its goals.

Chapter III
The Algos Center: Information Systems in a Small Non-Profit Organization **46**
Susan J. Chinn, University of Southern Maine, USA
Charlotte A. Pryor, University of Southern Maine, USA
John J. Voyer, University of Southern Maine, USA

This case reveals many problems facing small non-profit organizations, which primarily expend their resources on mission-critical activities, and allows readers to supply possible courses of action. Second, it provides an opportunity to evaluate how a consulting experience was handled and to make recommendations to ensure successful project implementation.

Chapter IV
Isobord's Geographic Information System (GIS) Solution **64**
Derrick J. Neufeld, University of Western Ontario, Canada
Scott Griffith, Tell Us About Us Inc., Canada

Isobord, a start-up company that is setting up a new strawboard production plant in Manitoba, Canada, is facing critical operational problems that threaten its future. A geographic information system (GIS)/relational database management system (RDBMS) solution is being explored, but budget and time constraints, as well as organizational inexperience, seriously threaten the project. An information technology decision must be made immediately if there is to be any hope of implementing technology to manage the first year's straw harvest.

Chapter V
Information Technology in the Practice of Law Enforcement **81**
Susan Rebstock Williams, Georgia Southern University, USA
Cheryl Aasheim, Georgia Southern University, USA

This case describes how the Charlotte-Mecklenburg Police Department began the rollout of a "mobile" information system that will eventually enable all information relating to incident reports, arrests, and investigations to be collected, distributed, and managed in a paperless, wireless environment. The strategies and approaches used to develop this system, the technologies employed, and, most importantly, the challenges faced in merging wireless, wired, database, and applications technologies while satisfying the user requirements of the police department are detailed in this case.

Chapter VI
Implementing Relational Database Systems: Implications for Administrative Cultures and Information Resource Management ... 104
Andreea M. Serban, Santa Barbara City College, USA
Gregory A. Malone, Cabrillo College, USA

This case describes the experiences of two institutions, University of Redlands and Cabrillo College, as they implement similar relational database systems. It describes the effects of the implementation process on the institutional administrative cultures, and the implications for information resource management.

Chapter VII
Public Sector Data Management in a Developing Economy 125
Wai K. Law, University of Guam, Guam

An island state government agency responsible for publishing monthly import/export data had problems meeting the monthly publication schedule. This case describes the initial investigation which reviewed problems of inefficiency, poor technical support, downsizing under budget reduction, and confusing data standards. A general deficiency in computer and information literacy gave little hope for internal information resource development. On the other hand, concerns for information privacy, shrinking budget, and control over data resources limited potential assistance from outside groups.

Chapter VIII
The Benefits of Data Warehousing at Whirlpool 135
Barbara J. Haley, University of Virginia, USA
Hugh J. Watson, University of Georgia, USA
Dale L. Goodhue, University of Georgia, USA

This case study briefly describes Whirlpool, the business need that suggested a data warehouse, the approval process, and the data warehouse that was built. It describes how the data warehouse is accessed, how users are trained and supported, and the major applications and benefits. The lessons learned also are described to benefit those companies that are implementing or thinking about implementing data warehousing.

Chapter IX
Developing a Homegrown Course Management System: Community/Course Action/Interaction Management System (CAMS©) **154**
Brian G. Mackie, Northern Illinois University, USA
Norbert L. Ziemer, Northern Illinois University, USA
Nancy L. Russo, Northern Illinois University, USA
Wayne E. Mackie, Saginaw Valley State University, USA

This case describes the development of a unique, student-centered, online course management systems (OCMS). The system grew from a fairly straightforward grade reporting system into a full-blown collaborative system within a short — in traditional information systems development terms — timeframe of approximately one year. Changes made to the system and the factors motivating the changes are discussed, as are challenges faced before, during, and after the development process.

Chapter X
Deliberate and Emergent Changes on a Way Toward Document Management **171**
Tero Päivärinta, University of Jyväskylä, Finland
Airi Salminen, University of Waterloo, Canada

A unit of Fortum Service Ltd. operates and maintains the Rauhalahti power plant in Central Finland. The unit launched a project pursuing coordinated organization-wide electronic document management (EDM). This case follows deliberate and emergent changes related to document management in the organization. The case shows that a shift from the paper-based era towards organization-wide EDM is a comprehensive change both affecting and affected by several components in the organization.

Chapter XI
Implementing a Data Mining Solution for an Automobile Insurance Company: Reconciling Theoretical Benefits with Practical Considerations **189**
Ai Cheo Yeo, Monash University, Australia
Kate A. Smith, Monash University, Australia

The insurance company in this case study operates in a highly competitive environment. In recent years it has explored data mining as a means of extracting valuable information from its huge databases in order to improve decision making and capitalise on the investment in business data. This case study describes an investigation into the benefits of data mining for an anonymous Australian automobile insurance company.

Chapter XII
Long-Term Evolution of a Conceptual Schema at a Life Insurance Company 202
Lex Wedemeijer, ABP, The Netherlands

This case study outlines the evolution of a highly inte-grated Conceptual Schema in its business environment. A gradual decline in schema quality is observed: size and complexity of the schema increase, understandability and consistency decrease. Contrary to popular belief, it is found that changes aren't driven only by "accepted" causes like new legislation or product innovation. The case shows that a real Conceptual Schema is the result of "objective" design practices as well as the product of negotiation and compromise with the user community.

Chapter XIII
Designing a First-Iteration Data Warehouse for a Financial Application Service Provider 227
Nenad Jukic, Loyola University - Chicago, USA
Tania Neild, InfoGrate Incorporated, USA

This case study describes the efforts behind designing a first iteration of an evolutionary, iterative enterprise-wide data warehouse for AIIA Corp., a financial application service provider. The study demonstrates the importance of the following steps during a data-warehousing project: a well-defined mission, effective requirement collection, detailed logical definitions, and an efficient methodology for source systems and infrastructure development.

Chapter XIV
A Case Study of One IT Regional Library Consortium: VALE — Virtual Academic Library Environment 244
Virginia A. Taylor, William Paterson University, USA
Caroline M. Coughlin, Consultant, USA

Historic models of library management are being tested and modified in the digital age because of several interrelated factors. Partially cost-focused models for delivering IT systems and information sources to library users are being developed. In this case, suggestions for alternative managerial strategies and economic models for IT regional library managers to pursue are given, based on the lessons to be gleaned from this experience and an examination of the literature describing other regional IT digital library ventures.

Chapter XV
Prudential Chamberlain Stiehl: The Evolution of an IT Architecture for a Residential Real Estate Firm, 1996-2001 267
Andy Borchers, Kettering University, USA
Bob Mills, Prudential Chamberlain Stiehl Realtors, USA

This case describes the evolution of an IT architecture for Prudential Chamberlain Stiehl Realtors (PCSR), a 14-office, 250-sales-agent real estate firm located in Southeast Michigan. Initially, the CIO of the firm concentrated on providing basic connectivity to sales agents and a simple World Wide Web (WWW) presence. Although this was accepted by users and moved the firm forward technically, management questioned the value of this technology. In the next phase of development, PCSR worked to build a "rich" set of applications that enhance the firm's relationships with clients and agents.

About the Editor 288

Index 289

Preface

Advances in database techniques and technologies continue to emerge and significantly improve throughout the fields of database applications and research. In recent years, the overall utilization of database technologies has exploded throughout organizations of all sizes and types. Today, almost every computer-based application relies heavily on the use of database technologies and techniques. Many organizations have been successful, and yet some have failed in the utilization of database technologies. Learning from success factors and reasons for failure can assist systems professionals and students in the field to learn how to develop and apply database technologies successfully throughout organizations worldwide. *Cases on Database Technologies and Applications*, part of Idea Group Inc.'s *Cases on Information Technology Series* presents many real-life examples and experiences of those involved in database research and database technology applications and management. *Cases on Database Technologies and Applications* presents a wide range of the most current development, design and analysis of databases, and will assist practitioners and students alike in learning about emerging issues, problems, and challenges in developing database applications without pitfalls.

The cases included in this volume cover a wide variety of topics focusing on database technologies, database research, systems analysis and design and the utilization of software engineering technologies in database applications and management. These topics include: library databases, executive information systems, data warehouses, non-profit organization information systems, geographic information systems, information systems for law enforcement practices, administrative cultures and information resource management, public sector data management, large companies' adoption of data warehouses, online course management systems, an electronic document initiative at a power plant, data mining solutions for an automobile insurance company, flexibility within data resources, data warehouses for financial application service providers, virtual academic library environments, and IT architecture for a residential real estate firm.

As more businesses, universities and organizations seek technological solutions to the growing volume of data and information in organizations, database technologies continue to stand as necessities and valuable instruments in managing data and producing valuable and effective information. Hopefully *Cases on Database Technologies and Applications* will provide practitioners, educators and students with important examples of database technology implementation successes and failures. An outstanding collection of current real-life situations associated with the effective utilization of database technologies, with lessons learned from the cases included in the publication, this publication will be very instrumental for those learning about the issues and challenges in the field of database technologies.

Note to Professors: Teaching notes for cases included in this publication are available to those professors who decide to adopt the book for their college course. Contact cases@idea-group.com for additional information regarding teaching notes and to learn about other volumes of case books in the IGI *Cases on Information Technology Series.*

ACKNOWLEDGMENTS

Putting together a publication of this magnitude requires the cooperation and assistance of many professionals with much expertise. I would like to take this opportunity to express my gratitude to all the authors of cases included in this volume. Many thanks also to all the editorial assistance provided by the Idea Group Inc. editors during the development of these books, particularly all the valuable and timely efforts of Mr. Andrew Bundy and Ms. Michelle Potter. Finally, I would like to dedicate this book to all my colleagues and former students who taught me a lot during my years in academia.

A special thank you to the Editorial Advisory Board: Annie Becker, Florida Institute of Technology, USA; Stephen Burgess, Victoria University, Australia; Juergen Seitz, University of Cooperative Education, Germany; Subhasish Dasgupta, George Washington University, USA; and Barbara Klein, University of Michigan, Dearborn, USA.

Mehdi Khosrow-Pour, D.B.A.
Editor-in-Chief
Cases on Information Technology Series
http://www.idea-group.com/bookseries/details.asp?id=18

Chapter I

LIBNET: A Case Study in Information Ownership and Tariff Incentives in a Collaborative Library Database

A. S. C. Hooper, Victoria University of Wellington, New Zealand

EXECUTIVE SUMMARY

In any cooperative database the participants contribute their data for their own as well as the benefit of the other members, usually with incentives from the database administrators. A South African library network company (LIBNET) provided a networked service to participating libraries. Member benefits included conversion of their catalogues into machine-readable form, significantly reduced costs through cooperative cataloguing and more efficient interlibrary loans through a union catalogue of the holdings of the participant libraries. This case study explores some of the issues influencing tariff determination in a cooperative database. Questions of data ownership and the provision of incentives for the uploading of data also raise legal and ethical issues. The case study provides a basis for exploring business strategy in collaborative database management.

ORGANIZATIONAL BACKGROUND

The Public Good Character of Information

Information is usually considered to be a public good (Braunstein, 1981; Spence, 1974). Certainly, that which falls outside the already established category of intellectual property is a public good, a shared resource that is enriched rather than diminished by policies that increase rather than decrease everyone's access to it (Ebbinghouse, 2004).

A pure public good is one that has two major characteristics — nonrivalous consumption and nonexcludability (West, 2000). Nonrivalous consumption means that the good or service is not diminished or depleted when consumed. If information is shared between two people, it is not diminished thereby, and both can have full use and benefit of it. Nonexcludability means that consumption of the good or service cannot be denied to people who have not paid for it. It is an important factor in controlling the spread of information by vendors wishing to market it, especially in an online environment where it can easily be downloaded and further distributed, processed or reused.

Information may have different value to different people with whom it is shared. Some consumers may be prepared to pay significantly more for a specific piece of information than others. And, of course, the time it is delivered can be an important factor in determining the value of information for a particular consumer. The manner in which information is provided plays a significant role in determining its characteristics as a public good. Printed information in book or journal form has physical characteristics that enable it to be priced and marketed as an artifact irrespective of the informational value of the contents to different consumers.

The implications of this are that, because it is difficult for a vendor of information to be reimbursed for the development and provision of the goods or services, or to control subsequent distribution, there is a reduced incentive for investing in the creation of the good. So, while there may be a demand for the information, no seller will offer it. Sometimes, public good providers create modified or less-efficient markets to generate the revenue that pays for the public good. Advertising revenue can be used to pay for public TV, Internet portals, search engines and other information products (West, 2000).

Alliance Forming for Information Provision

Because of the nature of information as a public good, very often it has fallen to governments to provide the good or service, either independently or in association with other providers. This concept is central to that of the knowledge economy in which the public good characteristic of information is used by governments to grow the competitiveness of the national economy through the development of knowledge and social capital. "E-Government is the use of information technology to deliver public services in a much more convenient, customer oriented, cost-effective, and altogether different and better way" (Holmes, 2001, p. 2). Increasingly, the way that governments make their services available is through online service provision, and, as such, they have become major players in the online database industry. "Digitising government can create a particularly lucrative new market" (Fountain, 2001, p. 5). By 1998, the electronic information services industry in the United States had become a $33.5 billion per annum market with an annual growth rate of 7.5% (Communications Industry Forecast, 2000). With so much at stake, it is hardly surprising that governments seek to benefit from their investment, or to control the process of data-ownership and the way that information is distributed or shared (Ebbinghouse, 2004).

By forming strategic alliances, individual organizations can increase their individual power with government and gain credibility, legitimacy and visibility. Many experts have regarded strategic alliances as the foundation for inter-organizational collaboration in the public and private sector, to reach new markets and technologies, to share risks and to gain complementary competencies. "When the knowledge base that supports an industry is hard to comprehend, still emerging and distributed across several organizations, then collaboration among firms, universities and national laboratories will reflect a strong and fundamental interest in access to knowledge rather than simply strategic calculation, resource sharing or transaction cost reduction" (Fountain, 2001, p. 75). In 1977, governments or not-for-profit agencies produced 78% of all databases, but by 1997 this percentage had dropped to 20% (West, 2000, p. 64).

The use of computers for the development of databases and catalogues was appreciated early in the evolution of business computing. Ease of sorting, ease of searching and the fast generation of reports found applications in many organizations dealing with large product lines or customer bases. The use of structured formats for electronic data interchange (EDI) facilitated the deconstruction of the original data and its use in different forms and for different purposes. Along with bankers, supermarkets, motor and aircraft manufacturers, librarians were quick to recognize the value of using computers to provide greater operational efficiencies. In tight financial times, the cost of harnessing the large networked computers needed for library systems was beyond the budget and technical expertise of most academic libraries. Academic administrators and politicians turned to collaboration as a means of accomplishing their goals (Patrick, 1972; Kemp, 1996; Kopp, 1998).

Especially in the 1980s and 1990s, a rapid increase in the number and cost of books and journals, combined with severe constraints placed on library budgets — especially in academic libraries — became a worldwide phenomenon, further exacerbated in those countries with volatile currency units (Hooper, 1990). The consequences of these problems were obsolete equipment, untrained personnel, out-of-date collections (Martey, 2002) and the resultant imperative to downsize/right-size, together with political pressure to collaborate (Kopp, 1998). It became imperative to find ways of making the most efficient use of the resources available by reducing duplication of book and journal purchases, especially on a regional basis, and optimizing interlibrary loan traffic to ensure the most efficient and effective use of those materials already available within the country.

> *Libraries are forming alliances for the purpose of identifying and addressing common needs arising from development in information technology, especially the growing importance of the Internet and the World Wide Web.* (Potter, 1997, p. 417)

This instinct to cooperate is part of the ethos of the library profession. The major driver of cooperative alliances among libraries has not been technology, except in so far as technology is an enabler of greater efficiency. Rather, the main drivers are economic considerations. These include sharing of resources, cooperative acquisitions, cooperative automation, shared cataloguing, and preservation and access (Gorman & Cullen, 2000; Hayes, 2003; Hooper, 1989).

The purchase of a book or journal requires the generation of data that is used not only for the order process, but forms the basis for subsequent entries. That data is structured according to author, title, publisher and other components, all of which might be required as the sort key in the generation of a report or for database search purposes. Collaborative data entry into a centralized networked database enables libraries to speed their order processes, make their catalogue entries more accurate and make more informed decisions about purchases, depending on the holdings of other libraries in the region. The same networked database could also form the central resource for cooperative catalogue development and the establishment of a regional or national union catalogue of library holdings, facilitating interlibrary loans and promoting networked communications among participant libraries.

The development of a centralized, networked database of the catalogue holdings of the major libraries in a region or in a country would provide operational efficiencies for participant organizations in the same way that banks, insurance companies and motor manufacturers promoted efficiencies through collaborative database development. Many of the problems associated with collaborative database development were the same — especially those relating to systems integration, data and content ownership, catalogue content management and the determination of tariffs for database use combined with incentives for participants to contribute their data. (Rayport & Jaworski, 2002, pp. 366-372). The reason for this is that, in collaborative databases, several information producers combine to generate the data for the online server/vendor to supply to the information consumer. These three players — producers, vendors and consumers — in the online information services market can have conflicting interests, especially when the information consumers are also the information providers and they establish the server/vendor for that purpose.

Inter-Organizational Systems and Library Consortia

Information technology has been used for many years to promote collaborative working opportunities, to share data and to control dispersed operations. The characteristics of inter-organizational systems (IOSs) that link numerous business partners have only recently been investigated because they form the basis for many electronic commerce business models. The reasons why organizations and businesses adopt IOS (or EDI as a prominent type of IOS) (Ahmad & Schroeder, 2001) show a marked similarity with those of libraries embarking on collaborative ventures. These include perceived benefits, external pressure including competitive pressure, and readiness in terms of financial resources and IT sophistication (Iacovou et al., 1995; Chwelos et al., 2001) Competitive pressure has also been highlighted by Premkumar and Ramamurthy (1995), Crook and Kumar (1998), Bensaou and Venkatraman (1996), Morrell and Ezingard (2001), and Maingot and Quon (2001), while industry pressure was noted by Bensaou and Venkatraman (1996), Iacovou et al. (1995), and Chwelos et al. (2001). Efficiency and effectiveness also feature as key drivers (Morrell & Ezingard, 2001; Ahmad & Schroeder, 2001).

Like library consortia, IOSs also raise the incongruity between the need for collaboration while still needing to compete (Johnston & Gregor, 2000). Creating congruence among the partners can be a key uncertainty and risk reducing strategy (Angeles & Nath, 2001). To do this, a participative rather than an authoritarian management and decision-making style is desirable among partners (Angeles & Nath, 2001). Nevertheless, the competitive aspects of IOSs also need consideration. IOSs affect competition in three ways: they change the structure of the industry and alter the rules of competition, they create competitive advantages, and can create whole new businesses (Siau, 2003). Furthermore, academic administrators and politicians have turned to this form of collaboration as a means of accomplishing their goals (Siau, 2003), which are very often competitive.

The origins of many of today's e-commerce business models can be found in those business innovations that recognized the value of networked computers for obtaining greater efficiencies and promoting collaborative contributions. Many of the problems and issues that were found to have been intractable then remain problems in contemporary businesses. Solutions found to these problems in earlier models can often lead to insights and solutions in today's businesses.

The Foundation and Promise of LIBNET

The South African library system is the most comprehensive and sophisticated network of information resources on the continent of Africa. Although very flawed, it gave birth to an impressive collaborative venture that has survived through dramatic political, economic and technological developments. In 1979, a committee examining the possibility of establishing a national computerized catalogue in South Africa concluded, "The cost and resources needed to establish a national catalogue from scratch would be prohibitive" (Laing, 1997, p. 53). The committee, largely made up of senior librarians and academics, was aware that the rate of growth of publication titles would double every 25 years. While very dependant on the importation of scientific and technical information, a small country like South Africa, with so many other more pressing demands on its national resources, needed to make the most efficient use of funds spent on its national bibliographic development and control. It made sense, therefore, to develop a national online catalogue of the bibliographic holdings of the major research and public libraries.

No individual library could afford to fund the development of such a facility, not even the State Library. As a statutory organization falling under the Department of National Education, the State Library considered that its responsibilities, defined before the days of computerized catalogues and online databases, would have included the functions of a national online catalogue. Indeed, over the years it had been responsible for the compilation of the *South African National Bibliography*, the SANB. This serial publication provided the bibliographic details of all South African publications deposited by publishers in the various Legal Deposit Libraries. The State Library also maintained the South African Joint Catalogue of Monographs that recorded many of the acquisitions and holdings of the major libraries in the country in order to support interlibrary loan requests. The Joint Catalogue was terminated in 1976 and published on microfiche. From 1979 onwards it was decided to publish the bibliographic records of the Joint Catalogue on computer tape (Musiker, 1986, p. 152). Accordingly, the State Library had an important role to play in the development of LIBNET because several of the functions that had hitherto been the statutory responsibility of the State Library would be taken over by LIBNET and developed in electronic form.

After months of investigation and consultation, LIBNET was established as a Section 21 (not-for-profit) utility company. The key enabler was a "pump-priming" grant from government and the 10-year subscription commitment made by the original members in the Memorandum of Agreement. There was some tentative enthusiasm about the direction in which library cooperation was going with the establishment of the fledgling company. Besides the State Library, the original members included universities, national and regional government departments, and municipalities that owned and ran the libraries intended to benefit from the collaborative venture. The subscribing libraries hoped that their expenditure on subscriptions and purchases would be offset by reduced numbers of acquisition and cataloguing staff, more efficient interlibrary loans transactions (with associated staff efficiencies) and more efficient information retrieval by consultant or reference staff. In addition it was hoped that the pressure on libraries to automate their management processes would be offset or delayed by participation in the LIBNET initiative. If nothing else, participation by members was a learning process that would facilitate subsequent decision making about library computerization — a way of putting their toes into the water without the pain of sudden and total immersion. And, of course, there were incentives to load their cataloguing data that would offset the cost of establishing their own computerized catalogues.

The original subscription commitment for 10 years made the member libraries shareholders in the company with the right to elect the board of directors at an annual general meeting of LIBNET. This was usually held, for convenience sake, at the annual conference of the South African Institute for Librarianship and Information Science. However, not all the directors were subject to election at the Annual General Meeting. Because of that library's important statutory responsibilities, the director of the State Library was a permanent member of the board of directors. In addition, the interests of the government were represented on the board of directors by a person nominated by the Minister of National Education. The managing director of LIBNET was *ex officio* a member of the board, while the members at the annual general meeting elected the rest of the directors. Largely they were drawn from the academic library sector, although an important component was the presence of senior businessmen who could bring their business and entrepreneurial acumen and expertise to bear on decisions before the board.

SETTING THE STAGE

Internally, the staff of LIBNET consisted of two main groupings — those responsible for developing the technological base of LIBNET's operations and providing the networked services, and those responsible for marketing the products and services as well as growing the clientele and membership numbers. This latter activity had a very positive side effect in that it made the LIBNET staff very much part of the professional library community in South Africa, and in fact, helped to create a sense of unity and camaraderie among the members.

This sense of participative ownership was essential to promote a constant flow of new cataloguing data of the highest possible quality being added to the database by all the subscribing libraries. It also provided LIBNET with the means to refine the services required by the members.

LIBNET's Technical Infrastructure

Initially LIBNET operated on the Washington Library Network software. Access protocols for LIBNET included an X.28 dial-up facility for IBM PCs; an X.25 packet switching as well as SNA and TCP/IP for dedicated data lines and point-to-point asynchronous communication with DEC VT-100 or compatible terminals. Any other data communications requirements were investigated to ensure as wide a range of access options for subscribers as possible (Laing, 1997, p. 54).

From the beginning the intention was to develop its own system using South African Machine Readable Cataloguing (SAMARC) records. The SAMARC format was based on the original MARC format developed by Henrietta Avram and her team in the Library of Congress in the 1960s and 1970s. It included some modifications made in the British UKMARC format as well as some idiosyncratic requirements to suit the multi-lingual South African situation. A great deal of time and effort went into developing the specifications and writing the software for LIBNET's new, home grown system until it was realized that it would not be as cost effective as originally intended. "Build or buy" decisions were very controversial at that stage, especially as the Open Systems Movement gained ground within the computer systems industry worldwide. Finally, in 1992, LIBNET rolled out their new system amidst some controversy. It was a turn-key system based on a library software package popular with university libraries in South Africa at the time. Running on a UNIX operating system, and therefore in line with current open-systems thinking, the system was accessible via X.28 dial-up facilities, via Telkom's dedicated data lines with X.25 packet switching, or with TCP/IP communications protocol on GOVNET, UNINET, and other networks available in South Africa.

Databases available were originally based on the Washington Library Network database, supplemented by the Joint Catalogue of Monographs developed by the State Library from records sent to them by the major libraries in the country, particularly the main university, and public libraries and the legal deposit libraries. With the implementation of its new system in 1992, LIBNET made available to its members a new "bouquet" of databases. These included the South African Cooperative Library Database (SACD), the Index to South African Periodicals (ISAP), the Library of Congress Database (otherwise known as the National Union Catalog [NUC]), the British National Bibliography (BNB) and Whitakers Books In Print. The Union Catalogue of Theses and Dissertations developed by Potchefstroom University and the South African National Bibliography were also available on the LIBNET database.

Jan's Problem

Jan's problem was not trivial. Two months earlier he and his friend Sid had both been at a meeting of the board of directors of the national bibliographic service provider LIBNET. Jan represented the LIBNET Users Committee on the Board, while Sid had been elected by the members at an AGM and had served since then for a series of three-year terms. They had served together on the Board for several years and flew to Pretoria for board meetings every two or three months. They were tall men, same age, same size, and archetypical representatives of the Boer and Brit elements of South African society. Yet the hostilities of the South African War were entirely absent in their dealings with one another. They were both university librarians of old and established research libraries. The good professional relationship they enjoyed started when Sid had been invited to serve as a professional advisor on the selection committee that recommended Jan's appointment. Since then they had consulted one another on matters of common concern, and served on professional committees and task forces. The trust and mutual confidence in each other's perspective and professional ability led to constructive decision making in various cooperative initiatives. They presumed that it was that trust and confidence that persuaded the LIBNET board to task them to find a solution to the data-ownership and tariff problem.

The fact that LIBNET had been established as a cooperative venture with government seed-money meant that the customers were also the information providers. Instead of providing all the funding, the government wanted to play an enabling role such that LIBNET would in due course become self-sustaining as a non-profit organization. As the database administrator, LIBNET sold its networking and database services to its members, using the information they had provided as the database content. To ensure high standards of data entry, LIBNET ran nationwide training programs and established quality control mechanisms to monitor input. It was in the interests of all members to ensure accurate data capture, and so incentives needed to be built into the tariff structure to reward those members that participated in the process.

The calculation on which the annual tariffs were determined had been a matter of concern to the LIBNET Board for several years. The larger libraries that were founding members of LIBNET paid an annual subscription and a usage charge based on EEs (enquiry equivalents) used. The EE was based on the number of searches conducted on the database. Associate members, who were usually the smaller libraries and other bodies, did not pay an annual subscription, but paid a monthly terminal connection fee and a tariff per EE used which was almost twice the EE charge of the larger subscribing library members.

However, these tariff arrangements did not take account of intellectual property rights and data ownership. A great deal of original intellectual work went into the process of data capture of bibliographic records. The library catalogue of any large research library represents a major investment for the institution concerned. It is the intellectual property of the institution and as such could be sold or negotiated in the same way that other intellectual property could be negotiated. Many academic libraries continued to spend additional funds on catalogue conversion projects in order to capture their cataloguing data retrospectively. This expenditure enabled them more quickly to establish their own machine-readable catalogue for the needs of their domestic library systems. To upload that data to a national bibliographic service utility such as LIBNET did not draw them any royalty payments. They got no benefit from the initial expense of data capture other than greater bibliographic control of their own domestic collection. However, the enriched online catalogue was an important marketing consideration that could be used by LIBNET to attract new members. Like many other members, Jan and Sid considered that their extra expenditure gave them a greater stake in LIBNET, and they felt that their extra contribution to LIBNET's development and welfare was not being recognized or appreciated. And, of course, the higher percentage of their libraries' bibliographic records that were on the database, the more likelihood that other libraries would want to borrow books from them on interlibrary loan.

Meanwhile, almost as an encouragement for this viewpoint, the State Library continued to develop and market its Joint Catalogue of Monographs and South African National Bibliography. Was there not a way in which other libraries, in tough budgetary times, might not recoup some of their expenditure in similar ways? LIBNET paid royalties to those information providers like the British Library for the British National Bibliography, the Library of Congress for its National Union Catalog and the Washington Library Network for its database. If LIBNET was deriving a benefit from the contribution of libraries such as those directed by Jan and Sid, surely there could be some reconsideration of the tariff determination by LIBNET?

The two-hour flight back to Cape Town after that Board meeting in Pretoria had done little to ease the minds of Jan and Sid. Who were the information providers? Who owned the database? Who was paying for what services and should their institutions not be getting some form of royalty or compensation for the added contribution they were making? In addition, how could a tariff policy be set that allowed libraries to reduce budgetary uncertainty ahead of time when the tariff policy was based on an annual subscription as well as connect-time pricing and/or per-record charges? How could all this be done without damaging LIBNET and its financial viability, or were there other strategic options available to them?

The Boeing 737 wove its way through tall towers of cumulus, like huge, airborne cities. Through the late afternoon sky, the sun's rays struck the white bulbous towers from the west, creating deep shadows and slowly redecorating the thick, puffy clouds in gold and pink as the land below melted into shadow. Not much chance of the data ownership and tariff problems melting in the same way. Although it was a privilege to be able to see the world from a perspective that few creatures in all of Earth's history had ever seen, one way or another, that privilege would have to be paid for.

CASE DESCRIPTION

Jan leaned back in his chair and looked across his desk and out the window. On the wall to his right hung a painting of a typical farming scene in red and brown and ochre — one of the university's art treasures with which he had been burdened as curator. Below it, but closer to him was his computer, its monitor and keyboard, and his telephone — his links to the outside world. Evidence, if it was needed, of the increasing reliance of libraries on the growth of information and communications technologies to streamline and enhance business services in all areas of endeavor.

It was now two months since he and Sid had flown home from Pretoria, and the problem that the LIBNET Board had referred to them had in no way been resolved in the intervening weeks. Within a few minutes, Sid would be arriving for a meeting to explore and, if possible, resolve the issues involved in tariff determination and data ownership. As usual for his meetings with Sid, Jan had scheduled a lunch break for about 12:45 p.m. in the university's staff dining room. The caterer had agreed to prepare freshly caught grilled yellowtail and roast seasonal vegetables as the main course with a light sorbet and fresh fruit compote to finish off. And two bottles of Pinotage were ready to provide some consolation for the mental effort they expected to expend. He was looking forward to the rest of the day, and hoped that the business end would be completed before lunch started.

"Good to see you, my friend!" smiled Jan, as he and Sid shook hands. After a brief word with Anne, Jan's personal assistant, the two men went into the committee room with every intention of being undisturbed until they had resolved the problem. To set the scene Jan reviewed the background that had given rise to the situation. For 10 years, academic library directors had been laboring hard to ensure the purchasing levels of materials for their libraries. A combination of publishing price rises that had impacted on university and other libraries throughout the world, and the falling value of the South African currency unit on international currency markets had increased their journals budget by a factor of three, while the book budget remained unchanged. The total acquisitions budget had almost doubled over a period of five years. Despite this, the actual buying power of the money was reduced by 20% in terms of the numbers of both book purchases and journals subscriptions. The academics were in an uproar and the university administrators were demanding closer cooperation on a regional basis between the two university libraries. "More bang for the buck" and "You must work smarter, not harder" were the clichés that rang around the meetings of the library committees of both institutions.

"I tell you, Sid, the combination of publishing price rises and the falling value of the South African Rand on international currency markets has increased our journals budget by a factor of three, while our book budget remains unchanged. And we have fought to maintain that situation!" Jan complained. "Clearly, closer cooperation in purchasing policies and more ready access to the holdings of each other's libraries would assist in easing the problem. But to do that we will need to ensure full bibliographic control of the book and journal holdings of both our libraries. That is not a trivial matter — and it will be expensive," observed Jan.

"Our options are to do it either through LIBNET, or through some form of cooperative regional bibliographic database as we have been discussing with our colleagues," suggested Sid. Arising from their earlier meetings over many years, both Sid and Jan were under pressure to promote regional cooperation — and that pressure came in the form of financial incentives from outside benefactors willing to help fund the emergence of a new social structure now that the years of apartheid and social isolation were ended.

"But LIBNET has made an important contribution over the eight years of its existence. We signed on for 10 years. We are committed to it for another two years at least. It makes sense to support and use it. But regional cooperation is also important. We can incorporate the benefits that flow from our LIBNET membership for regional advantage," suggested Jan.

"That's true. But I have to conserve resources and watch carefully the percentage of my library's budget that goes to LIBNET. The larger libraries that make up the foundation members of LIBNET pay not only our annual subscriptions, but also for the use we make of the system beyond the calculated maximum. If we cut back on use in order to save money, we're cutting back on the benefits to be gained from our subscription," reasoned Sid. "The tariff structure locks us in. Part of the problem is trying to budget ahead of time for our needs. I can't anticipate the EE usage, the connect time, or even the annual subscription sufficiently far in advance to reflect them accurately when the budget goes to the University Council."

"Yeah! But both your library and mine still have a lot of retrospective cataloguing to do before we reap the real benefits of LIBNET. In fact there are holdings gaps for libraries throughout the country. We have started a project to convert our card-based catalogues to machine-readable form starting with heavily used materials. What are you doing?" asked Jan.

"We've contracted with a commercial company operating out of Australia," said Sid. "They sub-contract to staff in the Philippines, and send copies of our catalogue cards for data capture. It's not entirely satisfactory because it involves a lot of checking for completeness, but I must say, mostly the quality of the data-capture is good."

He looked out of the window trying to imagine a team of Philippino data-capturers making sense of the catalogue cards they were working with. "Look, you can't expect them to use their initiative to fix obvious errors. That's not what they are paid for — and anyway they may not even understand what they are keying in. But it still reflects the initial investment in creative cataloguing made by the university over the years. It would be great if we could recoup that expenditure by selling off our records to some other library. You're not interested, are you? I'll give you a special price?" smiled Sid. "After all, there must be a high percentage of overlap between your holdings and ours."

"No way, my friend. We are doing our retrospective conversion in-house, simply to save money. Can you imagine what my bosses would say if I bought catalogue records from you?" He grinned back. The traditional rivalry extended to professional matters as well. For both, retrospective conversion projects were an important cost factor and not without their detractors among the academic Luddites.

"The urgent need is to establish a credible computer-readable catalogue for the needs of our domestic systems faster and cheaper than would otherwise be possible. That will give us a basis for any regional cooperation as well. With both our bibliographic databases loaded, we would have an immensely valuable regional resource," mused Sid. "But when we upload it all to LIBNET, what are we going to get for our troubles? More interlibrary loan requests and a whole lot of extra work! Why can't we get some additional form of recognition and compensation? After all, LIBNET is here to help us, but the spin-off of our membership means additional expense and work for us."

"How come? What are you trying to say?" asked Jan.

"Look. Although there are incentives built into the LIBNET fee structure, to upload all our new data to the national database still costs us more. Is that extra contribution being recognized or appreciated? If the State Library and Potchefstroom University can own their data, and even sell it to others, why can't we? After all, our additional data contributes to LIBNET's enriched online catalogue. That's partly what makes LIBNET attractive to new members. Other libraries join and then start using the records we provide to reduce their own cataloguing costs. Some benefit from the data we have uploaded. Others use the same data to save themselves the cost of buying books. They demand those books on interlibrary loan. It doesn't seem right that our extra expenditure on retrospective catalogue conversion places us in a position of being additionally exploited by increased numbers of interlibrary loan requests! It's nonsense! There should be some sort of royalty built into the LIBNET tariff structure to compensate us for our contribution — not just to LIBNET, but to the country as a whole."

"Ja! I see what you mean. Actually, this thing has been brewing a long time," replied Jan, getting into the thrust of Sid's argument. "Let's look at it from another perspective. The State Library is statutorily charged with responsibility for the development of the South African National Bibliography, and the director is therefore *ex-officio* a member of the LIBNET Board. He considers the records contributed by the State Library rightly belonged to the State Library. That includes the South African National Bibliography and the Index to South African Periodicals. Although they are all available through LIBNET, they belong to the State Library. On the other hand, the Executive Director of LIBNET would naturally want to protect his interests and would take the view that each subscribing library has a responsibility to load its bibliographic data onto LIBNET in terms of their Memorandum of Agreement — and the national interest. But the directors of the major research libraries, who like ourselves are also members of the Board, will consider that they should be getting some return on their investment, some compensation for the initiative they had taken to ensure that the national online catalogue will be completed faster to everyone's benefit. What is in it for us and them?"

"That's it. OK. Let's look at the major issues." Sid pulled out a document with his scribbled notes. That morning he had jotted several points down before driving over to Jan's library. These were the principles that he thought should drive any decisions about equity in this situation. "Let's take them one at a time as defendable issues or issues that may be of political or strategic importance to individual members of the Board." He read them out.

1. Each library owns the records that it has generated through its own creative efforts.
2. Each library also owns the records it has generated through paying for the data conversion process.
3. The State Library owns all records that it has contributed to the LIBNET database, even though many of those records were contributed by participating libraries sending in copies of their catalogue cards, or by legal deposit libraries contributing their acquisitions lists to the State Library.
4. Similarly, the Library of Congress owns the National Union Catalog that is accessible through LIBNET, and the British Library owns the British National Bibliography, also accessible through LIBNET.
5. LIBNET owns all databases that it has developed from the contributions made to it by subscribing libraries, or for which it has paid in agreement with the owners of other bibliographies.
6. Individual libraries have the right to decide whether or not to upload bibliographic data to LIBNET. Once uploaded, the records belong to LIBNET in terms of the subscription agreement, but they also belong to the originating library and may not be sold by LIBNET without permission or recompense.
7. Having paid for their subscriptions and the downloading of their own bibliographic records from LIBNET, individual libraries are entitled to establish their own domestic bibliographic database, but may not sell records downloaded from LIBNET.

8. Any library is free to sell, or otherwise make available, its own bibliographic records to any other individual or library, as it sees fit.

"Hey. That's good!" complimented Jan. "Let's go through each one and see if we can pick holes in them!"

From this set of basic principles, Sid and Jan debated their implications.

"What if the larger libraries withhold the uploading to LIBNET of their retrospective conversion records and recover their costs by selling them to other libraries? OK. In a way this would be going into competition with LIBNET and would be in breach of the original agreement we signed when we joined LIBNET."

"But by meeting that obligation, we are creating a stick for our own backs," grumbled Sid. "Increased interlibrary loans are a significant counter-incentive increasing staff pressure in a sensitive area. Not only must I deal with pressure on my materials budget, I must keep my staffing budget under control. The budget cuts affect both materials as well as staffing budgets."

"So what about a regional initiative?" asked Jan. "There is the financial incentive that flows from the possibility of overseas funding by benefactors. That could make a big difference to our situation. It will make good political sense too. We will be seen to be driving academic regional cooperation where many other initiatives have failed. Also, a smaller cooperative network would be easier to handle, would give more direct administrative control and would build on what we have already done through our earlier discussions and through LIBNET." He looked questioningly at Sid.

"Well, if LIBNET is unable to come up with some new and revised tariff structure that recognizes the contribution we are making, it could make sense for us to slowly withdraw our dependence on LIBNET and build a closer dependence on a regional cooperative structure. After all, we only have a year or so to go before our legal obligations to LIBNET end. As far as I am concerned, the financial constraints being placed on us by our respective administrations are such that all our options need to be considered. I am under a lot of pressure to reduce staff, improve services, increase book stock and take a lead in collaboration and regional rationalization." Sid looked pensive. It sounded like treason. After all the years of working on the promotion of LIBNET and of national and regional library cooperation, to suddenly turn to a narrow and self-serving strategic direction went against the grain. But he had to consider all the options that were open.

Jan looked at his watch. "Hey! It's lunchtime," he announced with a smile. "I have something good for you!" he said, thinking of the grilled yellowtail and the pinotage.

They gathered up their papers and with a sense of relief found their way out of the library and across the square to the university's staff dining room. Based on the discussion over lunch, Jan undertook to prepare a series of proposals for the next meeting of the LIBNET Board. He asked Sid to write up a memorandum on the basis of the day's discussions and forward it to him as soon as possible. He would then consult with his deputies before submitting his final proposals to the LIBNET Board.

The range and implications of their morning discussions ensured an ongoing debate over lunch and dominated their thoughts for the rest of that afternoon. On his way home, and while the issues were still fresh in his mind, Sid dictated a memorandum for typing the next day, so that it could be sent to Jan as a file attachment with the least possible delay. Both Jan and Sid felt they had had a very productive meeting — yet one that could have enormous repercussions for both the future of LIBNET, and also for academic library cooperation. It would probably have some important implications for the principles on which database development is funded and the way that the contribution of members is rewarded.

CURRENT CHALLENGES AND PROBLEMS FACING THE ORGANIZATION

The question of database ownership and the provision of incentives and rewards to the information providers were reflective of the changing needs of LIBNET members. Originally, they had required a networked union catalogue of the holdings of the nation's major research libraries. The cost of such a facility was beyond the budget of any one of the libraries, so they were happy to participate in and contribute to the development of this national utility.

After 10 years, however, three things had happened to change the perspective of the members:

1. LIBNET had successfully established the basis of that national catalogue. It had a modern networked system, a staff that nurtured high standards of contribution to the database, and simultaneously promoted the company's services nationwide.
2. The technology had changed, making online, real-time network access to a regional library system both affordable and desirable.
3. The political and economic climate of the country had changed. South Africa was no longer under siege. The academic boycotts, political and economic sanctions, and civil unrest that spread to the campuses of the major LIBNET members were over. Nelson Mandela was out of gaol. The first democratic elections had been held, and around the world, aid agencies and benefactors were keen to contribute to and participate in the remarkable emergence of what Archbishop Desmond Tutu had referred to as "the Rainbow Nation."

> What better contribution could be made than to democratize the nation's information resources by networking the major libraries on a regional basis so that their collections were accessible to all the citizens, whether or not they were students or staff?

With this option before them, it was understandable that Jan and Sid and their colleagues on the LIBNET Board of Directors started giving attention to who owned the LIBNET database. Their cash-strapped universities saw many benefits flowing from the injection of funds by overseas benefactors. Not only were there savings to be made from cooperative library acquisitions policies and cataloguing activities, but a unified circulation system and a reduction in duplicate journal subscriptions would be facilitated by a regional cooperative system. LIBNET was therefore under pressure to deliver at the same time as its initial "pump-priming" government funding, and the 10-year membership commitments of its founder institutions were coming to an end.

The resolution of the tariff and incentives structure became the catalyst that led on to the restructuring of the entire LIBNET business. On January 1, 1997, LIBNET sold its operations to a private company to enable it to expand into the commercial online market. Today, the new privatized LIBNET thrives as the most successful online information network in Africa. But it is very different in structure from its original conception — largely as a result of the factors driving the decisions outlined above.

The main reasons for "privatizing" LIBNET operations in the mid-'90s were:

- To bring in strategic partners through a shareholding structure,
- To create a vehicle for generating development capital, and
- To attract and keep the right type of staff members.

These intentions are now reflected in the current shareholding structure. The perspective has become one of an equal partnership between clients and staff. So the new LIBNET is evolving into a situation where staff and client shareholder groups will both have a 50% shareholding. The co-ownership concept, together with a creative share-incentive scheme, is making a huge contribution to its success. The business orientation of staff has increased beyond belief. Clients are benefiting through the ongoing improvement of products and services, while costs are controlled in the same process, because it is in the interest of the staff to run a profitable and competitive shop. Although there had been discussions at times with potential strategic partners to buy a stake in the company, that idea was abandoned several years ago without selling off any shares to outside investors. The traditional character of the company was therefore maintained without diluting the value of the shares.

The big challenge in doing business in the new South Africa is the Black Economic Empowerment and Affirmative Action law. The general line of thinking is that all businesses should have a 25% black ownership by 2010. Government itself is more concerned about real empowerment, such as people development, skills transfer, enterprise development, corporate social upliftment, and so forth. The record shows that there are, unfortunately, a small number of black businessmen in the country who are pushing the shareholding idea without contributing anything to the growth of the economy. As a result, LIBNET is still not listed on the Johannesburg Stock Exchange (JSE) and has no immediate plans to do so. The corporate scandals of the last couple of years have made the JSE less attractive (from a cost viewpoint) to apply for a listing. LIBNET doesn't need capital at present and shareholders are not prepared to sell their shares, so a listing does not make any sense. Accordingly, the new LIBNET intends to grow its black shareholding through the current structures of staff and client shareholders. Initially, shares were sold to staff at R0,20 per share at the time of privatization. Those shares were subdivided in the ratio of 10:1 five years later. The latest official valuation of the shares is about R0,50 to R0,60 per share. That is equal to 5 to 6 Rand per share before the subdivision.

Functionally, LIBNET has developed into a company with a primary focus on the maintenance and development of its traditional services (cataloguing support, interlending and reference services). These are still growing slowly, but the real performers are the newer products, such as electronic journals and the legal products (government and provincial gazettes, parliamentary monitoring and statutes). This has helped to spread the risks far better than before. Structurally, LIBNET has divided into two separate business units (Academic/Library, Corporate) to reflect the separate focuses, and these are functioning well with totally different marketing and support approaches. The core strengths remain the same — excellent relationship with clients backed by high-quality client support, and an excellent team of people doing the job.

The challenges facing the new LIBNET reflect the current economic development climate in contemporary South Africa. Apart from Black Economic Empowerment and Affirmative Action employment laws, these include doing international business with an unstable local currency, growing the markets and competing with larger international competitors.

REFERENCES

Ahmad, S., & Schroeder, R. G. (2001). The impact of electronic data interchange on delivery performance. *Production and Operations Management, 10*(1), 16-30.

Angeles, R., & Nath, R. (2001). Partner congruence in electronic data interchange (EDI)-enabled relationships. *Journal of Business Logistics, 22*(2), 109-127.

Bensaou, M., & Venkatraman, N. (1996). Interorganizational relationships and information technology: A conceptual synthesis and a research framework. *European Journal of Information Systems, 5*(2), 84-91.

Braunstein, Y. (1981). Information as a commodity. In R. M. Mason, & J. E. Crebs, Jr. (Eds.), *Information services: Economics, management and technology* (pp. 9-22). Boulder, CO: Westview.

Chwelos, P., Benbasat, I., & Dexter, A. S. (2001). Research report: Empirical test of an EDI adoption model. *Information Systems Research, 12*(3), 304-321.

Communications industry report (14th ed.). (2000). New York: Veronis, Suhler and Associates (as cited by Jain & Kannan, 2002, *op. cit.* p. 1123).

Crook, C. W., & Kumar, R. L. (1998). Electronic data interchange: A multi-industry investigation using grounded theory. *Information Management, 34*, 75-89.

Ebbinghouse, C. (2004). If at first you don't succeed, Stop!: Proposed legislation to set up new intellectual property rights in facts themselves. *Searcher, 12*(1), 8-17.

Fountain, J. E. (2001). *Building the virtual state: Information technology and institutional change.* Washington, DC: Brookings Institute Press.

Gorman, G. E., & Cullen, R. (2000). Models and opportunities for library cooperation in the Asian region. *Library management, 21*(7), 373-384.

Hayes, R. M. (2003). Cooperative game theoretical models for decision-making in contexts of library cooperation. *Library Trends, 51*(3), 441-461.

Holmes, D. (2001). *eGov: e-Business strategies for government.* London: Nicholas Brierley.

Hooper, A. S. C. (1989). Formal cooperative agreements among libraries: Towards a South African model. *South African Journal for Librarianship and Information Science, 57*(2), 125-129.

Hooper, A. S. C. (1990). Overlapping journal subscriptions as a factor in university library co-operation. *South African Journal for Librarianship and Information Science, 58*(1), 25-32.

Iacovou, C. L., Benbasat, I., & Dexter, A. S. (1995). Electronic data interchange and small organizations: Adoption and impact of technology. *MIS Quarterly, 19*(2), 465-485.

Jain, S., & Kannan, P. K. (2002). Pricing of information products on online servers: Issues, models and analysis. *Management Science, 48*(9), 1123-1142.

Johnston, R. B., & Gregor, S. (2000). A theory of industry-level activity for understanding the adoption of interorganizational systems. *European Journal of Information Systems, 9*, 24-251.

Kemp, G. (1996). Networking in South Africa. *Bulletin of the American Society for Information Science, 22*(6), 26-27.

Kopp, J. J. (1998). Library consortia and information technology: The past, the present, the promise. *Information Technology and Libraries, 17*(1), 7-12.

Laing, R. (1997). LIBNET (A Financial Mail Special Report). *Financial Mail, 144*(4), 53-64.

Maingot, M., & Quon, T. (2001). A survey of electronic data interchange (EDI) in the top public companies in Canada. *INFOR, 39*(3), 317-332.

Martey, A. K. (2002). Management issues in library networking: focus on a pilot library networking project in Ghana. *Library Management, 23*(4/5), 239-251.

Morrell, M., & Ezingard, J. N. (2001). Revisiting adoption factors of inter-organizational information systems in SMEs. *Logistics Information Management, 15*(1/2), 46-57.

Musiker, R. (1986). *Companion to South African Libraries.* Johannesburg: Ad Donker.

Patrick, R. J. (1972). *Guidelines for library cooperation: Development of academic library consortia.* Santa Monica, CA: System Development Corporation.

Potter, W. G. (1997). Recent trends in state wide academic library consortia. *Library Trends, 45*, 417-418 (as cited by Kopp, 1998, *op. cit.*).

Premkumar, G., & Ramamurthy, K. (1995). The role of interorganizational and organizational factors on the decision mode for adoption of interorganizational systems. *Decision Sciences, 26*(3), 303-336.

Rayport, J. E., & Jaworski, B. J. (2002). *Introduction to e-commerce.* New York: McGraw-Hill.

Siau, K. (2003). Interorganizational systems and competitive advantages: Lessons from history. *The Journal of Computer Information Systems, 44*(1), 33-39.

Spence, A. M. (1974). An economist's view of information. *Annual Review of Information Science and Technology.* American Society for Information Science.

West, L. A. (2000). Private markets for public goods: Pricing strategies of online database vendors. *Journal of Management Information Systems, 17*(1), 59-85.

APPENDIX

1. The Companies Act, No 61 of 1973

STATUTES OF THE REPUBLIC OF SOUTH AFRICA — COMPANIES
Companies Act, No. 61 of 1973

21. Incorporation of associations not for gain

1. **Any association**:
   (a) formed or to be formed for any lawful purpose;
   (b) having the main object of promoting religion, arts, sciences, education, charity, recreation, or any other cultural or social activity or communal or group interests;
   (c) which intends to apply its profits (if any) or other income in promoting its said main object;
   (d) which prohibits the payment of any dividend to its members; and
   (e) which complies with the requirements of this section in respect to its formation and registration, may be incorporated as a company limited by guarantee.
2. **The memorandum of such association shall comply with the requirements of this Act and shall, in addition, contain the following provisions:**
   (a) The income and property of the association whencesoever derived shall be applied solely towards the promotion of its main object, and no portion thereof shall be paid or transferred, directly or indirectly, by way of dividend, bonus, or otherwise howsoever, to the members of the association or to its holding company or subsidiary: Provided that nothing herein contained shall prevent the payment in good faith of reasonable remuneration to any officer or servant of the association or to any member thereof in return for any services actually rendered to the association.
   [Para. (a) amended by s. 4 of Act No 59 of 1978.]
   (b) Upon its winding up, deregistration or dissolution, the assets of the association remaining after the satisfaction of all its liabilities shall be given or transferred to some other association or institution or associations or institutions having objects similar to its main object, to be determined by the members of the association at or before the time of its dissolution or, failing such determination, by the Court.
3. **The provisions of section 49 (1) (c) of this Act shall not apply to any such association.**
   [Sub-s. (3) substituted by s. 3 of Act No 31 of 1986.]

4. **Existing associations incorporated under section 21 of the repealed Act shall be deemed to have been formed and incorporated under this section.**

2. The LIBNET Tariff Structure

LIBNET TARIFF STRUCTURE: GENERAL INFORMATION

1. **Current situation**

   The existing tariff structure is based upon the following:

- An annual membership fee of R9720 incorporating 18000 enquiry equivalents (EEs);
- A tariff of R0.49 per EE for the use of the system after the first 18000 EEs (0.43/ EE after 300000 EEs);
- Associated members do not pay any annual membership fee but they pay R0.70 per EE with a minimum usage of 200 EEs per month;
- Members receive credit for data contribution; and
- All other products are priced separately.

2. **Advantages/disadvantages of present system**

   Advantages

- Members pay in relation to their usage of the system; and
- Members who train their staff properly normally use fewer EEs per search.

Disadvantages

- Because the variable cost (the actual cost of processing and retrieving the information) is only a small percentage of the EE tariff, the more frequent users are funding an unreasonably high portion of the LIBNET fixed costs (this aspect was also emphasized by LHA Management Consultants);
- Users do pay for the usage of the system even if they don't retrieve any information;
- Members do not use LIBNET to its full potential, because of the "CASH REGISTER SYNDROME." Staff members are instructed to use LIBNET sparingly. It is difficult to determine the effect on the building of a cooperative database as a result of this behavior;
- The present system requires a complex accounting system;
- When users question their EE usage, it normally takes up a lot of time of skilled staff members to determine what the problem, if any, is; and
- Users don't know in advance what a specific search will cost them.

3. Financial Projections

Depending on certain strategic decisions to be taken by the LIBNET Board, the income required to cover the expenditure during the next financial year will be approximately R5 million.

The following tariff adjustments (based on the present tariff structure) would be required to provide that income:

Service Unit		:	R27 000	(R9720)
EE tariff:	GT 18 000	:	R1,00	(R0,49)
	GT 300000	:	R0,45	(R0,43)
Associate members		:	R2,00	(R0,70)

Most of the members will just cut back on their usage in order to stay within their budgets.

4. Alternatives

It is important to determine what the requirements of a fair and just tariff structure must be. Some thoughts on that are:

- A user must pay for the information received and not necessarily for the use of the system;
- The tariff structure must promote an increased use of the system;
- More frequent users must pay more than less frequent users;
- Less frequent users must pay more per transaction than more frequent users.

One very attractive alternative is to determine a fixed annual subscription fee with unlimited use of the system. The biggest problems would however be to find a formula to determine the annual subscription per member and to prevent abuse of this system.

Aspects that could be considered for inclusion in the formula are:

- The number of terminals per members;
- The size of the library based upon the number of books and periodicals or the staff complement;
- The number of databases (SACD, LC, UK, UCTD, etc.) being accessed; and
- Systems functions (enquiry, cataloguing, etc.) being used.

3. Revising the LIBNET Tariff Structure

LIBNET — CONSIDERATIONS FOR A REVISED TARIFF STRUCTURE

(Extracts from a document prepared by the ad-hoc sub-committee on tariffs)

Introduction

At present tariffs are based entirely on usage and this, together with the GOVNET tariff structure, inhibits libraries from using LIBNET to its full potential.

At the same time those libraries that are heavily involved and committed to LIBNET find themselves vulnerable to exploitation by libraries with a lesser commitment. Not only is their cataloguing data exploited, the identification of their holdings makes them the target of a greater degree of interlibrary loan requests than would otherwise be the case. At the same time libraries with a small contribution to LIBNET are protected from interlibrary loan requests and are able to exploit the libraries that contribute heavily.

The libraries that are directly or indirectly funded by the Department of National Education contribute 95% to LIBNET's running costs.... This situation will not change significantly when the original Memorandum of Agreement that established LIBNET comes to an end in two years time.

While libraries using LIBNET are conscious of cost, most of the cost savings or the benefit of using LIBNET are hidden.

4. LIBNET Organizational Structure

Table 1. LIBNET organizational structure

After many years as an academic library director, A. S. C. (Tony) Hooper now teaches information systems management at the Victoria University of Wellington, where he is program director for the Master's of Information Management degree.

This case was previously published in the *Journal of Cases on Information Technology*, 7(3), pp. 77-97, © 2005.

Chapter II

Evolution of an Executive Information System: The Replenishment Data Warehouse at JeansWear

Hamid Nemati, University of North Carolina, USA

Keith Smith, VF Corporation, USA

EXECUTIVE SUMMARY

This case highlights factors that provided the impetus for changing a successful EIS into a data warehouse at the VF Corporation. The data warehouse was developed to aid JeansWear, a division of VF, with its point-of-sale/replenishment activities. The data warehouse provides greater reporting and OLAP capabilities, giving replenishment analysts a detailed and synthetic view of the marketplace. It is estimated that about $100 million in 1998 alone might be attributed to the improved replenishment decision making due to the data warehouse. The case discusses the basic concepts and architecture of this data warehouse and outlines the development process and the problems that the development team had to overcome. It also examines the essential role that this data warehouse is currently playing in the success of VF Corporation. Finally, the case outlines and discusses a number of factors that should be considered and questions that should be asked prior to initiation of a data warehouse project in order to assure a successful outcome.

INTRODUCTION

This case is a description of how a successful executive information system evolved into a data warehouse at VF Corporation, the largest publicly held apparel manufacturer in the world (www.vfc.com). The case discusses the forces that necessitated the development of this data warehouse and the challenges that the development team faced in achieving its goals. The data warehouse project occurred in a very volatile corporate environment. VF Corporation was reorganizing, which included the merger, splitting, and reassignment of all of its divisions. The data warehouse was conceived before the reorganization mandate, but occurred during it. This data warehouse has been very successful. It is estimated that about $100 million in 1998 alone could be attributed to the improved decision making due to the data warehouse. In the context of the changing corporate landscape, it is pertinent that businesses be able to run important IS projects with longer time frames well. How VF handled this problem would be an important learning tool to IS students, as well as IS practitioners who want to learn more about developing an enterprise-wide data warehouse. This case is a useful teaching tool intended for an upper-level undergraduate course in IS or an MBA course in management of IT projects, as well as a graduate course in IS that covers topics in data warehouse design and development.

BACKGROUND

VF Corporation (NYSE: VFC, www.vfc.com) celebrates its centennial year as one of the largest apparel manufacturers in the world. From its founding in 1899 as a maker of gloves and mittens in Reading, PA, to its multi-billion, multinational profile as a manufacturer of several types of clothing, VF has enjoyed steady and healthy growth. Net income in 1998 was 388MM on sales of $5.47 billion, a rise of 11% and 5% respectively. Earnings per share growth in 1998 was up 15% to $3.17, well above the corporate goal of 8-10%. Return on average common equity in 1998 was 19.7%, continuing a run of return at or above 10% for 10 of the last 11 years. The book value per common share was $17.30 and management has set aside $147 MM to repurchase stock, citing its belief that VF stock remains an excellent value.

Like many textile companies in the U.S., VF has moved much of it's manufacturing out of the country. Fifty-seven percent of its sewing operations was non-domestic at the end of 1998. The company plans to increase this percentage in the near term, hoping to relieve pricing pressures and rising labor costs. VF plans are to grow sales to $7 billion with growth rates of between 8-10%. VF plans to reach these goals through its policy of "consumerization" launched in 1997. Consumerization keys on three growth areas: acquisitions, technology, and brand marketing.

VF's legacy of jeans manufacturing began with Wrangler WesternWear, introduced in 1947. In the 1950s, Wrangler acquired the Blue Bell Corporation, a maker of denim jeans and related products, based in Greensboro, NC. VF Corporation purchased Wrangler in 1987. At that time, VF owned the Lee brand. This move made VF the number two make of jeans in the U.S., behind Levi-Strauss, Inc.

The corporation is comprised of six operating coalitions, or business units. They are JeansWear, Intimates, Knitwear, Playwear, International, and WorkWear. The major brands are Wrangler, Lee, Vanity Fair, Jantzen, Healthtex and Red Kap. VF Corporation has several popular brands with strong customer name recognition. Its JeansWear division controls almost a third of the domestic market. Jantzen is the number one brand of women's swimwear, while Vassarette is the bra leader in mass merchandise stores. Red Kap, a manufacturer of occupational apparel, is the leader in that category.

VF Jeanswear's information services history dates to 1958. At that time, the Blue Bell Corporation installed a series of IBM computers in an effort to automate some manufacturing functions. These included plant production planning and fabric inventory. In 1963, Blue Bell automated part of the general ledger process and added some cost accounting as well. As with many corporations, Blue Bell remained IBM to and through the model 360 series to virtual memory to today. The major portion of JeansWear processing is on IBM mainframes still.

VF replenishment began in the early 1990s when the VP of information services left IS to start the replenishment area. The resulting replenishment executive information system and its data warehouse successor have brought VF to the forefront of replenishment technology. From its inception, replenishment at VF has been ahead of the trend, giving VF a strategic advantage. This advantage has been augmented by the development of software tools that allow information to be analyzed to greater depths, particularly in the fields of data mining and data warehousing.

SETTING THE STAGE

VF JeansWear is a vendor for a large number of retailers, ranging from Wal-Mart to a large number of independently owned and operated western wear stores. Each of these retailers has a different agreement as to how merchandise will be purchased, delivered, and replenished. Flow replenishment is the ability to adjust inventory and styles proactively in response to changing consumer tastes. That is, VF, notably its JeansWear division, had the ability to mange its own brands within a given retail environment. JeansWear must have a replenishment process that is very flexible and robust. Merchandise situations differ from retailer to retailer and store to store within retailer. Each requires a unique process for ordering, manufacturing, shipping, and stocking of VF goods.

The logistics of such a task are tremendous. Retail sales of individual items such as jeans are numerous and non-homogeneous. The clothing industry, and jeans manufacturers in particular, can no longer rely on marketing campaigns to create the demand for its products. The demand is often created by consumer tastes and must be recognized by the manufacturer and/or retailer. In addition, the splitting of the jeans market into niche segments has forced retailers to adapt quickly and accurately to changing consumer taste. Trends must be picked up very quickly and hence, individual sales are much more important than they once were. As a result, in early 1990s, the marketing strategy for JeansWear was changed from a push strategy, where the company could mold the image of the jeans wearer, to a pull strategy, where consumer demand forced changes in product development. Now trends are micro-trends that demand micro marketing. This has been VF's strong suit in recent years, due in large part to its successful product replenishment system.

The replenishment process begins with the stocking of jeans and/or other wear on the designated floor and shelf space allocated for their products. The goods are sold at a retailer's cash register. The sale is recorded electronically and the data passed to JeansWear via electronic data interchange (EDI) documents. By transmitting the point-of-sale (POS) information captured at the retail cash register on a daily basis via EDI, restocking times are significantly reduced. The inventory and sales information are analyzed carefully and fed into a complex set of product replenishment models. These models suggest which on-hand goods are to be shipped and then produce work orders for the remainder. The models also suggest changes to the stock mix or retail space layout, if needed. Goods are then allocated or manufactured and sent to the retailer accordingly. The system utilizing these models generates orders on a daily or weekly basis to restock VF goods, based on retailer preference.

Consequently, the replenishment process is complex and problematic. VF's solution to this problem was to develop a system that was designed to provide needed information to VF management to achieve their replenishment goals.

CASE DESCRIPTION

In the early 1990s, VF introduced its market response system, a decision support system that made true flow replenishment possible by utilizing EDI and POS information. The market response system was supported in part by an executive information system (EIS). This executive information system was a mainframe-based system that had some characteristics of a data warehouse (DW), such as the ability to inquire across dimensions such as time. The system captured POS data, integrated manufacturing capacity, and product availability. The system could generate orders on a daily or weekly basis to restock VF goods.

The Executive Information System

This executive information system was developed based on a close working relationship between VF and retailers. VF would manage dynamic, model stock programs at the store/SKU level, create purchase orders and ship to stores, each as needed. VF would also provide information on product performance. The retailer, in turn, would assist in establishing a model stock quantity and the method through which that model stock would be determined, provide POS data, and would allow purchase of VF products to be determined by the flow replenishment system. VF's system provided decision support information both for VF management and retailers. It offered three-dimensional views of POS data, drill-down capabilities, user customization features, and unlimited query capabilities. To VF and its associated retailers this provided a win-win move. The system reduced inventory costs, avoided the loss of sales due to stock-out, and provided the customer with the latest in fashion and quality. The system increased sales and inventory turns. It decreased inventory while, conversely, minimizing stock-outs. Total costs both to VF and the retailer decreased while sales (and therefore profit) increased.

Although the system provided numerous benefits, it had a number of limitations. Decision makers needed to perform *ad-hoc* analysis that required the use complex queries to help determine the best product replenishment strategies. However, the mainframe environment of this system was inflexible. Reports and on-line queries were not readily available to the decision makers and required the intervention of the IS group. To remain competitive, VF needed a system that would allow it to achieve its replenishment goals. Achieving these goals would be very profitable to the VF Corporation and also it would decrease customers' stock-outs. This would, in turn increase consumer goodwill between VF and its retailers, increasing profits for both. In addition, JeansWear needed greater reporting ability and the capability to perform true OLAP and data mining. The system provided neither. A data warehouse would satisfy these objectives.

A data warehouse provides integrated, subject oriented data of improved quality to support enterprise decision-making activities (Inman, 1996). The data warehouse process is iterative process and involves obtaining, cleaning, massaging, and summarizing data by using some extraction tool to speed up the information retrieval process (Inman, 1996). It has also been touted and developed as a response for the need to get information out of the traditional transactional databases in a useful and timely manner. A data warehouse can be utilized for storing data from operational systems for efficient and accurate responses to user queries (Bischoff, 1997). A data warehouse makes it easier, on a regular basis, to query and report data from multiple transaction processing systems and/or from external data sources an/or from data that must be stored for query/report purposes only (Berson & Smith, 1996). A data warehouse also provides the data foundation that is very conducive to developing decision support systems (Gray & Watson, 1997), including EIS. Inman (1996) states that "It is in the EIS environment that the data warehouse operates. The data warehouse is tailor-made for the needed EIS analyst. Once the data warehouse has been build, the job of the EIS is infinitely easier" (p 249). (See Berson & Smith, 1996 for a detailed description of data warehousing and OLAP).

DATA WAREHOUSE DEVELOPMENT LIFE CYCLE

Unlike other information systems projects that focus on a specific business issue of specific departments, an enterprise-wide data warehouse project may involve issues relating to the entire organization. It crosses the boundaries between business units and departments. As a result, development and implementation of data warehouse is a massive organizational undertaking. It involves issues ranging from technical to strategic and political. This makes the development and implementation of data warehouse unique to the organization and producing a generic approach to developing a data warehouse nearly impossible. It is said that a company cannot buy a data warehouse, it must construct it. However, as with any large scale IS project development, there are a number of development methodologies that companies can use to construct a data warehouse. In this section we highlight the development methodology used for constructing the data warehouse at the VF. Although this methodology is unique to VF, it however followed the general phases of a typical system development life cycle approach. Using this methodology, the development process proceeds through the *planning and analysis, design, construction, implementation and maintenance and operations* phases.

Planning and Analysis Phase

In 1996, a project known as RFSM (retail floor space management) was formed out of a "Best Practices" survey. Four new initiatives were developed to leverage better VF's core competency of flow replenishment. The initiatives were sales planning, micro-marketing, planogramming (a system that assists in decisions about the retail space and the specifics of store layouts by produces 3-D representations of the store) and the development of an improved replenishment system, a data warehouse.

The key ingredient of this data warehouse would be in its ability to provide information as needed to the end users, or its ability to provide "just-in-time" information for effective decision making. Specifically, a data warehouse implemented at VF must provide the following needed capabilities:

1. The ability to access and process large volumes of data.
2. Consistent, fast query response times.
3. A calculation engine that includes robust mathematical functions for computing derived data based on user-defined queries.
4. Seamless presentation of historical projected and derived data.
5. A multi-user read/write environment to support what-if questions.
6. The ability to be implemented quickly and adopted easily by the end users.
7. Robust data access security and user management.
8. Take over the functions of the executive information system.

In the fall of 1996, initial meetings were held for a feasibility study on the data warehouse project. The scope and objectives of the project were laid out and debated. In January 1997, the project scope document was completed and presented to upper management for review and approval. The scope document proved to be very accurate and was modified little during the project's course. Initial project time projections ran from a low end of six months to over one year. Since the primary thrust of the DW was to augment an already successful EIS system, it was hoped the extra functionality would not take an extended period of time.

The main person who needed to be satisfied with the design was the VP of replenishment services, whose staff would use the data warehouse the most. The important goals to replenishment services were to cover the functionality of the executive decision system, extend across all of JeansWear, be adaptable (scalable) to all coalitions, and allow true OLAP querying capabilities. The DW's primary focus (to the users) was to leverage better the replenishment data for individual stores and major retail chains.

Design Phase

In the design phase, once the development team has been identified, the detailed specifications of the data warehouse are determined. Specifically, in this phase, source data systems are identified; the physical data models are designed; and the design of data extraction, cleaning and transformation processes are mapped out. In addition, the design of end-user applications and their specifications are also determined.

After the project was accepted, the core members of the project team were determined. These were: the manager of the mainframe replenishment systems; the VP of replenishment services; the implementation manager of RFSM; and a relational database expert. Other faces came and went as needed. These included database experts, as well as consultants from IBM (these consultants, however, had minimal input and a negligible effect on the project).

Although much of the purpose of the data warehouse was already defined (i.e., replace and expand the EIS system), the task was not easy. There were many related decisions to be made. One important decision was to construct the database. The database decision was important. Wrangler's main databases had historically been hierarchical rather than relational. There had been for some time, however, a moderate DB2 (IBM's relational engine) presence. A hierarchical base for the DW was never considered. The data warehouse database design team at JeansWear felt its expertise was in the relational area and could obtain the needed functionality for the data warehouse from a relational model. They also felt that they had more experience in maintaining relational models both logically and physically. JeansWear felt that the users would find the relational model easier to use both from the standpoint of the software available, as well as understanding the nature of the data intuitively.

Construction Phase

The main objective of this phase is the technical implementation of the design. Specifically, during this phase, databases are constructed using vendor-specific platforms. The databases are subsequently optimized and populated using the data extraction processes designed earlier. The databases are then fine-tuned through an interactive process that involves the end users. At this phase, the metadata, which is a catalogue of the data stored in the data warehouse is also created.

JeansWear considered several database platforms: Oracle, Cognos, Informix, and others. The eventual winner was Informix, due to JeansWear's existing satisfaction with its current Informix applications. JeansWear considered the conceptual design of the Informix engine to be superior for the long run.

Informix is a fully relational database. It is UNIX-based and has several OLAP tools that can be used with it. It is a major player in the client/server relational database field, so the JeansWear decision really came from picking the best of the biggest. Vendors without a critical market share (VF JeansWear defined) were not considered.

The OLAP software was selected at this time, also. Again, there were several contenders. The decision was made to obtain BRIO Technology's BrioSuite software. This software was considered to give all the functionality of the other tools, but BRIO's main draw was its ease of use. At this time (Winter 1996-97), BRIO's software was noticeably easier to pick up and use. The learning curve was small. This was important to the users. It was thought that the use of BRIO would be broad based by nontechnical users, hence short learning times were desirable to get in and out fast. This data warehouse has become an essential tool to support the complex replenishment system in place at VF JeansWear today.

Implementation Phase

The main activities performed in this phase are testing and evaluation of the accuracy, robustness and reliability of the system output, end-user training and finally the rollout. In late winter 1996-97, the project was up in earnest. The database design was developed, hardware and software requirements detailed, and human resources for current and future phases allocated. Initial database servers were purchased, along with the Informix and BRIO software.

Since the users had been heavily involved with the construction of the data requirements, user training involved a review of the information available and its updating cycles. Users attended BRIO classes as well as getting instruction on SQL. The pieces were then in place to roll out the first application.

In early fall of 1998, the Wal-Mart data repository was placed into use. Wal-Mart is JeansWear's largest customer. Wal-Mart provides inventory and sales information in a very timely manner and is very stringent in its replenishment information and store design feedback. From the Wal-Mart implementation, other vendors have been added, most notably K-Mart, Sears, and other large retail outlets.

Physically, the data warehouse resides on two HP servers, with data approaching 1 terrabyte. The system runs in a UNIX environment. Storage space is always at a premium and the servers are in a constant state of need assessment and upgrading.

Operation and Maintenance Phase

The maintenance and operation phase involves managing the day-to-day operation of the data warehouse environment as well as planning for the future growth and evolution of the system.

Three people support the hardware/operating system software of the data warehouse. There are two Informix DBAs and the manager of the group. This group is responsible for design changes and ensuring that the data warehouse is loaded correctly and is available for users. A major update is performed every weekend, with other updates during the week. The information stored in the data warehouse is in conjunction with IBM's Inforem software to run the replenishment model. The data warehouse stores information from the replenishment model for analysis. After the model makes its recommendations, these plans are approved or modified, then goods are reordered.

In the user area, there are two data specialists. Their job is to create queriable tables for the users and to write specialized queries. They also assist in keeping the data warehouse functioning. This position requires substantial knowledge of the business and also technical expertise scales in understanding data structure and SQL.

The number and expertise of the users varies. JeansWear has product/brand managers, who in turn have staff. These individuals are the primary target audience for the warehouse. There are many brands within JeansWear, meaning the user community ranges from 20 upwards, but the information from the warehouse permeates through the company. Some users are more sophisticated than others in the use of the warehousing tool. Some are able to write their own queries and/or suggest new tables and data fields. Others strictly request queries to be written for them.

DEVELOPMENT CHALLENGES

This data warehouse project was a first for VF and most of the participants were treading in unknown waters. There is a price to pay for this. In this case, there were the aforementioned design changes, plus an underestimation of the resources (in time and personnel) required. JeansWear had limited experience in data warehousing, but was not comfortable with a consultant running the project, the data warehouse developed slowly. The project spanned multiple business units, also, adding another layer of complexity. This further slowed the progress. However, in this section, we will describe three major challenges that the development team faced.

Database Design Challenges

The first major challenge that the development team had to face was the design of the database. This database design should transform the legacy data resources into data warehouse structure. Given the decision support nature of the data warehouse, Kimball (1996) states that the Dimensional Modeling (DM) approach is the best way to design the databases. Kimball argues that the dimensional modeling offers the following advantages: (1) the dimensional model is predictable and standard. That is, the access of the data can be made using "strong assumptions" about the database, making access faster than using the cost-based optimizers of an E-R query; (2) since all dimension tables are equivalent, the query entry point to the fact table can be accomplished at any point; and (3) a dimensional model is "gracefully extensible". Kimball (1996) uses the term "gracefully extensible" to say that a dimensional modeling database has three characteristics: (1) existing fact and dimension tables can be changed by adding new data rows or via an SQL alter commands, (2) query and reporting tools do not have to be changed after such a change, and (3) old queries or reports will yield the same results after a change. See Kimball (1996) for an excellent description of the Dimensional Modeling Technique for developing a data warehouse. However, JeansWear had a limited experience with this design methodology. Their expertise was in relational modeling. Ultimately, JeansWear built the data warehouse upon the concepts of the Dimensional Model using relational tables.

The data warehouse is split into three databases: (1) large retailers, (2) small retailers, and (3) other or mass sales. The databases themselves are divided into sections referred to within VF as repositories. Each repository is assigned to a particular retailer. There are several tables for each repository. Table structures are common across repositories with important exceptions, but repositories do not share tables. Each repository is unique. This is important for the users. They can sign into a particular retailer and build or use the same queries to mine the database without worrying about separating one retailer's data from another. Separate repositories also make security easier to enforce.

The tables are relational and represent the fact/dimension organization of a dimensional modeling (DM) approach to data warehouse design (Kimball, 1996; 1997). This technique attempts to model the business process more closely by creating dimensional tables for business tasks, rather than creating relational data models (as the E-R technique suggests). Dimensional tables are tied to fact tables, which contain the majority of the data for inquiries. Dimensional tables are joined to dimensional table/fact table combinations in star joins, allowing the user to access data both faster and in a more business process logical way. Facts reside in separate tables, usually, with dimensions related accordingly. This allows users of the data warehouse to analyze the data in a dimensional manner, referring to the table elements as facts and dimensions, yet keep the advantages of the relational model. The VF replenishment warehouse contains information across many dimensions. Some of the dimensions are time, product, brand, and volume. Each dimension allows VF to further differentiate sales. A given data repository can be examined in many dimensions, singularly or in interaction.

Data Extraction, Cleaning and Transformation Challenges

The biggest challenge facing the data warehouse planing and development team was data extracting, cleansing and transforming. Inman (1996) estimates that in most data warehouse development projects, data extraction, transformation process can use up to 80% of the resources allocated to the entire project. Even quality data must be cleaned or scrubbed before use.

Even though the team pulled the data from JeansWear master files that had been in use for years, data integrity was always verified going back several years. To populate the warehouse, the data was obtained by extracting and transforming sequential files from the operational systems, creating sequential files to be loaded into the DW Informix database. The operational systems were a combination of online and batch programs that manage the daily business activity. Data captured via EDI was input into a legacy mainframe replenishment system. This data is passed to the data warehouse via download updates. Data was stored in both hierarchical and relational databases. These databases were processed nightly in the batch systems and sequential files were created reflecting the daily business activity. It is these sequential files that stored the sales, replenishment, inventory, orders, shipments, customer, and product information that were transformed into the files that refresh the warehouse.

The transformation process takes these files and creates both add and revision records, depending on the activity, for the DW. If a new sale comes in, a new fact is added. If a sales return occurred, the sales and inventory data must be revised.

The initial loads were complex and slow because all applicable sales history had to be processed into a suitable format. This required months of creating files from archived data. Overall, the process of extraction, transformation, and verification was time-consuming, but successful. A verification system was designed to cross-check the data warehouse and operational data.

After the mainframe processing is complete, the files (both dimension and fact) were sent to the RS/6000 via FTP. At this point, a database backup was performed, dimension data and fact tables refreshed, indexes were built, and the database restarted.

The period from January 1997 to late summer 1998 was spent mostly in data scrubbing and reanalysis. The database evolved through many iterative steps. Information needs changed and new fields were added. Although few information needs are fully accounted for at the beginning of an IS project, this database was more dynamic than usual.

Management and Strategic Challenges

Another major challenge facing the development team was not of a technical nature rather it was managerial. The problem was that the RFSM (retail floor space management) team was depending on the data warehouse as their source of information. Because many pieces of RFSM project were under development at the same time as the DW, many of the RFSM requirements were not identified until after development was underway. The impact of both of these problems was not understood before construction began.

The RFSM project required accurate and in-depth information concerning sales. The bulk of the needed information was in the legacy mainframe replenishment systems that fed the current EIS and would eventually feed the data warehouse. The current EIS could not supply the RFSM team with sales information the many different ways the team needed.

The other parts of the RFSM project requested other data fields and queries in addition to the original specifications. The database design of the warehouse became a constant moving target. The RFSM and the data warehouse teams added (and continue to add) new information to the DW.

Because of the growing importance of the DW, the quality of the data was constantly scrutinized. Information from the legacy system and the legacy system feeds was verified against the DW throughout the process. All numbers were challenged, especially the new fields created for the warehouse. The testing of numbers followed throughout development and was subject to a final systems check before production.

As stated before, the data warehouse was part of the retail floor space management project. Also, the folding in of Wrangler and Lee into VF JeansWear was a major undertaking. The management of the data warehouse required a variation from the normal IS project management standard.

The project was a success because of the great knowledge and experience of the IS staff and the project team concerning the business process. This meant that the design and project hold-ups in constructions were due to the unfamiliarity with data warehousing and not because of a poor business objective. This is significant and a discerning factor in why many data warehouse projects have failed.

This expertise allowed VF to run this project outside the normal project development paradigm. Normally, a central analyst would coordinate all activities from inception to implementation and probably beyond. For this project, different managers ran a portion of the project, usually when the project touched on their expertise or their IS group. The user presence was at a very high level, a director of brands at JeansWear. The committee which oversaw the project evolved as the project evolved.

ORGANIZATIONAL BENEFITS OF THE DATA WAREHOUSE PROJECT

The POS/replenishment data warehouse has had a significant effect on the JeansWear division at VF. It aids in the restocking of retailers' floor space with VF goods. In addition, it allows up-to-the-minute analysis of the movement of goods. The plans are to make its structure the basis of a company-wide data warehouse with POS/replenishment data. This EIS/data warehouse combination has been very profitable and strategically important to VF. It has slowed any erosion from designer and store brands and helped VF increase market share in the jeans business.

The POS/replenishment system, with its associated data warehouse, strengthens the relationship between VF JeansWear and its retailers. As VF better predicts demand needs for its products, its replenishment takes on a just-in-time look. Lead times for products were shortened, inventory levels (both for VF and the retailer) dropped, merchandise stocked out less, and the retail space used by VF was redesigned to best meet the customers' buying habits. This arrangement is beneficial to VF and its retailers.

Communication between VF and retailers has improved. Since both VF and the retailers had a large stake in the success of VF's replenishment plans, each provided and received information about sales. Some retailers made data collection changes (such as discerning whether goods were bought in a department or at a general, up-front check-out), so that VF could track sales with greater accuracy.

The improved communication is bidirectional. Smaller retailers provided information in the detail they were capable. The information shared with smaller retailers helps them develop their VF product section and similar goods. Large retailers, such as Wal-Mart, accumulate very detailed information in their own systems and pass it back to VF. VF uses this data both to predict demand, research requested demand, and verify current data.

Although there has always been some form of model stock analysis at Wrangler, the EIS and data warehouse input can be traced to around 1990. In 1990, Lee and Wrangler Jeans accounted for 18% of total jeans sales (Collett, 1999). By 1998, that figure had risen to 25%, in a $10 billion-per-year jeans market.

Analysts have pointed to VF's ability to micro-market its goods as the major reason that it has gained market share at a time when Levi's, its closest analogous rival, was losing ground to designer brands and private label brands (Collett, 1999). It is possible that Wrangler and Lee would have lost ground as Levi did without the Model Stock program. This is speculation, but not without a rational basis. Collett (1999) assumes that half of the increased market share has been due to VF's market-leading replenishment abilities.

An estimation of added profit attributable to the DW in 1998: the difference between an 18% market share and a 25% market share is 7%. Assigning half of this gain to the DW yields about 4%. This would yield $400M extra in sales, or approximately one-seventh of JeansWear sales. The VF corporate gross margin is 33%; here a conservative 25% is assumed. This means about $100 million in 1998 alone that might be attributed to the POS/replenishment program's success.[1]

Brand managers and their staff can mine the data warehouse, also, in ways that heretofore were not possible. Management reports that were not available before or not as accurate are available through the warehouse and BRIO's OLAP tools.

Additional benefits have been many. The most notable benefit is the closer manufacturer/retailer relationship between VF and its retailers. At some retailers, VF does its own retail space management. The retailer does not order from VF in the traditional way, VF tells the retailer what it will put on its floor and how, within certain mutually agreed upon constraints. This saves the retailer time and money, while maximizing sales: a win-win scenario.

There are many examples of the positive effect that this data warehouse has had on the overall operation of VF. The POS/replenishment data warehouse has completely replaced its predecessor, improved the replenishment function at

JeansWear and gives management a tool to recognize special business opportunities which they were not able to do before. The warehouse is still evolving and will continue to do so for quite some time, continuing to change and augment the way VF does business.

LESSONS LEARNED FROM THE DEVELOPMENT OF DATA WAREHOUSE

With the rapid advances in technology, companies have become very good at capturing huge amounts of data in their various transactional processing systems. Unfortunately, this has created a problem with how to get useful information out of these systems in an efficient and timely manner. Data warehousing is a new technology that addresses this problem. However, creating a data warehouse is not an easy task. A data warehouse implementation is extremely complex and takes a considerable about of time and resources to implement. Many data warehouse projects fail for one or more various reasons. A data warehouse is more of an environment than a product. Therefore the question "what are the key ingredients to creating the perfect data warehouse for the organization?" is a relative one. Different organizations have different needs, as well as internal talent and existing infrastructures (knowledge, hardware and other intangibles). There exists no blueprint for a guaranteed successful implementation.

What are the critical factors for a successful implementation? There is no set formula or a process that can be put in place to attempt to set up a moderate list of questions that can be asked. A successful data warehouse implementation requires complete and correct answers to the following questions:

1. What is the Business Case for Developing a Data Warehouse?

What appears to be on the surface a very easy question is the most important one. It is hard to get somewhere until the somewhere is decided. Answering this question leads to what the focus should be. What are possible goals? And what are the user expectations from the data warehouse project? There may be a specific business problem to be solved using a data warehouse. Since such problems are often not enterprise-wide, the corporate answer may be to implement a data warehouse instead of a complete data warehouse. This will have many effects, the most notable one being the scale of the project. Smaller companies or those companies who wish to employ logical incrementalism to their business practices tend to favor this approach.

With VF, the objectives were clear: the replacement of the EIS that supported the POS/replenishment function while adding OLAP capabilities. The difficult work of focus had, in effect, been decided a decade early with the first EIS system. The details of the business requirements may not be known. A data warehouse may show business opportunities missed before. Here follows the second question. Once the focus of the warehouse has been determined, the resources must be evaluated, both tangible and intangible.

2. Does an In-House Expertise in Data Warehousing Exist?

For companies contemplating developing a data warehouse, this may not an easy question to answer, but it is imperative that the in-house expertise be carefully assessed. The development and maintenance of a data warehouse project is enterprise dependent. Hence, there is no one-solution-fits-all approach to developing a data warehouse. It can be said that developing a data warehouse is an art and not a science. Since the art of data warehousing assumes that there must be artists to complete the project, then a company must evaluate its internal resources toward this end.

The importance of the artist cannot be overstated. As in any art, it is the artists themselves that make or break such a project. The most important elements in a warehouse project are the principals assigned to the project, the level of their business knowledge, the meaning of the goals decided upon, and the technical expertise of the individuals. All good projects are evolving entities, so individuals that can recognize problems or opportunities and adjust accordingly are invaluable to data warehousing implementations.

There are two considerations in choosing the major project participants. First, does the system have executive and user support? To achieve this, a cross-functional team from the user population should be assembled to participate in the development process. It is crucial that the users from business areas are on board from the start of the project. Secondly, the level of competence of the users should be assessed. How well do they understand the business area(s) they support? Do they see the big picture? Do they have any understanding of what a data warehouse may or may not be able to do? Are they literate about technology? This will determine the depth and the eventual successful use of the warehouse.

Another important consideration here is the IS group's expertise in the data warehouse development should be accurately assessed. Does the IS group have the technical knowledge to pull this off? Do they understand the business well enough to be conversant with the users? Can enough resources be allocated to the project to make it successful?

These are some of the questions that must be answered before going forward. This will determine the depth and the quality of the information that can be obtained from the warehouse. If the in-house IS group lacks the necessary experience in developing a data warehouse, the use of outside consultants should be considered. Consultants are best used to offer temporary guidance in a project or perform highly specialized, usually one-time tasks, for a project. However, an outside consultant should not be put in charge of the entire project without consultation with the IS group.

One of the essential ingredients for VF's success in their data warehouse project was the quality of the staff that participated in it. Their knowledge of the current EIS, the goals of the data warehouse, and their understanding of the business process overcame the usual problems in data warehouse construction. The strength of the data warehouse implementation at VF was the knowledge of all parties concerned. The management experience and expertise in both information technology and the user area was substantial. This in-depth knowledge kept the project on track and solved problems that have doomed other DW projects. The excellent working relationship between users and IT staff kept communication lines open and progress steady. This allowed VF to implement a successful DW without a substantial amount of outside resources.

3. What are the Data Considerations in Populating the Data Warehouse?

Data extraction, transformation for a data warehouse is a tedious and time-consuming part of the entire project. In the case of VF, databases were not designed originally to support data warehouses, therefore the data that can be provided is rarely in a usable form. Sales history may not show the continuity of brands where such brands were replaced, for example. Either, but preferably both, the user or the IS staff must understand all these connections.

Again, VF had a substantial advantage. They had been gathering and storing data for the POS EIS for years. Although cleaning and transforming the data for the DW model was a substantial task, the building blocks were available. VF did not need to begin storing data once it had identified which data it wanted, the data was already available.

With these questions answered, the project is ready to begin. From this point, data warehouse projects have the usual stages of information gathering, data/project design, project construction and implementation. The most unique part of a data warehouse construction is the design and loading of the database. We have discussed the design — the loading, however, is another matter. Obviously, if the legacy data has a relational structure, then the move to a relational-based DW will be easier. If not, the cleansing of the legacy data will be a major undertaking. A good amount of time must be allotted for this task.

This area was the major task of the VF data warehouse construction. Almost all of the data that would feed the warehouse was in flat files or relational databases. VF underestimated the amount of time needed because it is impossible to judge the time needed adequately. Too many variables exist for data warehouse construction to lend itself to the traditional methods of project estimation.

Below is a list of the factors that led to the successful development of the data warehouse at VF:

1. Established a solid business case for developing a data warehouse.
2. Secured executive and user support for the data warehouse.
3. Assembled a cross functional team from the user and IS population.
4. Designed the system as an integrated part of the corporate strategy.
5. Developed a project plan and determined the areas of expertise required to achieve the goals of the project.
6. Researched hardware and software solutions and tools carefully.
7. Managed and monitored the data warehouse continuously.

CURRENT CHALLENGES/PROBLEMS FACING THE ORGANIZATION

The single most important key to surviving and prospering in an increasingly competitive world in the 1990s and beyond is the ability to analyze, plan and react to ever-changing business conditions in a much more rapid fashion. To do this, managers need more and better information. At VF, the data warehouse has become an integral part of this. It also provides an infrastructure that enables managers to complete ad-hoc analysis that would have been impossible to do with the EIS system. However, although the rewards can be substantial, the hard and fast rules of successful data warehousing are minimal. Here is the paradox of data warehousing: a data warehouse can be critical to the identification of problem business areas and the discovery of new business opportunities, yet the warehouse design and construction is often a discover-as-you-go process. This lack of hard rules makes successful data warehouse projects a riskier proposition than the usual IS project. It should be undertaken with great care.

The data warehouse has continued to evolve. Monthly meetings continue on the status and plans for the warehouse, user data needs and data integrity. The warehouse has been a victim of its own success in that users are asking for more data fields and more input into the presentation of the data (usually through SQL views).

The data warehouse is constantly expanding. New fields are added. Sales generate more transactions that must be stored and analyzed. SKUs change. The management of the data as a whole and storage of that data is an ongoing project. New queries are added regularly. As POS data and new fields are added, new ways of looking at information arise. Analysts are developing these new queries. More retailers are added with regularity to the data warehouse. The major retailers were implemented first. Each retailer is unique. Most queries can be used for all retailers; however, analysts also look for different ways to look at each individual retailer.

Due to the success of the warehouse, VF is looking to expand the warehouse concept across all coalitions and to expand its use within JeansWear. Currently, VF is moving to enterprise resource planning (ERP) systems using SAP. This integration of data may eventually aid the cross-development of other data warehouses. The replenishment data warehouse will continue to be a vital part of the overall retail floor space management project. The DW is an evolving project, changing to meet the needs of a developing retail market. Resources will be needed to maintain and enhance the databases and provide new queries.

The database was designed with scalability in mind and should be able to reach across divisional lines should VF desire. This would allow VF to leverage its superior replenishment technology, via the DW and other initiatives, throughout all distribution channels. These synergies are part of an overall corporate strategy.

In the late 1990s, VF undertook an ambitious enterprise resource planning (ERP) project using SAP software. VF has invested heavily in leading edge systems to support the growth they envision and, at the same time, reduce costs. The move to common systems across the organization will allow the coalitions to work together more closely and share information more efficiently.

The SAP project is the largest single software project VF has ever attempted. It requires a very large amount of resources. Other software projects must compete for limited resources, as in any corporation. This is a challenge to future growth of the warehouse. Also, the eventual implementation of the ERP software presents the challenge of integration where it is possible and productive

REFERENCES

Berson, A., & Smith, S. (1997). *Data warehouse, data mining, & OLAP*. New York: McGraw-Hill.

Bischoff, J., & Alexander, T. (1997). *Data warehouse practical advice from the experts*. NJ: Prentice Hall.

Collett, S. (1999) Levi shuts plants, misses trends. *ComputerWorld*, *33*(9), 16.

Eric, T. (1997). *OLAP solutions: Building multidimensional information systems*. New York: Wiley & Sons.

Gray, P., & Watson, H.(1998). *Decision support in the data warehouse*. NJ: Prentice Hall.

Inman, W. H. (1996). *Building the data warehouse*. New York: Wiley & Sons.

Kimball, R. (1996). *The data warehouse toolkit*. New York: Wiley & Sons.

Kimball, R. (1997, August). A dimensional modeling manifesto. *DBMS Magazine*.

ENDNOTE

[1] These figures are only estimates of the authors and reflect no VF internal studies or opinions. Many factors have contributed to VF's jeans apparel success outside of the replenishment system. This paper has only tried to quantify in some rational fashion the financial impact of the system. The authors have not been privy to any VF financial information beyond VF annual reports.

Hamid Nemati is an assistant professor of information systems at Bryan School of Business and Economics, University of North Carolina at Greensboro. He has also served on the Faculty of the College of Business Administration, Georgia State University. He received his doctorate degree from the University of Georgia. He also holds a BS in physics and an MBA from the University of Massachusetts. He has extensive professional experience as an analyst and has consulted with a number of major corporations. His current research and publications are in the areas of decision support systems, data warehousing, data mining, and knowledge management.

Keith Smith is a senior systems analyst for VF Corporation in Greensboro, North Carolina. He has 17 years of experience in information technology. He has worked for Wachovia, Sara Lee, and VF. He holds a Bachelor of Science in mathematics from Wake Forest University, a Bachelor of Business Science in accounting from Guilford College, and a Masters in Business Administration from the University of North Carolina at Greensboro. He is currently enrolled in the Master's in Information Technology and Management program at UNCG.

This case was previously published in the *Annals of Cases on Information Technology Applications and Management in Organizations*, Volume 2/2000, pp. 148-168, © 2000.

Chapter III

The Algos Center: Information Systems in a Small Non-Profit Organization

Susan J. Chinn, University of Southern Maine, USA

Charlotte A. Pryor, University of Southern Maine, USA

John J. Voyer, University of Southern Maine, USA

EXECUTIVE SUMMARY

Two systems faculty from a university was contracted to perform an analysis of information systems at the Algos Center, a small non-profit charitable organization which provides support for children and their families facing losses. The Center specifically requested help in integrating its fundraising and accounting software packages or exploring alternative software solutions. It also needed to generate reports required by the board of directors and United Way. Finally, the Center requested help in designing a family database to capture and track statistics about the families receiving services. As the team analyzed the Center, they discovered many underlying issues that would form part of their recommendations to the staff. This case makes two contributions. First, it reveals many problems facing small non-profit organizations, which primarily expend their resources on mission-critical activities, and allows readers to supply possible courses of action. Second, it provides an opportunity to evaluate how a consulting experience was handled and to make recommendations to ensure successful project implementation.

ORGANIZATIONAL BACKGROUND

The Algos Center is a non-profit organization based on the east coast. (Because we are using a pseudonym to describe the organization, the Web site address cannot be revealed). It was founded in the 1990s by an individual who helped a young relative deal with her aunt's death; he saw a need for a Center that would help and support grieving children. The Center's mission is just that: to aid grieving children, teens, and their families through outreach, education, and peer support. The model for this organization is the Dougy Center, which was the first center in the United States to provide peer-based bereavement support groups for grieving children (Chappell, 2001; http://www.dougy.org/about.html).

In support of the mission, the Center sponsors many program activities, but bereavement peer support is the primary service provided (Rubin & Witztum, 2000; Stroebe, Strobebe, & Hansson, 2002). Approximately 170 children, teens, and adults attend these support groups every week. Trained volunteers conduct the groups. The volunteers seek to provide a safe environment for participants to express their feelings; they do not attempt to be counselors or therapists. A professional consultant or staff member also attends these meetings. All participants are welcome, even if they cannot afford the suggested monthly pledge donation. Groups are divided into age categories: 3 to 5, 6 to 8, 7 to 12, teens, and young adults (up to age 30). Adult family members participate in support groups as well.

A related program, the Life Care Program (LCP), offers support groups for children and teens dealing with family members facing terminal or life-threatening illnesses. This program was started in the mid-1990s in collaboration with several hospices, hospitals, and nursing and cancer associations. While the bereavement peer support program is ongoing, LCP is offered in six-week sessions.

Two other major programs are offered. The Diversity Peer Support Program provides peer support in association with Kennedy Elementary School, which has a very diverse student body. Many of the students come from war-torn backgrounds and have lost family members. The second program, Community Extensions, is aimed at helping schoolchildren who are faced with a loss, and at assisting adult organizations and businesses dealing with grief issues. Other Center services include presentations to organizations by trained volunteers, and sponsorship of an annual bereavement conference. In addition, the Center offers referrals to mental health professionals, gives telephone support, and sends brochures and other written materials to callers.

The Center is governed by a 25-member volunteer board of directors. The executive director, appointed by the board, manages three full-time staff, six part-time staff members, and five unpaid interns who are university students. More than 100 volunteers assist with the events and support groups. Because there are so few full- and part-time staff, the organizational structure is very flat and informal; most of the staff has direct access to the executive director (see Appendix A for the organization chart). The Center is a public, non-profit charity (a 501 (c) (3) organization) that relies on contributions from individuals, grants from foundations, and United Way allocations, as well as corporate sponsorships and special fundraising events, to support its operating budget. The Center sponsors many activities throughout the year including a pet walk, fun run, golf tournament, and a gala event featuring dinner and an auction. Appendix B shows its statement of income, expenses and changes in net assets for its most recent fiscal year.

Non-profit organizations such as this Center rely to a large extent on individual donations; successful fundraising necessitates tracking the funds that are received from each donor (Klein, 2004). Information is also needed to evaluate the effectiveness of each fundraising event. Non-profits often use specialized fundraising software for this purpose (Davis, 2002). In addition, the organization's accounting software must be set up so that donated funds or grants that are restricted in purpose can be carefully monitored to ensure that the funds are used only for their designated intentions (Gross, Larkin, & McCarthy, 2003). The board of directors typically wants expense information organized in the same way as the budget is prepared, generally by expense category such as salaries and rent, to ensure that the organization's expenses do not exceed the board's authorizations (Trussel, Greenlee, Brady, Colson, Goldband, & Morris, 2002). In addition, funding organizations such as United Way and government agencies, such as the IRS, require that expenses be reported by program type. Many non-profits thus have greater record-keeping requirements than do for-profit enterprises of comparable size (Cutt, Bragg, Balfour, Murray, & Tassey, 1996).

SETTING THE STAGE

Janet Tucker and Caryn Powell, two professors at a local university, both had a strong interest in non-profit organizations. Dr. Tucker was a professor of MIS with an emphasis in systems analysis, while Dr. Powell was an accounting professor with an emphasis in accounting information systems. They put out a general offer to conduct an information system needs assessment for any local non-profit organization in support of the university's mission of community involvement. The assessment could include problem or opportunity identification, project selection, a feasibility study, identification of project risks, and development of recommended courses of action (Block, 2000; Coates, 1997).

The Algos Center responded quickly to the solicitation, and, after a brief phone call with the executive director, a preliminary meeting was scheduled with the key organization members: Elizabeth Medford, Executive Director; Vicki Hume, Development Director; and Dawn Lopez, Operations Manager. Tucker and Powell put together an outline for their first meeting. They wanted to get a sense of what information systems issues the Center was facing, and to set the goals and boundaries for what they were offering to do. They wanted to clarify that they were not proposing to design and implement any new information systems, but rather to evaluate how information was being collected, stored, and reported, and to develop recommendations to improve the systems (Burt & Taylor, 2000). They wanted to set up a schedule to collect data and they also wanted to make sure that the board of directors would approve of their involvement (Cornforth, 2003).

At the initial meeting, Elizabeth Medford, Vicki Hume, and Dawn Lopez explained some of the major issues they had been having with their information systems. The first issue concerned the software they were using for fundraising, Paradigm (http://www.mip.com/software/fundraising/paradigm.htm), and their accounting software, QuickBooks (http://quickbooks.intuit.com/). Vicki said she was having a hard time getting the reports she needed out of Paradigm. Both Vicki and Elizabeth acknowledged that there were inconsistencies in how data (notably expense codes) were being entered in each program. Dawn believed that they were not taking full advantage of Paradigm's features. They liked QuickBooks, but they wanted to see if there were features in it that they could be using better, or if there was a way for the two packages to work together. This is a concern that many non-profits have when they attempt to use off-the-shelf software (Jones, 2000). Dawn noted that they were currently entering duplicate data in both systems.

The second issue concerned reports that the Center was obligated to produce for the board of directors and United Way. As is true of many non-profits, the Center received revenue not only from hundreds of individual and corporate donations, but also from various funding sources, such as United Way. These fund providers need detailed information about how the money is spent (Bradley, Jansen, & Silverman, 2003). Non-profits also require accurate financial and program data in order to plan for future growth — an especially critical need for organizations like the Center with limited technological expertise (Smith, 2002).

The third issue involved a database project that Dawn was starting. She wanted to design a family database that would allow the Center to track bereavement meetings and to generate statistics. The database would be useful to the Center, and it would also facilitate reporting to United Way. For example, United Way required demographic data that the Center staff had had trouble compiling other than manually (Cutt et al., 1996).

Elizabeth indicated that the Center was growing, and there was a need to prepare for the growth they were expecting. Tucker and Powell were offering their services pro bono, but they did ask Elizabeth if they should be mindful of any financial constraints when developing recommendations for purchasing software or equipment. Elizabeth said not to worry about it. Elizabeth also asked for confidentiality when viewing any information about their clients. However, she and the rest of the staff agreed to be very open about sharing documents and other agency information with the university team.

After their meeting, Tucker and Powell immediately drafted a letter to Elizabeth, which in essence was the consulting contract (Block, 2000). The agreement was to review their software, reports, and database design, and to evaluate alternative approaches to the integration and growth issues that had been discussed. The letter stated that the Center's current environment would be assessed through interviews, document collection and review, and an analysis of their computer systems. The project, starting in July, was to terminate in the fall with a formal report of recommendations.

CASE DESCRIPTION

Gathering Fundraising and Accounting Software Requirements

Tucker and Powell decided to meet first with Dawn Lopez, operations manager, to get an overview of how Paradigm (the fundraising software) and QuickBooks (the accounting software) were being used. Dawn was glad to show the team what she did. The team immediately got the impression that Dawn, as an information technology manager, worked hard to keep the Center's operations running, even though she worked part-time while pursuing a degree at a two-year technical school. Administrative Assistant Alicia Austin recorded donations in Paradigm, and then, Dawn recorded the donated amounts in QuickBooks. Dawn stated that she believed Paradigm could be used to record information about the volunteers that the Center wanted but was not currently collecting. She also showed the team how she produced reports in QuickBooks.

Dawn provided the team with a document describing deposit and data entry procedures. The team noticed that the names used for the same donation types entered in Paradigm and in QuickBooks were not consistent. For example, QuickBooks used "publications" and Paradigm used "booklets" to describe the same thing. The team observed Dawn as she demonstrated how deposits were entered into QuickBooks. At month's end, she manually compared the deposit report generated in QuickBooks with the list of donations entered in a Paradigm report. They usually did not match, and Dawn had to discover where the discrepancies were. In the case of one particular discrepancy, it was not easy for her to show the team how she had resolved it; she had simply attached a sticky note to a printed report saying that the discrepancy had been resolved. It seemed to the team that there was much less duplication of data in the fundraising and accounting programs than had originally appeared to be the case. The total dollar amount of a group of donations deposited at one time was entered as a single transaction in QuickBooks; the individual donations and data relating to each donor were recorded only in Paradigm. In another instance, the team observed Dawn entering a contribution that was designated to cover expenses as a negative expense, instead of as contribution revenue that would offset the relevant expense. Dawn admitted that although she was responsible for entering data into QuickBooks, she had no formal training in accounting. This is a common problem for non-profits with limited staff; they may not have been trained to enter data properly (Barrett & Greene, 2001). The team and Dawn also discovered that Paradigm only supported exporting data to a limited number of programs such as dBase, old versions of Excel, and a comma delimited ASCII format. There were no export options to QuickBooks. Dawn had not been successful trying to export data.

After meeting with Dawn, Tucker and Powell believed that meetings with both Vicki Hume and Elizabeth Medford were needed. They wanted to know how Vicki was using Paradigm, what reports she was producing, and what information she needed that she was not able to produce. From Elizabeth, they wanted to learn more about United Way reporting needs.

The team met with Vicki Hume and inquired about the donation category and expense code discrepancies between QuickBooks and Paradigm. Vicki replied that the staff had simply not gotten together to standardize the codes, and furthermore, that some codes were "deliberately" entered differently in the two software packages. She said she would prefer a solution where the Center could use QuickBooks for all their work, but she realized that fundraising software would be needed to handle event tracking, a feature usually absent from a general purpose software application.

As development director, Vicki was a heavy user of Paradigm. She generated two important reports: one segmented donors into categories to use in generating mailing lists; the other was an analysis of contributions, which she used to track the progress of fundraising campaigns and to analyze donation trends (see Appendix C for a sample report). In order to produce reports, it was necessary to generate queries; some reports also required subqueries. For many reports, Vicki kept getting an error message that the subquery could not return more than one row. The team asked Vicki to keep track of specific querying problems over the next few weeks. Vicki agreed with Dawn that there were many functions in Paradigm that were not being used, and that it was hard to figure out which fields would print out. She also had to resort to calculating many aggregate functions (e.g., counts, averages) manually. When the team asked if she consulted the user's manual to help solve some of these problems, she remarked that the user's manual was missing. Concerning vendor support, Vicki said she believed they paid a flat rate for a specific number of calls per year, and to ask Dawn for details.

During a subsequent meeting with Dawn, Vicki presented the team with a Paradigm query she had tried to run without success. Vicki also said that she wanted an audit trail of who made each update to the data in Paradigm to see who might be to "blame" for poor data entry. Later, back at the university, the team re-ran the query using test data on their office computer and found that it worked perfectly. During their next visit, they examined some of Paradigm's features with Dawn and found an error log tool. The error log displayed error codes and SQL statements that appeared to fail because of data entry problems (e.g., attempts to put two values into a single-valued field). Dawn learned that she could contact the vendor to acquire SQL scripts that could be run to "kick out" problem data. Dawn had never previously looked at the error log.

Tucker and Powell asked Dawn for more information about Paradigm documentation and user training. First, the team inquired about the missing Paradigm manual; Dawn said it was available, and that Vicki would often say that something was missing when, in fact, it was not. Dawn loaned the manual to the team and the CD-ROM updates. The CD had updated pages that were supposed to be printed out and inserted into the manual, but although the pages had been printed out, Dawn lacked the time to insert the pages. It was later discovered that the CD actually had the complete manual on it, but that several computers (including Vicki's) lacked CD-ROM drives. The team then asked about the Paradigm training Dawn had received. Training is often a major component in successful technology adoption, but can often be a shortchanged component in a resource-constrained non-profit organization (Barrett & Greene, 2001; Hecht & Ramsey, 2002; Light, 2002). Staff personnel need to be cross-trained in the event that one staff member should leave. The staff also needs ongoing training to take advantage of upgrades in software, hardware, networking, etc. (Smith, Bucklin & Associates, Inc., 2000). Both Dawn and Alicia had taken a training course. The training emphasized building queries that served as the basis for generating reports. Dawn told the team that she could call the vendor for unlimited support and that all of the updates came bundled with the support contract.

Center Reporting Requirements

Elizabeth discussed reports requested by the board of directors with the team. To produce one of the reports required by the board, the treasurer had to export information from two QuickBooks reports into an Excel spreadsheet; from there, he had to manually prepare the report in the desired format. Elizabeth hoped it would be possible to produce this report more easily, saving the treasurer much effort. Elizabeth also explained that the board needed to have monthly reports that listed expenses by functional classification (e.g., for salaries, rent, depreciation, and utilities) in the same format in which the budget was prepared (see Appendix D for a sample report). This format would improve the directors' ability to compare expenses with budget authorizations. United Way required not only expenses by functional classification, but also wanted management expenses to be distinguished from program expenses (see Appendix E for a sample United Way report). The Center wanted to set up the accounts in QuickBooks so that the data could be retrieved more easily by both functional classification and program. In addition, Elizabeth explained that increasing reliance on grants meant that in the near future, the Center would need to start tracking the use of restricted purpose funds across fiscal years. There was no one on the staff who knew how to do this in QuickBooks.

The Family Database Project

Elizabeth explained that the Center needed a database because United Way required a lot of demographic information about the Center's clients, such as age, ethnicity, etc. She provided the team with the Center's intake form that clients fill out and a copy of the United Way's information requirements. Elizabeth said there were two important reports that would be "nice to have." First, she wanted a report that provided the reasons why families sought out the Center; this report would enable the staff to analyze who did or did not use the Center and why. The second was a report that would show the growth in demand for services over the years. Dawn provided the team with a description of the types of information they wanted from the database. Some of the desired information would require data the Center did not currently collect. She also provided a copy of her plan to set up the database in Microsoft Access (http://www.microsoft.com) including a list of tables and attributes (see Appendix F for her data model).

Tucker and Powell analyzed the forms and compared them to both Elizabeth's reporting requests and to the requirements Dawn had provided for future report generation. The Center's intake form lacked some of the fields (e.g., ethnicity) for information that Elizabeth needed for United Way reporting. In addition, some of the information, such as income that United Way requested was included on the intake form, but was not being filled in.

The team spent additional time seeking clarification from Dawn about the data the Center wanted to track, as well as assessing her database design skills and her preliminary data model. Dawn said she had taken an online course in Microsoft Access and had gotten an A in it; however, the concept of foreign keys was new to her. As the team worked with Dawn on redesigning the data model, they discovered that the Center also wanted to use the family database to track attendance at various group sessions; however, facilitators were not taking attendance at group meetings. The Center also wanted to track phone calls using the family database; thus, Dawn had included phone calls in her original data model. The Center wanted every cold call as well as calls from participating (current) clients to be included in the database. There was no policy about how long the Center planned to keep the data. Pamela Russell, family coordinator, kept a manual phone log, so the team decided that talking with her would be in order (see Tribunella, Warner, & Smith, 2002, for a rigorous discussion of database design).

The team then paid a visit to Pamela to look at the phone log. They discovered that Pamela kept a manual log of all calls, but that she was instructed to check off only one action (outcome) per call (see Appendix G for the phone log form). For example, if she mailed program information to a caller and provided an outside referral, she could only select one of those outcomes. At the end of every month, she manually tallied up the different actions and then summed those totals for the reporting year (Tribunella et al., 2002, discuss more systematic data gathering approaches).

CURRENT CHALLENGES/PROBLEMS FACING THE ORGANIZATION

Given the number of technology issues they found, Tucker and Powell were impressed with the way the Center's staff managed to keep their operations running as smoothly as they did. They were further impressed when they saw the hardware the Center was using. The file server was a donated PC that was rapidly running out of disk space. During the team's visits, Dawn was able to acquire another PC that she hooked up to the first one as a cluster. Most of the computer equipment in the Center had been donated; in fact, one of the team members wound up donating her five-year-old computer, and it was gratefully accepted. They were particularly impressed with the staff, especially Dawn. Not only was Dawn going to school and working at the Center part-time, she was also heavily involved (as were the rest of the staff) in fundraising activities. She even served as a bereavement support facilitator.

As Tucker and Powell studied the Center, they kept thinking about what they would put into their final report of recommendations, and what kinds of reactions they would receive. The Center, as an organization with a small staff and limited resources, was acting as an "adopter" of technology; that is, the type of organization that is simply operating in a survival mode and "making do" with existing technology (Fried, 1995). A major challenge facing many consultants working with non-profits is that they encounter a culture where non-profits shortchange themselves on technological resources, so that they can devote most of their resources to the primary mission (McCarthy, 2003). Tucker and Powell also knew that some of the Center's staff was aware that technology might be better harnessed to support their mission activities, but the staff did not have a plan in place for realizing this goal. Some of those technology goals would mean that the Center would experience radical changes in its business processes (Amis, Slack, & Hinings, 2004). Was the Center ready for change? The team also reflected on how they might evaluate their own efforts as consultants and as change agents (Bergholz, 1999). They had tried to function in the role of facilitator, which involved empowering clients to "own" changes in technology use and to mobilize and support client initiatives (Winston, 1999); however, they wondered if instead their role had been more of a traditional one or as an advocator. In the traditional role, consultants functioning as change agents focus on the implementation of technology, while advocators create a business vision and pro-actively function as champions for change (Winston, 1999). Was their position as facilitator a good match for a client in the adoptive mode? Had they been effective consultants to the Algos Center to date? How could they be useful to the Center in the future?

REFERENCES

Amis, J., Slack, T., & Hinings, C. R. (2004). The pace, sequence, and linearity of radical change. *Academy of Management Journal*, *47*(1), 15-39.

Barrett, K., & Greene, R. (2001). *Powering up: How public managers can take control of information technology*. Washington, DC: CQ Press.

Bergholz, H. (1999). Not-for-profit consulting. *Journal of Management Consulting*, *10*(3), 13-16.

Block, P. (2000). *Flawless consulting*. San Francisco: Jossey-Bass.

Bradley, B., Jansen, P., & Silverman, L. (2003). The nonprofit sector's $100 billion opportunity. *Harvard Business Review*, *81*(5), 3-11.

Burt, E., & Taylor, J. A. (2000). Information and communication technologies: Reshaping voluntary organizations? *Nonprofit Management and Leadership*, *11*(2), 131-143.

Chappell, B. J. (2001). *My journey to the Dougy Center*. Amityville, NY: Baywood Publishing.

Coates, N. (1997). A model for consulting to help effect change in organizations. *Nonprofit Management and Leadership*, *8*(2), 157-169.

Cornforth, C. (Ed.). (2003). *The governance of public and non-profit organizations: What do boards do?* London: Routledge.

Cutt, J., Bragg, D., Balfour, K., Murray, V., & Tassie, W. (1996). Nonprofits accommodate the information demands of public and private funders. *Nonprofit Management and Leadership*, *7*(1), 45-68.

Davis, C. N. (2002). Look sharp, feel sharp, be sharp and listen — Anecdotal excellence: People, places and things. *International Journal of Nonprofit & Voluntary Sector Marketing*, *7*(4), 393-400.

Fried, L. (1995). *Managing information technology in turbulent times*. New York: John Wiley & Sons.

Gross, M. J., Larkin, R. F., & McCarthy, J. H. (2003). *Financial and accounting guide for not-for-profit organizations* (6th ed.). New York: John Wiley & Sons.

Hecht, B., & Ramsey, R. (2002). *ManagingNonprofits.org*. New York: Wiley.

Jones, R. A. (2000). Sizing up NPO software. *Journal of Accountancy, 190*(5). 28-44.

Klein, K. (2004). *Fundraising in times of crisis*. San Francisco: Jossey-Bass.

Light, P. C. (2002). *Pathways to nonprofit excellence*. Washington, DC: Brookings Institution Press.

McCarthy, E. (2003, August 18). A confluence of technology and philanthropy. *The Washington Post*, p. E5.

Rubin, S., & Witztum, E. (Eds.). (2000). *Traumatic and non-traumatic loss and bereavement: Clinical theory and practice.* Madison, CT: Psychosocial Press/International Universities Press.

Smith, Bucklin & Associates, Inc. (2000). *The complete guide to nonprofit management* (2nd ed.). New York: Wiley.

Smith, S. R. (2002). Social services. In L. M. Salamon (Ed.), *The state of nonprofit America* (pp. 149-186). Washington, DC: Brookings Institution Press.

Stroebe, M. S., Strobebe, W., & Hansson, R. O. (Eds.). (2002). *Handbook of bereavement*. Cambridge: Cambridge University Press.

Tribunella, T., Warner, P. D., & Smith, L. M. (2002). Designing relational database systems. *CPA Journal*, *72*(7), 69-72.

Trussel, J., Greenlee, J. S., Brady, T., Colson, R. H., Goldband, M., & Morris, T. W. (2002). Predicting financial vulnerability in charitable organizations. *CPA Journal*, *72*(6), 66-69.

Winston, E. R. (1999). IS consultants and the change agent role. *Computer Personnel*, *20*(4), 55-73.

APPENDIX A

Organization Chart for the Algos Center

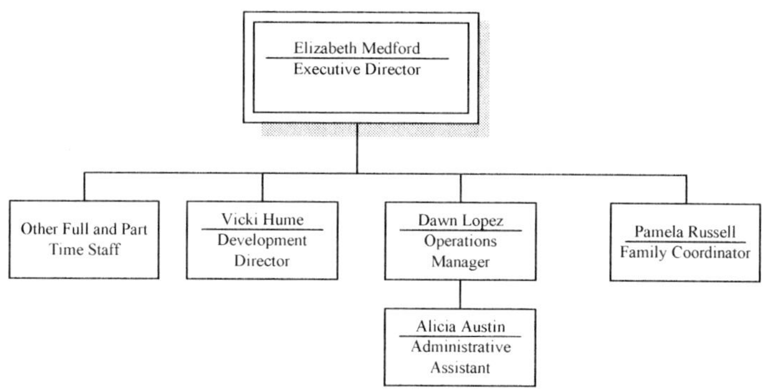

Note: Any of these staff positions may supervise volunteers on an informal basis.

APPENDIX B

Financial Statement for the Year July 1, 2001 through June 30, 2002

Income:	
Contributions	$152,009
Special Events (less net expenses)	$99,173
United Way/Designated Donations/Allocation	$99,312
Foundations and Grants	$108,929
Investments	($27,214)
Other Donations	$32,770
Donated Services	$10,645
Net Assets released from the restricted fund (scholarship fund payment)	$1,073
Total Support Revenue:	$476,697
Expenses:	
Program Expenses	$342,153
Management and General	$91,083
Fundraising	$32,546
Total Expenses:	$465,782
Increase in unrestricted net assets:	$10,915
Decrease in restricted net assets:	($3,893)
Net assets, beginning of year:	$368,155
Net assets, end of year:	$375,477

APPENDIX C

Sample Paradigm Report

Donors who gave amounts (gifts or pledge payments) greater than or equal to $50, between 7/1/00 and 6/30/02 (for the 2001/2002 Annual Appeal, AA01, or Core Support 01 Campaigns)

Name	***Donor Address***	***City***	***State***	***Zip***	***Gift Amount***	***Date***	***Gift/ Pledge Payment***	***Campaign***
John Johnson	678 Long Lane	Smithfield	MD	xxxxx	$200	3/13/2002	Pledge Payment	Ann. Appeal 01/02
Susie Smith	1040 Taylor Road	Chelmstown	MA	xxxxx	$75	4/20/01	Gift	AA01
Mr. & Mrs. Thompson	123 Main Street	Union	NY	xxxxx	$150	11/20/00	Gift	Ann. Appeal 01/02
Mr. & Mrs. Thompson	124 Main Street	Union	NY	xxxxx	$50	5/4/01	Pledge Payment	Core Support 01

APPENDIX D

Sample Expense Report

	Jul-03	Aug-03	Sep-03
Expense			
60000 - Personnel			
60100 - Salaries and Wages	19,356	20,211	9,863
60105 - FICA	1,045	1 ,091	1,073
60115 - SUTA	46	54	49
60125 - Health Insurance	1,143	1,158	1,150
60130 - Simple IRA Contribution	385	412	400
60140 - Other Insurances	980		
Total 600000 - Personnel	22,955	22,926	22,535
60200 - Building			
60205 - Cleaning	250	250	250
60210 - Insurance	500	500	500
60215 - Real Estate Taxes			2,500
60220 - Rent	495	495	495
60225 - Utilities	618	798	329
60290 - Other Building	100	48	31
Total 60200 - Building	1,963	2,091	4,105
60300 - Office & Administration			
60305 - Accounting & Payroll	325	325	325
60310 - Audit			2,900
60312 - Credit Card/Bank Fees	75	64	89
60315 - Equipment Maintenance	300	300	300
60320 - Office Supplies	283	196	421
60325 - Postage	334	308	471
60335 - Technical/Sftwr Support	275	275	275
60340 - Telephone	256	289	271
60390 - Other Office & Admin	68	123	83
Total 60300 - Office & Administration	1,916	1,880	5,135

APPENDIX E

United Way Report

FISCAL YEAR _______ EXPENSES FOR CURRENT YEAR ALLOCATION	GRAND TOTAL 1.	MANAGEMENT 2.	PROGRAM SERVICES 3.	 4.	 5.	 6.
22. Salaries						
23. Employee benefits						
24. Payroll Taxes, etc.						
25. Professional Fees						
26. Supplies						
27. Telephone						
28. Postage and Shipping						
29. Occupancy						
30. Rental/Maintenance of Equipment						
31. Printing and Publications						
32. Travel Conferences						
33. Miscellaneous (Include Insurance here)						
34. Payments to Affiliated Organizations						
35. Depreciation*						
36. Major Equipment/Mortgage*						
37. SUBTOTAL EXPENSES	$0.00	$0.00	$0.00	$0.00	$0.00	$0.00
38. Less Expenses for activities financed by: Restricted Revenue........................						
Depreciation Expenses*..................						
Major Equipment/Mortgage*.............						
39. **TOTAL EXPENSES FOR ACTIVITIES FINANCED BY**	$0.00	$0.00	$0.00	$0.00	$0.00	$0.00
40. **DEFICIT/SURPLUS** (Line 21, page 6 minus Line 39)	$0.00	$0.00	$0.00	$0.00	$0.00	$0.00

*United Way does not fund these costs. However, for financial reporting purposes, please include them on this line, then remove them in Line 38.

APPENDIX F

Dawn's Data Model

Tables and Relationships

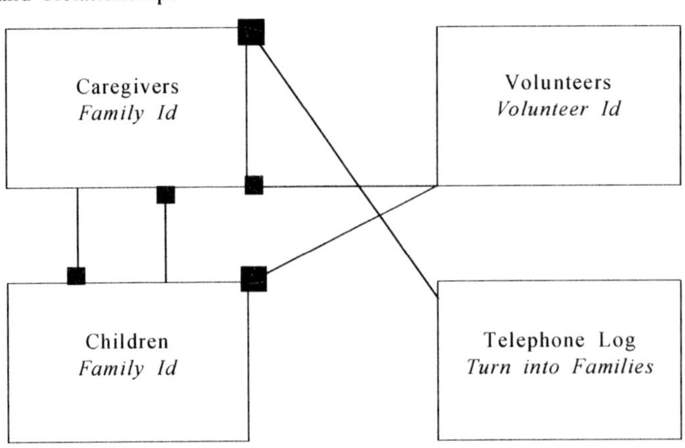

APPENDIX F (cont.)

Fall Breakdown:

Caregiver Table

Family Id
Primary Affiliation - combo box
Adult 1 Last Name
Adult 1 First Name
Adult 1 Telephone
Adult 1 Employer & Title
Adult 1 Gender
Adult 1 Nationality
Adult 1 Date of Birth
Adult 2 Last Name
Adult 2 First Name
Adult 2 Telephone
Adult 2 Employer & Title
Adult 2 Gender
Adult 2 Nationality
Adult 2 Date of Birth
Address
City
State
Zip Code
Email Address
Intaker 1 - links to Volunteer Id
Intaker 2 - links to Volunteer Id
Intake Date
Appropriate for Groups - Yes/No
If Yes, which group - combo box
If No, reason why - combo box
Referral Source
Currently Attending - Yes/No
Start Date 1
End Date 1
Start Date 2
End Date 2
Current Night of Service
Current Co-Facilitator 1 - links to Volunteer Id
Current Co-Facilitator 2 - links to Volunteer Id
Previous Night of Service
Previous Co-Facilitator 1 - links to Volunteer Id
Previous Co-Facilitator 2 - links to Volunteer Id
Name of Deceased
Relationship to Deceased
Cause of Death
Date of Death
Date of FirstCall - could link to telephone log
Wait List - Yes/No
Policies given - Yes/No
Mailings to receive - combo box
Relation to children attending - combo box

Children Table

Family Id - links to caregivers
Primary Affiliation - combo box
Last Name
First Name
Intaker 1 - links to Volunteer Id
Intaker 2 - links to Volunteer Id
Intake Date
Appropriate for Groups - Yes/No
If Yes, which group - combo box
If No, reason why - combo box
Currently attending - Yes/No
State Date 1
End Date 1
Start Date 2
End Date 2
Current Night of Service
Current Co-Facilitator 1 - links to Volunteer Id
Current Co-Facilitator 2 - links to Volunteer Id
Previous Night of Service
Previous Co-Facilitator 1 - links to Volunteer Id
Previous Co-Facilitator 2 - links to Volunteer Id
Name of Deceased
Relationship to Deceased
Cause of Death
Date of Death

Volunteer Table

Volunteer Id - links to group members
Primary Affiliations - combo box
Volunteer Preference
Other Interests - combo box
Training Date
Current Night of Service - combo box
Current Co-Facilitator - links to Volunteer Id
Current Age Group
State Date 1
End Date 1
Previous Night of Service/Volunteering 1
Previous Co-Facilitator 1 - links to Volunteer Id
Start Date 2
End Date 2
Previous Night of Service/Volunteering 2
Current Co-Facilitator 2 - links to Volunteer Id
Start Date 3
End Date 3
Date of Birth
Gender
Nationality
Employer & Title
Referral Source
In-Services Attended - text area

Telephone Log Table

Last Name
First Name
Relation to Grieving Chile
Business/Organization Name
Address
City
State
Zip Code
Telephone 1
Telephone 2
Email Address
Type of Caller
Type of Service Provider
Referral Source

APPENDIX G

Center Phone Log

PHONE LOG

Date____________________

Time____________________

	Verbal Program Info.	Info. Sent	Phone Support	Referral to our program	Referral to other center	Referral to other resource	Total
Family							
Agency/ School							
Individual							
Volunteer							
Other Center							
Student							
Other							

Susan J. Chinn, Assistant Professor of MIS at the University of Southern Maine, holds a PhD from Kent State University and an MS from Virginia Commonwealth University. She spent several years in industry as a programmer/analyst and consultant. Dr. Chinn has taught systems analysis, systems design, expert systems, programming languages, and introductory undergraduate and graduate MIS survey courses. Her research interests include information technology in non-profit organizations, organizational use of the Internet, and tools and techniques for systems analysis and design.

Charlotte A. Pryor, Assistant Professor of Accounting at the University of Southern Maine, holds a PhD from the Pennsylvania State University and a CPA certificate. Professor Pryor teaches accounting information systems, and managerial, governmental, and not-for-profit accounting. For a number of years, Dr. Pryor was the chief accounting officer for the Washington, DC region of the National Park Service and treasurer of the Potomac Appalachian Trail Club. She is a member of the AICPA and the IMA. Her research interests primarily involve accounting education and accounting and information systems issues in small businesses and government and non-profit organizations.

A frequent adviser to public and private concerns, John J. Voyer, Professor of Management at the University of Southern Maine, is the author or co-author of several monographs and journal articles. He has made numerous refereed presentations before professional organizations in his field, serves as a reviewer for a number of academic journals in management as well as for conference papers, and is a former member of the editorial board of Group and Organization Management. Dr. Voyer has held the title of Price-Babson Fellow (2000), Sam Walton Fellow (2003) and has participated in the Art and Practice of Leadership Seminar (Harvard Kennedy School of Government, 2003).

This case was previously published in the *Journal of Cases on Information Technology*, 7(2), pp. 1-15, © 2005.

Chapter IV

Isobord's Geographic Information System (GIS) Solution

Derrick J. Neufeld, University of Western Ontario, Canada

Scott Griffith, Tell Us About Us Inc., Canada

EXECUTIVE SUMMARY

Isobord, a start-up company that is setting up a new strawboard production plant in Manitoba, Canada, is facing critical operational problems that threaten its future. Isobord's product is a high quality particleboard substitute that uses straw, rather than wood, as the main raw manufacturing material. To achieve viability, Isobord must develop processes to carefully coordinate and manage its straw baling, stacking and hauling operations. Through effective information systems, Isobord has the potential to reduce the amount of equipment it needs to purchase to meet straw harvest requirements. A small investment in optimization technology could yield considerable cost savings if the efficiency of capital equipment can be improved. A geographic information system (GIS)/relational database management system (RDBMS) solution is being explored, but budget and time constraints, as well as organizational inexperience, seriously threaten the project. An information technology decision must be made immediately if there is to be any hope of implementing technology to manage the first year's straw harvest.

BACKGROUND

"... Like Rumplestiltskin, Isobord is spinning straw into a wealth of new opportunity!" The room erupted with applause as Gary Filmon, premier of the Province of Manitoba, Canada, dramatically concluded his speech welcoming Isobord Enterprises Incorporated to the small town of Elie, Manitoba. The ceremonial ribbon cutting on November 8, 1996, officially certified Elie as Manitoba's latest boomtown and home to the world's first large-scale strawboard production plant.

The new 215,000-square-foot Isobord plant is designed to produce over 130 million square feet of premium-quality strawboard per year. What makes the Isobord operation unique is its reliance on an annually renewable agricultural by-product, straw, as the primary raw material input. Most particleboard plants rely on wood as the primary input.

When it is completed, the Isobord facility is scheduled to process 200,000 tons of wheat straw per year to produce its high quality strawboard product. Initial runs of the product quickly earned great praise in consumer markets, due to the superior physical and mechanical properties of the straw-based board. Specifically, because Isobord uses straw fibers and nontoxic, environmentally-friendly isocyanurate resins in the manufacturing process, the final product performs better than standard wood-based particleboard in terms of water resistance, moisture swell, elasticity, internal bond, weight, density, strength, moldability, and screw retention. U.S. consumers of particleboard were so excited about Isobord's product that they agreed to purchase 75% of the output before the plant was even constructed!

According to Gary Gall, Isobord's president, "The beauty of the Isobord product is that it utilizes an annually renewable natural resource that was previously considered to be an agricultural by-product. By utilizing the straw we can simultaneously help to combat the negative effects of straw burning, and create a sustainable business in Manitoba." Until Isobord came along, Manitoba farmers were forced to burn straw after the harvest each fall. With the Isobord option, farmers can now sell the straw, reduce their workload, and cut down on air pollution in one fell swoop.

SETTING THE STAGE

Isobord, a start-up company headquartered in Toronto, Ontario, is in the process of developing a strawboard processing plant in the fertile Red River Valley of Manitoba, a location some 2,000 kilometers away from the head office. Isobord's ability to create a sustainable operation in Manitoba is largely dependent upon the abilities of its management team. Unfortunately, while fundraising, production and promotion have all received consistent attention by senior Isobord executives, the problem of harvesting straw has been essentially ignored. These executives seemed to believe that the straw would deliver itself to the new Isobord plant.

Feasibility studies were subsequently conducted by consultants to quantify the costs associated with collecting straw. Unfortunately, Isobord lacked an internal figure who understood both agriculture and the technical aspects required to coordinate the logistics of a massive straw harvest. Furthermore, Isobord had not yet retained any in-house information systems expertise. This lack of resources was paired with a technology-averse attitude of senior managers within Isobord, brought on by prior bad experiences with IT projects.

CASE DESCRIPTION

Isobord's success hinges on the availability of straw. Without straw there can be no board. At full-scale production Isobord will consume 400,000 wheat straw bales per year. The quantity of straw demanded by Isobord far exceeds any previous efforts at straw collection. As such, Isobord must carefully devise strategies to undertake the collection of straw resources. If straw resources become depleted, Isobord will lose revenues of approximately $200,000 for every day that the plant is shut down.

The initial business plan was based on the assumption that if Isobord offered to buy the straw, farmers would be willing to collect and deliver it to the plant. After all, farmers typically had problems getting rid of straw after the harvest each year (with heavy crops, straw was particularly difficult to reincorporate into the rich soils of the Red River Valley). As a result, farmers often resorted to burning as the only viable straw removal alternative.

Isobord saw this as a golden opportunity: instead of burning, farmers could sell their straw. This would reduce the negative environmental/air quality effects of burning (smoke created by burning straw is particularly stressful to children and people with respiratory ailments such as emphysema or asthma). The plan was simple and logical. Isobord would help alleviate burning problems by purchasing the wheat straw from farmers.

During the winter of 1995, Isobord offered farmers $30 per metric ton of straw delivered to the plant. By doing so, they placed an economic value on a material that previously enjoyed no real market. Wheat straw, which had been used in small quantities for animal bedding, could now be sold in large quantities for a guaranteed price. Isobord was certain they would receive a warm welcome from the local community: they were providing a vehicle for farmers to simultaneously dispose of their straw and to make money.

What Isobord officials failed to consider was the effort required to collect and deliver the straw. As they quickly learned from the farmers, it is far easier to put a match to straw than it is to bale, stack, and haul large loads of low value goods to a distant plant. Compared with a typical $160/acre wheat crop,[1]

Isobord's offer of \$30/metric ton (effectively, \$30/acre[2]) did not provide sufficient economic incentive to persuade farmers to collect and deliver straw bales. Farmers would need baling equipment, stacking equipment, loaders, and trucks — all different from the equipment required for harvesting and transporting grain. By the time all the work was completed, farmers claimed they would be losing money by selling straw to Isobord. The farming community quickly became disinterested in Isobord's proposals. They were not willing to act as the manpower, equipment suppliers and logistical controllers for Toronto's high rollers. Isobord's simple dream of 'build it and they will come' had crumbled.

Plan A had failed: straw would not be baled and delivered directly by farmers. But the first endeavor was not a total failure. Isobord management had learned a great deal about straw collection through its interactions with the farming community. Clearly, obtaining straw would require more focused efforts.

CURRENT CHALLENGES/PROBLEMS FACING THE ORGANIZATION

If the project was to continue, Isobord would have to get very serious about straw collection. To make its business case to investors, Isobord had to demonstrate the availability, affordability and annual sustainability of the required 200,000 ton straw supply. The banks insisted that Isobord provide contracts stating that farmers would supply straw, at a stated price, for a five-year period. If Isobord could not produce proof of a guaranteed straw supply at a known price for a minimum time period, the banks would not continue to contribute money to the project. Once the straw supply was committed to Isobord by the farmer, it would have to be baled, stacked and transported to the plant. Management insisted that regardless of the chosen straw collection method, it must fit within the established budget of \$30 per metric ton.

In the spring of 1995 the firm encouraged a group of farmers to set up the Straw Producers Cooperative of Manitoba to help develop the straw supply base. The Co-op was made up of a board of 10 directors, each of whom was responsible for promoting the Isobord project to a district in southern Manitoba. The Co-op's chief objective was to convince farmers to sign straw supply contracts with Isobord.

Soon after the Co-op was formed, Isobord President Gary Gall decided that additional efforts should be focused on organizing the straw collection operations. Gary contacted Rudy Schmeichel, a motivated independent start-up consultant from Toronto who had just completed a contract with Lifetech, a new biotechnology company. Rudy accepted the Isobord challenge and moved to Manitoba in July of 1995. He was met at the Winnipeg airport by Scott Griffith,

Isobord's only Manitoba staff member. Scott drove Rudy to the Elie office, located on the main floor of an old three-story house that had previously been a convent. From the convent, Rudy and Scott began their crusade to organize the Straw Division.

Rudy quickly made contacts in the community. He spent considerable time in the coffee shops listening to the locals talk about the Isobord project. He began to get his bearings and soon established a place for himself in the community. From his "field research" Rudy began to devise a plan to bring straw from the field to the plant. Major operations included: (1) baling the swaths of wheat with a baling unit (i.e., a tractor pulling a baling machine that gathers loose straw into standard-sized 4'x4'x8' bales); (2) stacking the bales with a bale forwarder (i.e., a tractor that collects bales and stacks them at the edge of the field); and (3) dispatching a loader and multiple trucks to the field to pick up the bales and haul them to the plant.

BALING AND STACKING LOGISTICS

Each baling unit can process up to 36 bales per baling hour, travels (between fields) at a maximum speed of 30 kph, and costs approximately $250,000. Each bale forwarder can process up to 90 bales per hour, travels at a maximum speed (between fields) of 90 kph, and costs approximately $220,000. Since the capabilities of bale forwarders exceed those of baling units, it made sense to organize equipment into "baling crews" consisting of one bale forwarder and two or more baling units. Baling crews communicate with the central dispatch office using two-way VHF radios.

While the straw collection process may appear fairly simple initially, Isobord faces a number of serious constraints. First, the maximum time available for baling is estimated to be only 600 hours per season, based on expectations regarding typical planting and harvesting schedules,[3] climatic conditions,[4] available daylight hours and anticipated equipment breakdowns. Rudy estimated that approximately 75% of the 600 available hours will be spent baling, although this could range anywhere from 90% to 60%, depending on how efficiently dispatch is able to route the baling crews.

A second constraint is that straw must be collected from a wide geographical area: approximately 6,000 targeted fields are randomly distributed over a 50-mile radius of the plant. Operators will be required to navigate an expansive network of unmarked municipal mile roads; finding an unknown field might be compared to finding a house in a city where the streets have no names — or perhaps to finding "a needle in a haystack." Furthermore, very few landmarks exist on the Manitoba prairies to help vehicle operators find their way. If operators get lost, they could waste hours of valuable baling time. Stephen Tkachyk, an Isobord baling crew chief, had experience navigating country roads at night. He stated that if you get lost at night, your best bet is to go to sleep in the truck and find your way in the morning!

Hauling Logistics

Several trucking companies were asked to provide quotes for hauling services. Because of the unique nature of this hauling job, all of them requested additional information. To provide quotations the trucking firms wanted to know the following:

- The number of loads that would be hauled from each location
- The distance to be hauled
- The location of the pickups
- The routes to be traveled

To accumulate the necessary information, Rudy suggested that "trip ticks" be created that defined the route from each field to the plant. Rudy needed the distance numbers as soon as possible so that the trucking companies could provide quotations, so Scott began developing handwritten trip ticks. However, with over 300 Co-op members, many of whom farmed multiple wheat fields, this process quickly became tedious. Furthermore, given the shifting nature of wheat field locations due to crop rotation, it was apparent that these "one-off" trip ticks would become outdated very quickly.

An Initial Solution

To organize routing of baling crews, it was first necessary to determine where Co-op members were located. Scott purchased maps of Southern Manitoba and began marking the Co-op member locations using colored pins. Unfortunately, initial information provided by Co-op members only indicated locations of farm houses, not wheat fields. Isobord would need to know specific wheat field locations in order to provide baling service (legal field descriptions are designated by section-township-range coordinates, e.g., field SW-12-07-02-W is on the southwest quarter of section 12-07-02, west of the central meridian).

Over the next few weeks, Scott developed a system that would be easier to change as Isobord's needs changed. Using an Apple Macintosh computer and drawing software, he divided Isobord's straw collection area into a number of grid sections. Each grid section had a designated exit point, and the single best route between the grid exit point and the plant's straw storage site was identified. The best route between each particular field and the grid exit point was then determined on a field-by-field basis. The result of this exercise was a series of grid maps that included relevant roads, a section grid,[5] towns, hydrography, and the locations of Co-op members' farmhouses.

A grid section reference identifier and distance-to-plant data were then added to each Co-op member's database record. The grid mapping process sped up the calculation of trucking distances, and provided a graphical reference base for all Co-op member locations. When the grid maps were complete Scott produced reports using Microsoft Access that summarized distance to be traveled, routes to be taken, and number of loads to come from each location (number of loads was determined as a function of acres under contract from each Co-op member).

When a field is ready to be baled, a Co-op member will now call Isobord's dispatch office to schedule baling. The farmer will provide his name, the number of acres to be baled, and the legal description of the field. Dispatch operators will then prioritize the calls and assign them to a specific baling crew. The baling crew will navigate to the new field using detailed grid maps. The goal of the dispatch operators will be to minimize each crew's travel time, in order to maximize productive baling time.

Isobord had minimal technology available to coordinate baling efforts. Isobord was only about 10 employees strong, and Scott, a Management student who was just starting to learn how to program, was the only employee with any knowledge of software development. Isobord's information systems consisted of one PC running Windows 95 and a Macintosh that Scott brought from home to create the digital maps. Scott used Microsoft Access to create prototype databases. During the prototyping stage no formal systems methodology was used to guide development. Systems were developed based on theoretical concepts as to how a baling operation of Isobord's magnitude could be organized. During development the software was continually revised as new ideas surfaced. Based on the lack of in-house expertise and resources, Scott began to seek out a third-party solution.

Information Technology Options

Scott saw the value of using computers to help solve Isobord's straw collection problems, and so he did further research to learn what information technologies were available to help administer dispatch operations. He learned that systems used for computerized dispatch typically utilize two technologies. The first, relational database management systems (RDBMS), are used to create the custom interface required for entering, manipulating and storing data. The other dispatch technology commonly used, geographic information systems (GIS), are used to store and manipulate digitized map data. GIS map data consist of real-world latitude and longitude coordinates, which may be input to the system using available paper map data, or via global positioning systems (GPS) receivers. When combined with RDBMS technologies, GIS can be used to attach meaningful attributes to map elements (e.g., a user could display a particular city on a map as a circle, and then attach population, land area, and tax base data to the circle). The appendix contains a technical note describing GIS technology in more detail.

A RDBMS and GIS combination would allow Isobord to administer and control all information relevant to straw collection, such as:

- Information pertaining to all Co-op members, including wheat field locations, and summaries of accounts payable for harvested straw
- A record of all calls received requesting baling service
- Activity records for all field operations
- Inventory of all machinery, parts and supplies
- Payroll for employees who provide baling services

The GIS component of Isobord's system would consist of two main parts: map data and analytical capabilities. To map out Co-op members' field locations and coordinate machinery, Isobord requires "quarter-section grid" data (which defines all sections of land in Manitoba by their legal description), and "road network" data (which details all provincial and municipal roads throughout Isobord's dispatch area). Other map datasets (e.g., provincial hydrography, rail lines, towns and cities) would be useful for navigation purposes. The ideal GIS would display incoming calls, color-coded to indicate priority, on a digital map of Isobord's straw collection area. Thus, dispatch operators would have a constant visual representation of current operations, and would be able to assign baling crews in such a way as to minimize travel time.

By using a true GIS, Isobord could track important information about baling operations on each farm field visually. The field would be displayed on a digital map and each field point could be tied to all the data pertaining to the field. Dispatch operators viewing a field location on a map could access data pertaining to that field including when the farmer called to have the field baled, such as field size (number of acres), type of wheat straw planted on the field (spring, winter, durum), and type of combine used to harvest the straw. This information would allow Isobord's dispatch operators to make decisions quickly based on current information. The power of easily accessible spatial and operational data through a GIS/RDBMS system would provide dispatch operators with the means to optimize the effectiveness of the baling fleet.

Isobord's GIS should also be capable of analyzing the shortest and/or fastest path between any two points on a map. During calculation, the GIS should take into account variables such as the number of turns required to travel from one place to the next, the speed limit, and the road conditions for each segment of road. The user should also have options to classify roads (paved, gravel, or clay), define speed limits, or even remove a road from any route calculations (e.g., if it is unfit for travel due to flooding).

GIS Prototype

Scott believed GIS software would be perfect for managing Isobord's straw resources and maximizing baling crew efficiency. He began to develop an experimental, prototype GIS application using Microsoft Access. The grid maps previously created on the Macintosh were imported into the Access database and attached to Co-op member records. For each Co-op member, the dispatcher could now click an icon to load up a map of the relevant grid section.

While the prototype system admirably demonstrated the benefits of using a GIS, its functionality was limited. The map 'data' were actually static and discrete graphical images, rather than dynamic GIS datasets, so that any change in a Co-op member's field locations required a change to the underlying graphical image. In a true GIS, digital maps would be derived from data contained in an underlying GIS dataset; any changes to the data in a true GIS dataset would automatically be reflected in the map displayed. Furthermore, the prototype did not contain analytical functionality, therefore shortest route calculations could not be performed.

By this point Scott had developed a solid understanding of how straw collection logistics could be organized in order to maximize the utilization of equipment. However, he suspected that, as a new company, Isobord's ideas about how to manage operations would evolve significantly over the first few years of operations. As a result, Scott thought that retaining in-house control over software design would enable Isobord to implement a flexible solution that could be modified as the business of straw collection evolved. Scott therefore intended to internally develop database components in Microsoft Access, and then link that data to a commercial GIS tool. This solution would allow for flexibility in database design, while providing the analytical capabilities such as route optimization and thematic mapping offered by a full-scale GIS package. By performing some of the work in-house, Isobord would be able to control costs during the prototyping stage, and easily implement changes to software and processes as the art of a massive straw harvest became a science. At this point, Isobord approached three GIS consulting firms to discuss the possibility of creating a dispatch information system.

Firm #1: International Operating Systems (IOS)

With only three employees, International Operating Systems (IOS) was a small but innovative information systems consulting firm. IOS offered to sell Isobord a package called Bentley MicroStation (www.bentley.com), a geoengineering software application with GIS capabilities. MicroStation provided basic database and mapping capabilities, and IOS was willing to further develop the analytical capabilities required by Isobord.

While Scott was impressed with IOS, he had concerns about the complexity of the MicroStation proprietary programming language and the package's limited database functionality. To create a robust and user-friendly application, the MicroStation GIS would have to be linked to an Access database. The link was theoretically possible through ODBC (Open Database Connectivity — a standard database communications protocol), but IOS had never actually linked a MicroStation application to an Access database.

IOS developed a proposal for Isobord that included development of base map data in MicroStation and a basic link to the Access database. IOS asserted that it would need to develop the road network dataset and portions of the quarter section grid dataset. IOS would also need to create and identify river lot locations. The total development cost would be $20,000, including the MicroStation application, dataset development, an initial MicroStation-Access link, and a two-day training session on MicroStation for one Isobord staff member.

Firm #2: DataLink Mapping

Further research revealed a second small GIS consultant, DataLink Mapping (infoweb.magi.com/~datalink). DataLink specialized in developing GIS applications using MapInfo (www.mapinfo.com), a Microsoft-endorsed application. As with the MicroStation application, MapInfo could be linked to an external database via ODBC. MapInfo's documentation explicitly indicated that it could be integrated with Microsoft Access. It was also compatible with other database products through ODBC.

As with IOS, the DataLink proposal indicated that the road network data were not yet available from the Province of Manitoba. Thus, MapInfo could provide a solid base for displaying Isobord's geographic data, but could not perform shortest route calculations. Also, while integration of MapInfo with an external Access database was theoretically possible through ODBC, DataLink had not experimented with this MapInfo feature. DataLink produced an informal quotation to supply MapInfo, complete with the quarter section data, river lots, and hydrography, for $8,800.

Firm #3: Linnet Geomatics

An official at Manitoba Land-Related Information Systems recommended that Scott contact Linnet Geomatics (www.linnet.ca), a data warehousing, surveying and systems development firm. After discussing the situation with Isobord, Linnet put together a detailed proposal that included acquisition of hardware, software, datasets, and all required development and training to provide a "complete business solution." Scott was surprised to learn that both DataLink and IOS would be purchasing all or part of their GIS datasets from Linnet.

Linnet wanted to aid in the development of an administration system to help Isobord monitor and control their operations. Linnet had already developed an extensive production management system to help Louisiana Pacific, an oriented strand board (OSB) plan in northern Manitoba, monitor all aspects of its operations (e.g., to plan cutting, schedule hauling, pay invoices, track materials usage), and was eager to apply this knowledge to Isobord.

Linnet's proposal to Isobord was presented in standard systems development life cycle format. It included requirements and design, prototyping, application development, implementation, training, testing, and troubleshooting. The total price tag before taxes was $295,000. Throughout the quoting process, Linnet representatives repeatedly stressed that they only build systems that provide benefits to the client.

Scott further questioned Linnet about the possibility of using global positioning system (GPS) technology to monitor the movements of Isobord's baling fleet in real time. With GPS, Isobord could continuously monitor all of the equipment in the field; equipment operators would never get lost because the dispatch operators would always know their exact location. The GPS system would require a base receiving station equipped with a base-station monitoring device to relay all incoming GPS coordinates to a computer terminal. GPS units would cost approximately $2,200 per unit, plus $40,000 for a base station at the plant.

Linnet planned to develop the entire application using PowerBuilder to create the user interface and Oracle as the back end database. The GIS functionality would be developed within ArcView. All of Isobord's data would be stored in the Oracle database and accessed by both the PowerBuilder App and the ArcView App through ODBC. Linnet touted the benefits of Oracle and PowerBuilder as scaleable platforms capable of running systems throughout an enterprise. Their staff consisted of over 65 employees including several professional developers who consistently used Oracle/PowerBuilder and ArcView to provide solutions for clients.

Overall Evaluation of Technical Alternatives

Regardless of the solution chosen, Isobord would have to create a formal plan for the information system. The process of designing the structure of the database would be controlled largely by Isobord employees — and its success would hinge on their ability to communicate the system requirements to the chosen vendor. Through prototyping Isobord had created a working entity-relationship diagram for the project and had also documented the overall process flow for operations. At this point Scott and Rudy were the only individuals within Isobord who understood the intricacies of baling, stacking and hauling logistics. Unfortunately their knowledge was based on theory rather than experience. At this point they would have to invent the process and the supporting technology in parallel to complete an information system in time for the first straw harvest.

Time was required following initial development to test the system by simulating the conditions during a straw harvest. By populating the system with farm location data, and then running a series of test queries, Scott and Rudy hoped to verify that the functionality of the software met operational requirements. Typically farmers could provide a legal description of their land. The description would adequately identify field locations for about 75% of the Co-op members. For the other 25% of field locations, Isobord's dispatch office would require a paper map to ensure that the fields could be properly digitized and added to the GIS.

As a final provision, users would need to be trained in the operation of the dispatch information system. The software would have to be intuitive and user friendly if it was to be successful. This demanded that the software and hardware solutions had to be both stable and not overly complex. Scott had heard mixed reviews about Microsoft Access. Professional developers he spoke with frequently said "it's a great place to start, but it has its limitations. It's not good for multi-user systems beyond 10 clients or so, and it has a slow database engine so you need to watch your table size...." Beyond Access, the other technologies suggested by technical consulting firms were foreign to Scott. It was clear that new IT skills would have to be developed rapidly regardless of the solution chosen.

THE DECISION

Certain Isobord executives had become so enthused about the prototype system that they wanted to go ahead and use it for the first year. Other key players believed that it would be preferable to do things manually first, before investing in any information technology. Scott recommended implementing a real GIS system on a smaller scale in 1997, when straw harvested would be used mainly as buffer inventory, so that the bugs could be identified and fixed before straw collection became mission-critical in 1998.

Budget constraints made the acquisition of expensive software problematic. The original budget had been prepared with the understanding that farmers would bale and deliver straw themselves. With Isobord undertaking straw collection operations, the realities had changed considerably. It was difficult to finance a software project that was not even anticipated during initial budgeting.

It was late February 1997 as Rudy paced back and forth through the upstairs chapel in the convent, searching for answers. He knew that equipment purchases were dependent on his ability to coordinate the logistics of straw collection, but how could he quantify this decision? How many baling and forwarding units should be purchased? How should dispatch operations be managed? What information technology solution should he recommend? He needed to come up with an action plan now to be ready for straw collection in five short months.

REFERENCES AND FURTHER READING

Research Articles:

Dennis, A. R. (1998). Using geographical information systems for decision making: Extending cognitive fit theory to map-based presentations. *Information Systems Research, 9*(2), 194-203.

Fung, D., & Wilkes, S. (1998). A GIS approach to casino market modeling. *Journal of Applied Business Research, 14*(4), 77-88.

Smelcer, J. B., & Carmel, E. (1997). The effectiveness of different representations for managerial problem solving: Comparing tables and maps. *Decision Sciences, 28*(2), 391-420.

Watad, M. M. (1999). The context of introducing IT/IS-based innovation into local government in Columbia. *Journal of Global Information Management, 7*(1), 39-45.

Practitioner Articles:

Millman, H. (1999). Mapping your business strategy. *Computerworld, 33*(3), 77.

Pack, T. (1997). Mapping a path to success. *Database, 20*(4), 31-35.

Reed, D. (1998). Mapping up customers. *Marketing Week, 21*(10), 47-50.

Web Sites:

Backman, L. (19 October, 1998). ESRI — About GIS. *ESRI Online*. Available at http://www.esri.com/library/gis/

Interactive GIS demos, including JAVA and Shockwave applets. Available at http://abent0.ecn.purdue.edu/caagis/gispage1.html and http://www.zip2.com

Isobord. Available at http://www.isobord.ca

Linnet Geomatics. Available at http://www.linnet.ca

MapInfo. Available at http://www.mapinfo.com

Trimble Navigation Limited. (1998, May 8). Trimble GPS Tutorial. Available at http://www.trimble.com/gps/aa_abt.htm

ENDNOTES

1 Assuming $4/bushel, 40 bushel/acre average yield.

2 Assuming 1 metric ton/acre average yield (1 metric ton is approximately 2,205 lbs).

3 Straw harvesting must fall within the August-October window.

4 Rain or snow can make fields inaccessible, and straw cannot be collected if its moisture content exceeds 16%.

[5] The section grid outlined each section of land (one square mile). Each section is identified by a legal land description (section-township-range).

APPENDIX: A TECHNICAL NOTE ON GEOGRAPHIC INFORMATION SYSTEMS

Geographic information systems (GIS) allow users to integrate databases with computerized maps. By integrating maps with traditional databases, GIS software can produce visual representations of complex data. The visual aspect of GIS is its key strength. Virtually any data can be mapped to create a picture that captures the nature and extent of the relationship between the data and its geography. For example, GIS is often used by marketing organizations to plot demographic data for regions within a given city or postal code. This form of analysis allows users to create maps that display regions that fall within required demographic parameters.

GIS have been embraced by many organizations as a tool for generating competitive advantage. It is most commonly used for strategic planning, natural resource management, infrastructure management, routing and scheduling, and marketing. Telecommunications companies in particular have embraced GIS solutions. For example, Ameritech Cellular and Germany's Deutsche Telekom have exploited the power of GIS software in comparing potential site locations for new communications towers. Factors such as physical characteristics of the land, interference from other communications devices, height restrictions, weather patterns, consumer demand, and even the probability of floods, tornadoes, and other natural disasters are all analyzed by the GIS model to help define optimal locations for new towers. John Smetanka, director of R&D for On Target Mapping, knows the importance of GIS in telecommunications planning. He commented that, "When you map out all the variables, sometimes there are only one or two places a tower can be built. Maps are critical to having plans approved."

GIS are also used for information management. Deutsche Telekom is converting all paper-based drawings of their telecommunications networks into digital data. The geography of their networks are currently shown on over 5 million paper drawings and schematics. The digital versions of these documents will be integrated into a GIS data warehouse that will eventually hold 3 terabytes (i.e., 3 trillion bytes) of information. By using a GIS rather than a conventional database. Deutsche Telekom is able to record precise spatial locations for every component within their communications infrastructure. This capability makes the maintenance of drawings and physical components much easier.

The potential applications of GIS may be limited only by the imagination of its users. Proponents believe GIS will become a universal business tool. GIS applications require powerful computers that until recently were not readily available. With cheaper, faster computing power infiltrating businesses, GIS is now accessible to mainstream users.

GIS Data

Map data are stored in two different formats. Raster data are used to store images such as aerial photographs, and are extremely demanding on computer systems in terms of storage and processing requirements. Vector data are used to represent spatial lines and points, such as the highways, roads and rivers found on common paper maps, and require less much storage space and processing power.

A major challenge currently facing GIS users is the acquisition of data. GIS software provides users with the power to perform complex data analysis, but map data (raster or vector) are unfortunately not always readily available, and developing new datasets is time-consuming and expensive. Data to build a GIS dataset usually come from three sources: paper-based maps, aerial or satellite photographs, and/or global positioning system (GPS) receivers.

Paper maps. Data from maps can be input using a digitizing tablet. Digitizing a map is a painstaking process of tracing each line with a digitizing tablet, clicking to create individual points, and then joining the points to create vectors that represent the lines on the map. The quality of a GIS dataset developed from paper maps is directly dependent on the quality of the original map, the number of points used to define each line, and the skill of the digitizer operator. It is also possible to scan the original map to create a raster image, and then use computer software to automatically generate a vector image. This approach is becoming more popular, but requires significant computer processing power.

Photographic and satellite images. In addition to simple aerial photographs, satellites can take pictures of the earth using a wide array of imaging techniques. Data collected from satellites include pictures taken within the visible light spectrum, ultraviolet light (UV), and near infrared (NIR) light. Electromagnetic energy can also be measured using satellites. GIS software can use these different forms of spatial data to generate images.

Global positioning systems. GPS receivers use satellite positioning to derive precise coordinates for a point on the earth. GPS receivers convert signals from orbiting satellites into latitudinal/longitudinal position, velocity, and time estimates. Data from a minimum of four satellites are required for these estimates. Coordinates for any type of landmark can thus be derived and then stored for translation into map data. Data can also be transmitted in real time from the GPS receiver to a base station. By joining these point coordinate data to create vectors or lines, a map can be created that displays the precise path traveled by the GPS receiver. This technique is often used to define roads. Collecting GPS data can be time-consuming because it requires collection of information at the physical location on the ground. However, the data collected using GPS is considered better than data collected by other means, since it relies on actual coordinate data rather than data interpolated from a paper map.

The Power of GIS

Once raw map data have been acquired, attributes are attached to map points and stored in an integrated database package for later reference. As many attributes as necessary can be attached to each line or point on the map. This allows users to create complex graphical structures such as road networks, and then keep track of details such as road names, speed limits, surface types, highway classifications, street signs, and number of accidents per segment.

Once detailed data have been attached to the GIS, the user can begin to unleash its analytical capabilities. For example, one add-on GIS application called Network Analyst allows users to determine the best possible route between any two points on the road network with two simple mouse clicks (taking into account variables such as speed limit, traffic patterns, number of turns required on route — and even assigning different times for left and right turns). The capability of GIS as a routing tool has been embraced by organizations such as emergency services, taxi companies, bus companies, package delivery companies, and trucking companies. FedEx now uses a GIS to plot carrier stops to optimize carrier efficiency, and save time and money. Routing is only one example of the analytical capabilities available through GIS.

Challenges

One of the greatest challenges facing users of GIS is the lack of data standardization. Different software vendors use different file formats, and problems arise when users try to integrate datasets with varying scales to create a digital map. For example, the dataset that defines all roads within a certain area may be of 1:50,000 scale, while the bridges on these roads may be at 1:20,000. When the two datasets are layered, the bridges may not appear on the roads. In this case, many users choose to adjust the bridge data so that the bridges appear over the roads. Unfortunately, this practice degrades the quality of the bridge data, resulting in a picture that is more visually appealing, but less precise than the original. Errors are introduced each time a dataset layer is added and altered, and the reliability of the data is increasingly degraded. Scale matching is one of the most challenging aspects for GIS data developers.

GIS critics have warned of possible abuses of this technology. In the marketing arena, for example, GIS have been criticized as counterproductive. When marketers use GIS to uncover specific target or niche groups, they can introduce greater costs by trying to reach small segregated populations. Direct marketing relies largely on economies of scale to achieve penetration. Chris Greenwood, Director of a GIS consulting firm, noted that when you drill down into a market, you may end up spending the same money as a mass mailer, yet you will reach a smaller population. Greenwood believes that "The trick is to get the geographical scale to match the potential business benefit ... In my experience, people try to buy better geography than the underlying business issues require."

This case was previously published in F. Wang (Ed.), *Geographic Information Systems and Crime Analysis*, pp. 214-235, © 2005.

Chapter V

Information Technology in the Practice of Law Enforcement

Susan Rebstock Williams, Georgia Southern University, USA

Cheryl Aasheim, Georgia Southern University, USA

EXECUTIVE SUMMARY

In February 2001, the Charlotte-Mecklenburg Police Department began the rollout of a "mobile" information system that will eventually enable all information relating to incident reports, arrests, and investigations to be collected, distributed, and managed in a paperless, wireless environment. The system, dubbed Knowledge-Based Community Oriented Policing System (KBCOPS), began as a "grass roots" project within the police department to reduce paperwork, increase data accuracy, share knowledge and information, and promote a problem solving analytical framework. The system has been under development for seven years, from concept to implementation. The strategies and approaches used to develop this system, the technologies employed, and, most importantly, the challenges faced in merging wireless, wired, database, and applications technologies while satisfying the user requirements of the police department are detailed in this report.

ORGANIZATIONAL BACKGROUND

The Charlotte-Mecklenburg Police Department (CMPD) is the principal local law enforcement entity for the city of Charlotte, NC, and surrounding Mecklenburg County. CMPD serves a population of nearly 700,000 citizens in an area covering more than 550 square miles, and employs nearly 2,000 people, including sworn police officers and civilian support staff. Civilian personnel are assigned to a variety of clerical and administrative support functions related to but not directly involved in the practice of law enforcement activities. CMPD is headquartered in a state-of-the-art building in the downtown area of the city. This facility was designed and constructed to support the computing and data communications needs of CMPD.

CMPD is commanded by the chief of police with the aid of the deputy chief of administrative services, deputy chief of support services, deputy chief of field services and deputy chief of investigative services. There are many units in CMPD. Figure 2 in Appendix A contains a full organizational chart for CMPD. Technology services, a division of administrative services, manages existing information systems and is responsible for the design and implementation of new IT applications. In addition, they manage strategic planning and crime analysis and provide training for all police department personnel.

The operating budget for CMPD in FY2005 is approximately $146 million. Administrative services, which includes but is not limited to technology services, accounted for approximately 20% of the overall budget. CMPD's operating budget over the three most recent fiscal years is shown in Table 1.

CMPD prides itself on being a community-oriented law enforcement agency whose mission is "to build problem-solving partnerships with our citizens to prevent the next crime" (FY2004 & FY2005 Strategic Plan, p. 57). As stated in the 2004-2005 strategic plan, "the Police Department's problem solving efforts are predicated on the availability of accurate and timely information for use by employees and citizens" (FY2004 & FY2005 Strategic Plan, p. 57). Since 1995, CMPD has recognized that IT will be one of the most important crime fighting tools of the 21st century and has emphasized the commitment to making information one of its most important problem-solving tools. The strategic plan recognizes that IT will play an integral role in achieving the strategic goal of "making Charlotte the safest large city in America" (FY2004 & FY2005 Strategic Plan, p. 31).

SETTING THE STAGE

CMPD was established in 1994 when the city and county police departments of the Charlotte-Mecklenburg area merged. At about that same time, CMPD hired a new chief of police, who recognized the potential of information

Table 1. CMPD budget summary

	FY2003	FY2004	FY2005
Field Operations	$71,695,470	$72,321,646	$75,522,528
Investigative Services	$14,963,920	$14,388,016	$14,915,761
Special Services	$26,353,258	$25,119,778	$25,827,326
Administrative Services	$27,513,572	$28,886,714	$29,827,691
Total Police Services	**$140,526,220**	**$140,716,154**	**$146,093,306**

technology as a problem-solving tool in the practice of law enforcement — particularly in the areas of crime analysis and computerized mapping. To further this cause CMPD commissioned a nearby university to conduct an in-depth needs analysis in 1995. CMPD also hired a planning director to lead the effort of updating or replacing antiquated systems, and more importantly, to identify new systems that would improve the quality of policing. As a result of the needs analysis, an information systems master plan was created in 1996. The master plan called for the establishment of an infrastructure, followed by the development of mission-critical databases. Top priorities included the creation of a wireless network, an improved dispatching system, and a new report management system.

The information system requirements of CMPD are many and varied. Major systems include those that support: (1) administrative and personnel functions; (2) dispatching and 911 emergency services; and (3) incident reporting, case management, arrest, investigative, and crime analysis activities. The system that supports the information requirements encountered in the daily activities of law enforcement is of primary interest in this case. This mission-critical system includes, but is not limited to, incident reporting, case management, arrests, investigation, and crime analysis. The Knowledge-Based Community Oriented Policing System (KBCOPS) was designed and developed to support these activities.

Prior to the rollout of KBCOPS, daily law enforcement activities were carried out in a paper-laden environment. The processes of reporting and investigating incidents were not linked. When an incident was reported, a patrol officer was dispatched to perform a preliminary investigation. During this investigation, the officer took notes on a small paper notebook. When the officer returned to headquarters, often several hours later, he would file a paper report detailing the incident based on his notes and memory of the details of the case. The paper report was given to the appropriate supervisor for approval. The reports were sometimes returned to officers for revision before approval. Reasons for returned reports included spelling errors, grammatical errors and lack of sufficient information about the incident. Patrol officers quickly became aware of which supervisors were more likely to accept their reports without revision. In addition, reports were often resubmitted to a different supervisor due to shift changes. One problem arising from resubmission to a different supervisor was that the new supervisor was not aware of the initial rejection of the report and the reasons for the rejection. Once the report was approved it was sent to the Records Department. The Records Department was responsible for entering some of the information from the report into a database, archiving the report and routing a copy to the proper investigative unit. The supervisor for the investigative unit then assigned the case to a detective. The time frame from reporting an incident to assignment to a detective was four to five days.

In the pre-KBCOPS environment, systems across CMPD did not effectively link to each other. As a result, when a detective discovered a pertinent piece of information upon investigation of the case, the patrol officer who originally investigated the case was not usually notified and there was no mechanism for the notification to take place. If an officer wanted to look at crimes with similar characteristics, the paper reports for those crimes would have to be pulled from the archives by the Records Department and the cases would be analyzed manually by the detective. Information needed for crime analysis, which identifies patterns that might lead to the prevention of the next crime, was not readily accessible across units.

Although information technology supported the collection of data needed in daily law enforcement activities prior to the rollout of KBCOPS, it did not meet the needs of the department with respect to sharing, assimilating, and reviewing these data. It also fell short of fulfilling the chief's vision of IT-enhanced law enforcement. Efforts to create KBCOPS began in 1996. The development and implementation of this new system is the subject of the case described in the following section.

CASE DESCRIPTION

When a police officer responds to an incident in the field an incident report is filed. The first portion of KBCOPS implemented at CMPD — the Incident Reporting subsystem — supports the electronic capture, storage, and retrieval of these reports. Functionality has since been added to support case management activities, arrests, investigative activities, and crime analysis. The following sections describe the features of the system in more detail as well as the required infrastructure, the process used to develop the application, and user perceptions of the system.

The KBCOPS Application

The Incident Reporting subsystem rolled out in February 2001 and consists of modules for creating and approving incident reports. The Incident Reporting subsystem captures all information needed to file an initial police report. This includes data pertaining to suspects, vehicles, victims, witnesses, relationships between suspects and victims, the role a person plays in a crime (victim, suspect or witness) and prior offenses. Accurate, complete, and timely information is critical to subsequent arrest and investigative activities.

KBCOPS runs in a client/server environment. The client runs on laptops issued to police officers in the field, in what is essentially a browser window. Officers use the client software to create police reports *while they are in the police car* rather than waiting until they return to their division office or police headquarters to complete their reports. The ability to capture the data at or near the source, as opposed to hours afterwards, is a significant benefit of KBCOPS because it pushes better investigation at the scene and improves the quality of the information contained within the incident report. Confidence in the merits of this system is so strong that upon initial rollout of the Incident Reporting subsystem officers graduating from the police academy were issued three items: a flak jacket, a weapon, and a laptop.

To complete an incident report an officer fills out a series of forms that are generated as Web pages. Figures 3 through 5 in Appendix B provide examples of forms used in an incident report. Each form is submitted via a wireless link to a server at headquarters (HQ). Context-sensitive field-level and form-level intelligence and workflow routing capabilities are built into this application. Context-sensitive field-level intelligence means that given a specific piece of information the system automatically knows which remaining pieces of information are needed and, in many cases, what the range of acceptable values for those fields can be. Forms are also context driven — which means the next form generated is dependent on the entries on the previous form. This kind of built-in intelligence enables the system to check for errors, omissions, and inconsistencies. Officers must correct these errors before the report can be submitted. The length of time needed to complete an incident report depends upon the nature of the crime but typically ranges from thirty minutes to two hours.

The information submitted by officers in the field is immediately available to other authorized users of KBCOPS. Once a report is filed its contents cannot be modified. Each time changes or additions to an existing report are needed a copy of the report is generated. Changes are appended to the copy and it is saved as a new report. Each previous version remains intact, ensuring that CMPD never loses a version of the incident report — an important consideration for data integrity.

Once an incident report has been submitted, it must be reviewed by a supervisor. If the report is rejected the supervisor provides comments as to why. Reports are often rejected due to spelling and grammatical errors. The supervisor's comments and submission history of the report are recorded, which prevents officers from submitting the same report to another supervisor for approval without first making the corrections suggested in the previous supervisor's comments. Figure 6 in Appendix B shows the screen the officers view to determine the status of their reports. After the report has been approved, a rule-based feature routes the report to the proper investigative unit. These rules are quite complex — requiring knowledge of statutes, policies and specifics of the crime, offender(s) and victim(s). Prior to the development of the system routing a report to the appropriate investigative unit could take days or weeks. Now, the report is routed in a matter of hours.

The Case Management subsystem, which went live in August 2001, extended these capabilities to allow tracking of a case from initial incident all the way through the arrest and investigation procedures. The officer in charge of the investigative unit responsible for the case can view the case summary, assign investigators to the case, or re-route a case to another unit. The Case Management subsystem allows supplements to be added to a case. A case supplement provides an officer with a copy of the original report to change as needed. Both the copy and the original are kept to track the progression of the investigation. When a supplement is added to a case all officers involved are automatically alerted to the new information. Supervisors can make a supplement required, in which case officers are notified when a supplement is past due. Figure 7 in Appendix B illustrates the screen officers view to manage their cases.

The Incident Reporting and Case Management subsystems facilitated the process of completing and tracking police reports. However, users remained unable to retrieve information from the database in any way other than report format. The KBCOPS database contains a wealth of information that can be used to identify and apprehend perpetrators and to identify patterns and trends in criminal behavior. In August 2002 search capabilities were added. Officers, detectives, and other users can now use a large number of search options to retrieve information from the database. Searches can be based on the type of crime, date ranges, patrol division(s), method of operation (MO), physical characteristics of the suspect, weapon(s) used, or any combination of a wide range of variables. Figures 8 and 9 in Appendix B show examples of typical searches.

In addition to search capabilities, several other new features have recently been implemented. For example, the data captured in KBCOPS can be rolled up into the format required for the National Incident-Based Reporting System (NIBRS). NIBRS (NIBRS Implementation Program, 2002) is a nationwide tracking system used to solve crimes that occur across individual police department jurisdictions and across state lines. Although many local police departments have records management systems to capture data about crime incidents, they are unable to use those systems to report to NIBRS because the data are in an incompatible format, not coded in a NIBRS-compliant manner or not all of the mandatory NIBRS elements are captured. A feature that will provide a direct interface to NIBRS is currently underway.

Additional enhancements are being planned. One of these will integrate KBCOPS directly with other local, state, and federal law enforcement systems, as well as hospitals, pawnshops, utility companies, and other entities that possess potentially vital information. Additionally, GIS and global positioning system components will be integrated into KBCOPS to provide street file overlays on the officer's laptop. Finally, a juvenile arrest subsystem will be added in the near future. Handling crimes involving juveniles is complex because statutes and policies for dealing with juvenile offenders and victims differ significantly from those that do not. For example, fingerprints are not taken from juveniles for positive ID, making it nearly impossible to link crimes involving the same juvenile offender. The juvenile arrest module is scheduled for rollout in March 2004. Table 2 summarizes the currently implemented and planned components of KBCOPS.

Table 2. Components of KBCOPS

Incident Reporting System	
Key Functionality	**Key Features**
Create Incident Reports	Context-sensitive intelligence
Approve Incident Reports	Checks for errors/inconsistencies
Assign Case to Investigative Unit	Rule-based assignment algorithms
View/Track Status	Status screens
Add Supplement	Automated version control
Case Management System	
Key Functionality	**Key Features**
View Case Summary	Complete history of all versions
Assign Investigator(s) to Case	Automated alerts for new data
Re-Route Case to Another Unit	Supplements can be required
Add Supplement	Notification of past due supplements
Search Capabilities	
Key Functionality	**Key Features**
Search by Type/Date of Crime	
Search by Patrol Division	
Search by Method of Operations	
Search by Suspect/Multiple Suspects	
Search by Weapon/Vehicle	
NIBRS Reporting	
Key Functionality	**Key Features**
Roll-up crime data for federal reporting	Collects/edits information for NIBRS
	Produces error reports
	Formats monthly data for submission
Juvenile Arrest System*	
Key Functionality	**Key Features**
View Case Summary	Complete history of all versions
Assign Investigator(s) to Case	Automated alerts for new data
Re-Route Case to Another Unit	Supplements can be required
Add Supplement	Notification of past due supplements
Planned Enhancements	
Interfaces with other law enforcement entities	
Interfaces with hospitals, utility companies, pawnshops, and so forth	
Interface with GIS components to provide street overlays	

* *Scheduled to roll out in March 2004*

The KBCOPS Infrastructure

KBCOPS supports nearly 2,000 users. Category 5 (CAT5) cable is used within HQ for local area network (LAN) connectivity. CAT5 provides data transmission speeds of up to 100 million bits per second (Mbps) over normal telephone wire. Fiber extends to district offices up to 18 miles from HQ via a synchronous optimal network (SONET). SONET (Tomsho et al., 2003) is a wide area network technology that is used to allow dissimilar long-distance networks to transmit voice, data and video at speeds in multiples of 51.84 Mbps using fiber-optic media. Within the headquarters building and at district offices, CAT5 cable drops are available every 10 feet each with quad jacks supporting two data connections and two voice connections. This wiring infrastructure provides maximum data connectivity and work area layout flexibility.

The KBCOPS infrastructure initially included 1,500 laptops in the field (one issued to each patrol officer), more than 100 laptops at police headquarters for staff and support personnel, and some 500 desktop computers. Laptops are now issued to vehicles rather than to officers. Currently, over 700 police vehicles are equipped with trunk-mounted modems that support wireless data communication to and from headquarters. Servers and data switches were installed to support the implementation along with the required conventional wired connectivity. CMPD worked with a local wireless data provider to achieve a 99.9% coverage rate in the community. Approximately 53 towers are used to enable communication via TCP-based cellular digital packet data (CDPD). TCP (Tomsho et al., 2003) is an acronym for transmission control protocol, the primary protocol for transport of data packets over the Internet. CDPD (Tomsho et al., 2003) is a mobile computing technology used for wireless Internet and e-mail access. CDPD "sends packets of digital data over unused cellular voice channels at a rate of 19.2 Kbps" (Tomsho et al., 2003, p. 599). Although these towers are shared with cellular phone service providers, the frequencies over which CMPD transmits data do not compete with those used by cellular phone customers.

The Development and Implementation Process

The development process for KBCOPS has been lengthy and costly-running five years from concept to rollout of the Incident Reporting subsystem at a cost of nearly $4 million. Although a majority of this cost has been offset by grant funding, the remainder has been supplied through departmental funds.

The development of KBCOPS was based upon the systems development life cycle (SDLC). The SDLC is a process for understanding how an information system can support the needs of a business, then designing, building, and implementing the system (Dennis & Wixom, 2002). As shown in Table 3, the SDLC consists of five fundamental phases: planning, analysis, design, implementation, and support.

Table 3. Systems development life cycle phases

SDLC Phase	Purpose
Planning	Assess project feasibility; establish budget, schedule, and project team
Analysis	Study the business needs; determine system requirements; develop system models
Design	Create a detailed system specification (interface, database, program and network designs)
Implementation	Build the system, test the system, and place it into operation
Support	Maintain and enhance the system through its useful life

Planning for KBCOPS began in 1996 with the creation of the information systems master plan. Shortly thereafter, efforts to understand the business needs began with one year spent determining the system requirements. System developers and consultants worked with a functional area expert from within CMPD to map the required processes to design specifications.

The development team consisted of nine people — including applications developers, database administrators, systems administrators, project managers, consultants, and network/mobile communications experts. Coding for the Incident Reporting subsystem was finished in April 2000, and system validation testing was conducted in July and August of that year. As a result of these tests new functionality was added and a long test/fix cycle ensued.

Despite early success in the requirements analysis and process mapping phases of development, the project soon suffered a variety of problems. These problems were primarily attributed to the creation of inadequate design specifications, failure to control project scope, and lack of a strong technical project leader. In addition, a number of organizational changes were taking place, including the retirement, in 1999, of the Chief of Police. Both the retiring Chief as well as his replacement supported the development of KBCOPS.

As development of the system progressed the project experienced "scope creep." Scope creep — the identification of new requirements after the project was initially defined — is one of the most common reasons for schedule slippage and cost overruns (Dennis & Wixom, 2002). In 1998 a new director of information technology was hired, and the project was "re-scoped" with clearly identified project phases. An experienced technical project manager was brought on board to work with and oversee the development team. A formal development plan was established with a heavy emphasis on system validation testing. The design specifications were revised and new requirements defined. A great deal of progress on the KBCOPS application soon followed.

Design specifications were developed using Oracle Designer/Developer — a computer-aided software engineering (CASE) tool that supports the tasks associated with the system development process. The use of CASE tools has been shown to reduce development time (and costs) and improve software quality (Dennis & Wixom, 2002). The Incident Reporting subsystem is comprised of more than 1,000 modules (screens, reports, PL/SQL code segments, etc.) and 240 tables. JavaScript and HTML were used for the majority of the client application on the laptops, with PL/SQL running on the Oracle server.

At the time the KBCOPS application was developed the limited bandwidth (19.2 Kbps) available for the wireless transmission of data caused lengthy delays for officers filling in forms using the wireless connection from the field. Changes in the system architecture, including moving to JavaScript on the client side and redesigning transaction confirmation screens (referred to as "Success" screens) were required to address these delays. The use of JavaScript allows some validation of information entered into the forms (such as ensuring required fields are not blank) to be handled on the client machine, instead of sending the form over the wireless connection to the server for all validation (Gosselin, 2000).

The rollout of the Incident Reporting subsystem — the first subsystem to go live — was conducted over a six-week period. Two of the 12 patrol divisions went live each week. During this time period new incident reports were entered both in KBCOPS and in the old system to provide backup in the event of a major latent bug in the system. No major problems were found and duplicate data entry was soon discontinued.

CMPD used a proactive support strategy to assist officers during the implementation of the Incident Reporting subsystem. Officers and other users received 16 hours of initial training to learn how to use the system. A technical team of 12 full-time and six split-time people supported officers in the field. If an officer had questions or problems that could not be handled remotely, support personnel would go to the officer in the field to assist. Some support personnel were stationed at HQ, some at district offices, and others were mobile and thus able to respond quickly to an officer's questions at the incident site.

Today, support is handled by a team of four people at HQ. There is no longer a need to assist officers in the field as the system has become more familiar. KBCOPS has become an integral part of training on "report writing" within the police academy. Approximately 16 hours of the two weeks spent on report writing is dedicated to KBCOPS. Officers identified by their peers as "power users" help fellow officers when questions arise. The rollout of new features and subsystems now utilizes the "big bang" approach rather than a phased approach going division by division. Incremental changes are not viewed as significant enough to require a more conservative approach.

Development and implementation of new subsystems is ongoing. In September 2002 the director of information technology was replaced. Despite this change in leadership support and enthusiasm for the application, it has continued.

A summary of how a case was processed before KBCOPS versus after KBCOPS is provided in Table 4. Due to the automatic storage of fields in the

Table 4. Before and after comparison of processing of a typical case

Event	Before KBCOPS	After KBCOPS
Incident reported	• Officer dispatched to scene	• Officer dispatched to scene
Preliminary investigation	• Officer interviews witnesses and records information in paper notebook	• Officer interviews witnesses and records information in paper notebook
Incident report	• Officer files a paper report after returning to headquarters	• Officer files a report on-line while in the patrol car
Approval of report by supervisor	• Officer submits paper copy of completed report to supervisor • Report may be returned due to errors • Report revised and submitted (possibly to different supervisor) • Supervisor may not be aware of previous supervisor's comments	• Officer submits the report wirelessly • The system alerts the supervisor of a new report • Report may be rejected due to errors • Each supervisor's comments are saved by the system as part of the report
Report to Records Department	• Paper report sent to Records Department to be entered into database and archived	• Report does not go to Records Department but is automatically stored in the database
Assign to investigative unit	• Records Dept. sends a paper copy of the report to investigative unit • Supervisor of investigative unit assigns it to a detective • Often takes 4-5 days from reporting of an incident to assignment of a detective	• System alerts investigative unit to the report • Supervisor assigns a detective to the case electronically • Often takes 24 hours or less from reporting of an incident to assignment of a detective
Investigation of case	• Detective updates paper case file • Only those with access to paper file see updates • Cases with similar characteristics pulled and analyzed manually	• Detective updates case electronically • All versions maintained • System alerts officers involved to updates • Cases with similar characteristics analyzed using search capabilities

report to the database and the automatic routing of the approved report to the appropriate investigative unit by the system the time from reporting an incident to assigning an investigator has been reduced from four to five days to less than 24 hours.

A timeline of the major events that took place during the development and implementation of the KBCOPS application is provided in Table 5.

Table 5. Timeline for KBCOPS application

Year	Event
1994	CMPD established after merger of city and county police departments
1996	CMPD created an IS master plan
1996	Efforts to create KBCOPS began
1998	New director of IT and experienced technical project manager hired
1999	Chief of Police who initiated project retired
2000 (April)	Initial coding for incident reporting subsystem completed
2000 (July)	System validation testing on incident reporting subsystem
2001 (February)	Incident reporting subsystem goes live
2001 (August)	Case management subsystem goes live
2001	Compression software installed
2002 (August)	Search capabilities added to system
2002 (September)	New director of IT hired
2004 (March)	Juvenile arrest module projected to go live

User Perspectives of the KBCOPS Application

In November 2003 several users were interviewed to determine their perceptions of the KBCOPS application. The participants came from two groups, patrol officers and detectives. The interview questions were drawn from the technology acceptance model (Davis, 1989) and the information systems implementation literature (Burns, Turnipseed, & Riggs, 1991). The interview protocol can be found in Appendix C. Example comments from each group are provided.

Detectives' comments:

In the beginning, the time it took was huge. The compression utility has made a big difference. I am excited about it now. From an administrative point of view, it is great.

Newer officers do not seem to have a problem with the system. Older officers still have some resistance.

Investigation has improved. It used to take 4 or 5 days to assign a case to an investigator. Now it takes less than 24 hours. Also, being able to do searches is a big timesaver. We can identify patterns and trends. Our case clearance rate has improved greatly.

There is a big learning curve. Officers try to take shortcuts to get through the system. The reason the officers take so many shortcuts is there are so many screens to go through. Narratives aren't being done as well as they were before. Quality of data is still one of the biggest problems.

Patrol officers' comments:

The availability of information is a big plus. The ability to do searches transformed the system from one that seemed worthless to one you can use. Once you see how the information you enter is used, you understand why they need it. Seeing the big picture really makes a difference.

We were trained on how to use the system, but we didn't understand why we had to use it or how it would alter the investigation process.

The time it took to enter all that data seemed futile before. Now I use the search capabilities every day.

Entering information one screen at a time is a big problem. You can't see the big picture. Some screens ask for information you did not know you had to collect.

Spellchecking takes too long. You can't do intermediate saves in KBCOPS. If the system goes down while entering information, you lose the whole screen. I use Word so that I can undo, use the spellchecker and do intermediate saves.

CURRENT CHALLENGES/PROBLEMS FACING THE ORGANIZATION

Despite the success of the project, CMPD faces ongoing challenges with respect to the KBCOPS application. These challenges stem from technology, user, budgetary issues and aligning IT with community policing objectives.

Technology Issues

At the time this case was written bandwidth in the wireless environment was limited to 19.2K, with an effective bandwidth of 10K. Compression software was installed to improve bandwidth, reducing delays by 60%. However, officers continue to experience delays in uploading and downloading forms.

The system manages approximately one million inbound mobile requests per month and supports 200-250 simultaneous users. The system has thus far proven to be highly reliable, experiencing fewer problems than the internal LAN within CMPD. However, reliability could become an issue in the future as new modules are added and the number of simultaneous users increases.

Although there have been no security breaches to date, security of the wireless implementation must continuously be evaluated. Initially, security issues required almost two years to resolve. The current solution includes user authentication with two levels of encryption. User authentication is the process of identifying authorized users (Newman, 2003). The most common method is through the use of user names and passwords. Encryption prevents a person with unauthorized access to data from reading them (Newman, 2003). Two independent vendors ensure an end-to-end secure connection. The commercial wireless provider encrypts data across its channels, and an additional layer of priority encryption and compression is performed by a leading software-based security system running on CMPD servers. Maintaining security across the network will be an ongoing challenge for CMPD as new encryption standards and better authentication techniques become available.

As with any IT application, the need to manage and integrate emerging technologies is an ongoing challenge. Although there has been relatively little need for maintenance or replacement of equipment, this will become a necessity in the future.

User Issues

Restructuring CMPD's business processes forced changes in the daily activities of police officers. These changes continue to meet with some resistance. If not managed properly, user resistance can lead to attempts to undermine the system (Jiang, Muhanna, & Klein, 2000). Thus, finding effective ways to deal with user resistance is vital to the continued success of the project.

Although many users are satisfied with the system, pockets of user resistance are visible. Some officers see the system as pushing extra work on them. KBCOPS requires them to spend a significant amount of time entering information that populates the incident database — a database that is subsequently used primarily by detectives. Although the implementation of search features has helped, some patrol officers still question the value added by the system.

Additionally, the software has some shortcomings that frustrate users. Specific issues include the delay time for submitting forms, the inability for the officers to save a form before it is submitted, and the lack of support for spellchecking. The last two issues are particularly problematic for forms that require narratives. As a temporary solution, many officers enter their narratives in Word so that they can save their work intermittently and use the spelling and grammar features. They then copy the narrative to the required form. Although this workaround accomplishes the task, it takes extra time and leads to frustration.

Another challenge is created as officers become familiar with the system and take "shortcuts" to avoid filling in extra forms. Entering certain information in one form may generate many additional forms to fill in. Additionally, officers sometimes fill in the required fields in a form and leave non-required fields blank. Consequently, the information stored is sometimes incomplete and inaccurate, compromising the quality of the data and the resulting investigation. The shortcuts and incomplete forms also lead to problems between officers who enter the information and the detectives that depend on it.

Training is one of the most important parts of any change management initiative and is one of the most commonly overlooked (Dennis & Wixom, 2002). Training and a willingness to combine knowledge and skill sets across functional lines are critical success factors for implementation of large systems (Benji, Sharman, & Godla, 1999; Gauvin, 1998). Research suggests that training improves the likelihood of user satisfaction, increases organizational effectiveness, and improves employee morale (Barney, 1991; Peters & Waterman, 1982; Rosenberg, 1990; Ulrich, 1991). Although CMPD trains officers on the use of KBCOPS, training focuses on how to use the system rather than why it should be used and how it fits into the bigger picture of crime investigation.

Budgetary Issues

Continual feedback from users has led to a two-year backlog of requested enhancements. CMPD's ability to respond to these requests is threatened by the drying up of federal grants that to this point have largely underwritten the development of the system. Federal funds previously directed to local police initiatives are being eliminated or redirected to homeland security. Replacement of these funds will be a challenge (FY2004 & FY2005 Strategic Operating Plan).

Further evidence of budgetary problems is reflected by unfunded CMPD budget requests of $1,409,074 in FY04 and $917,009 in FY05 (FY2004 & FY2005 Strategic Operating Plan). Unfunded requests directly affecting KBCOPS included installation of LAN switches and other networking equipment to enable direct access to the system.

At a more technical level, system enhancements present challenges in establishing effective ways to deal with configuration management, defect tracking, quality assurance, and test planning. Developers identified these as areas of concern. Lack of code/version control and inadequate testing are classic implementation mistakes (McConnell, 1996). Continued success of the project will require finding solutions to these problems.

Figure 1. Index of crime rates per 100,000 of population

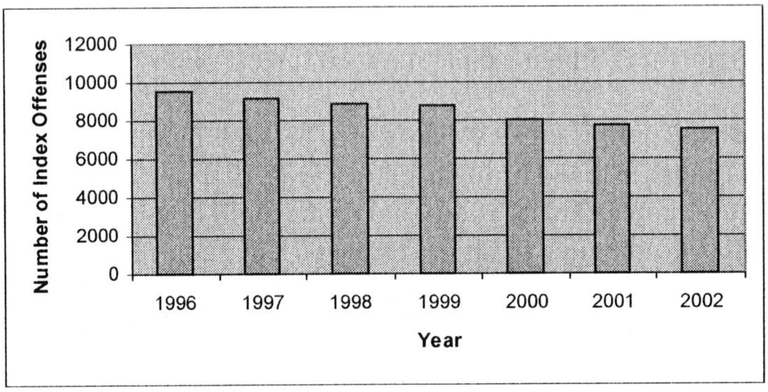

Aligning IT with Community Policing Objectives

Through the development and implementation of KBCOPS, CMPD has migrated from using IT in a reactive manner to employing IT in an active role for sharing knowledge, facilitating collaboration, and promoting a problem-solving analytical framework. The ultimate goal of KBCOPS is to improve the quality of policing. Although a causal relationship cannot be shown, crime rates decreased steadily between 1996 and 2002, as shown in Figure 1.

CMPD recognizes that it will be difficult to continue to reduce crime. Police will have to expand the number and scope of partnerships to solve new problems. CMPD must identify new ways in which KBCOPS and IT in general can support strategic initiatives and continue to improve the quality of policing.

REFERENCES

Barney, J. (1991). Firm resources and sustained competitive advantage. *Journal of Management, 17*(1), 99-120.

Benji, P., Sharma, M. K, & Godla, J. (1999, Summer). Critical issues affecting an ERP implementation. *Information Systems Management,* 7-14.

Burns, M., Turnipseed, D., & Riggs, W. (1991). Critical success factors in manufacturing resource planning implementation. *International Journal of Operations and Production Management, 11*(4), 5-19.

Davis, F. D. (1989, September). Perceived usefulness, perceived ease of use, and user acceptance of information technology. *MIS Quarterly,* 319-340.

Dennis, A., & Wixom, B. (2000). *Systems Analysis and Design.* New York: John Wiley & Sons.

FY 2004 & FY2005 Strategic Operating Plan. (n.d.). Retrieved November 25, 2003, from http://www.charmeck.org/NR/rdonlyres/ebfoi6vj2zxo3fizpg57kgvuw4oylbc52onaniem63x4s2rweqz6oogoohigtncpeyky6lcxy35tnlaswait6msbirb/Section+1+-+Final+FY2004+SOP.pdf
Gauvin, G. (1998). Plan to succeed. *Manufacturing Systems,* A44-A48.
Gosselin, D. (2000). *JavaScript.* Cambridge, MA: Course Technology.
Jiang, J., Muhanna, W., & Klein, G. (2000). User resistance and strategies for promoting acceptance across system types. *Information & Management, 37*(1), 25.
McConnell, S. (1996). *Rapid development.* Redmond, WA: Microsoft Press.
National Incident-Based Reporting System (NIBRS) Implementation Program. (2002, December 26). Retrieved November 25, 2003, from http://www.ojp.usdoj.gov/bjs/nibrs.htm
Newman, R. C. (2003). *Enterprise security.* Upper Saddle River, NJ: Prentice Hall.
Peters, T. J., & Waterman, R. (1982). *In search of excellence: Lessons from America's best-run companies.* New York: Harper & Row.
Rosenberg, M. J. (1990). Performance technology: Working the system. *Training and Development, 44*(1), 43-48.
Smith, D. (1996). *Taking charge of change.* Reading, MA: Addison-Wesley.
Tomsho, G., Tittel, E., & Johnson, D. (2003). *Guide to networking essentials* (3rd ed.). Boston: Course Technology.
Ulrich, D. (1991). Using human resources for competitive advantage. In I. Kilmann (Ed.), *Making organizations competitive.* San Francisco: Jossey-Bass.
Varshney, U., Vetter, R., & Kalakota, R. (2000). Mobile commerce: A new frontier. *Computer, 33*(10), 32-39.

APPENDIX A

Figure 2. Organizational chart

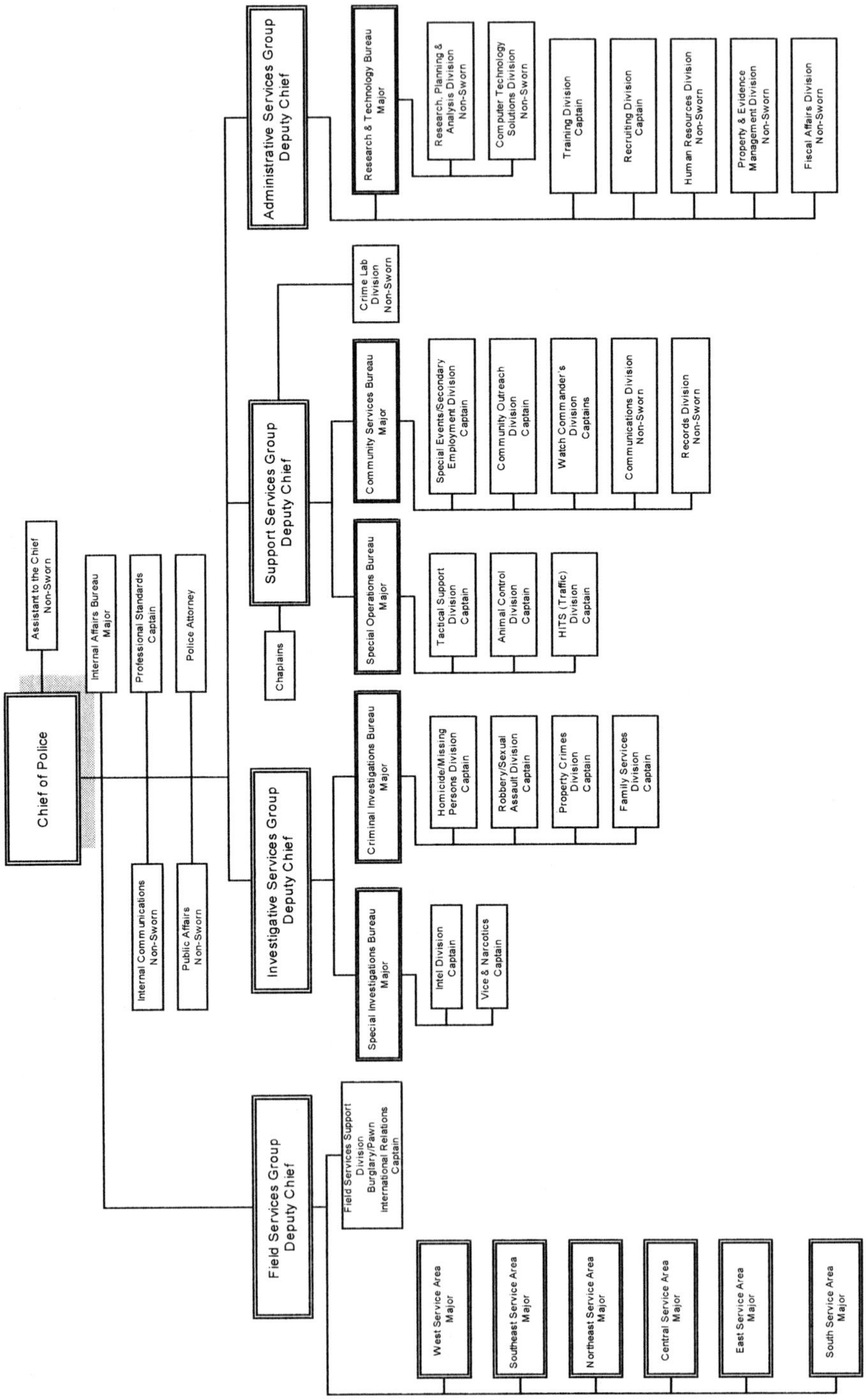

APPENDIX B

Figure 3. Incidents screen — Collects information about the date/time and location of the incident

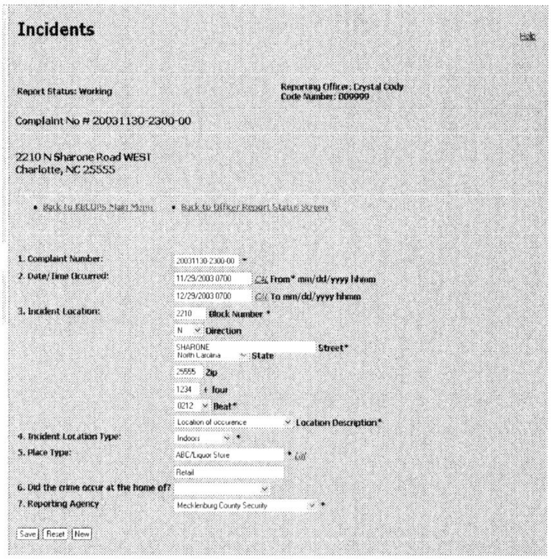

Incidents

Report Status: Working

Reporting Officer: Crystal Cody
Code Number: 009999

Complaint No # 20031130-2300-00

2210 N Sharone Road WEST
Charlotte, NC 25555

1. Complaint Number: 20031130-2300-00 *
2. Date/Time Occurred: 11/29/2003 0700 From* mm/dd/yyyy hhmm
12/29/2003 0700 To mm/dd/yyyy hhmm
3. Incident Location: 2210 Block Number *
N Direction
SHARONE Street*
North Carolina State
25555 Zip
1234 + four
0212 Beat*
Location of occurence Location Description*
4. Incident Location Type: Indoors *
5. Place Type: ABC/Liquor Store *
Retail
6. Did the crime occur at the home of?
7. Reporting Agency Mecklenburg County Security *

Save Reset New

Figure 4. Incident demographics — Collects other details about the incident including the clearance and case status

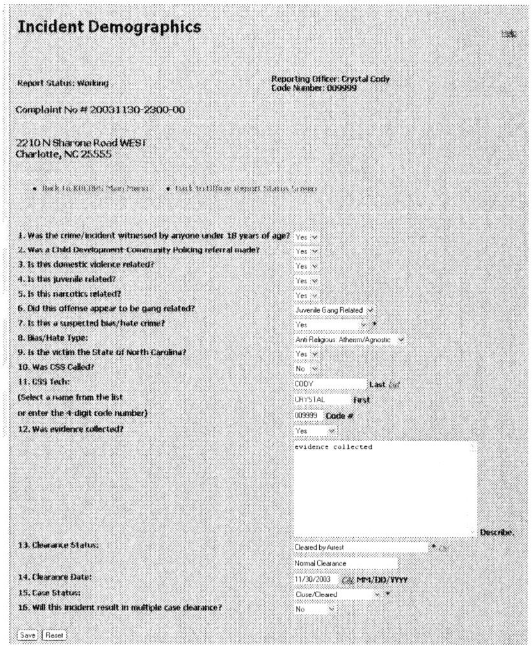

Incident Demographics

Report Status: Working

Reporting Officer: Crystal Cody
Code Number: 009999

Complaint No # 20031130-2300-00

2210 N Sharone Road WEST
Charlotte, NC 25555

1. Was the crime/incident witnessed by anyone under 18 years of age? Yes
2. Was a Child Development-Community Policing referral made? Yes
3. Is this domestic violence related? Yes
4. Is this juvenile related? Yes
5. Is this narcotics related? Yes
6. Did this offense appear to be gang related? Juvenile Gang Related
7. Is this a suspected bias/hate crime? Yes *
8. Bias/Hate Type: Anti-Religious: Atheism/Agnostic
9. Is the victim the State of North Carolina? Yes
10. Was CSS Called? No
11. CSS Tech: CODY Last
(Select a name from the list CRYSTAL First
or enter the 4-digit code number) 009999 Code #
12. Was evidence collected? Yes
evidence collected
Describe.
13. Clearance Status: Cleared by Arrest *
Normal Clearance
14. Clearance Date: 11/30/2003 MM/DD/YYYY
15. Case Status: Close/Cleared *
16. Will this incident result in multiple case clearance? No

Save Reset

Figure 5. Suspect description — Collects descriptive information on the suspect

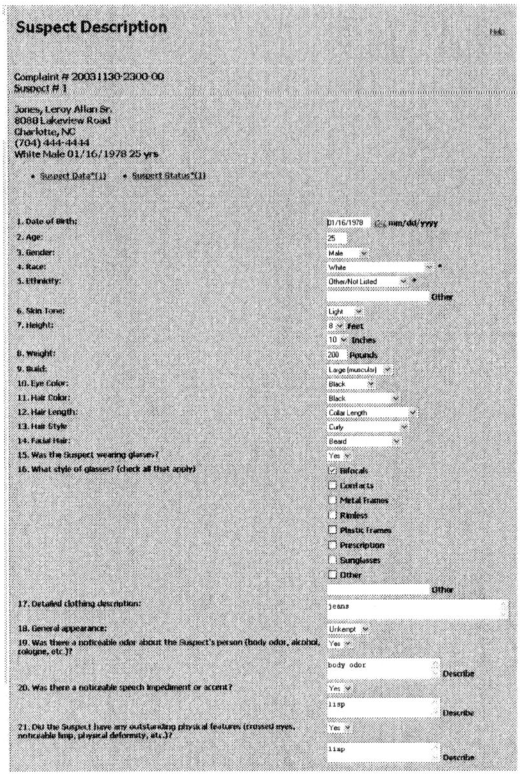

Figure 6. Officer report status — Allows officers to manage reports

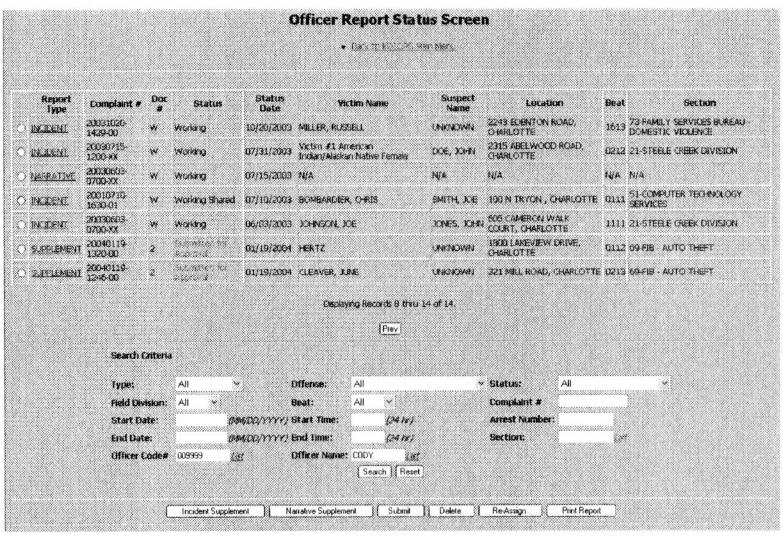

Figure 7. Case assignments — Enables officers to manage their cases

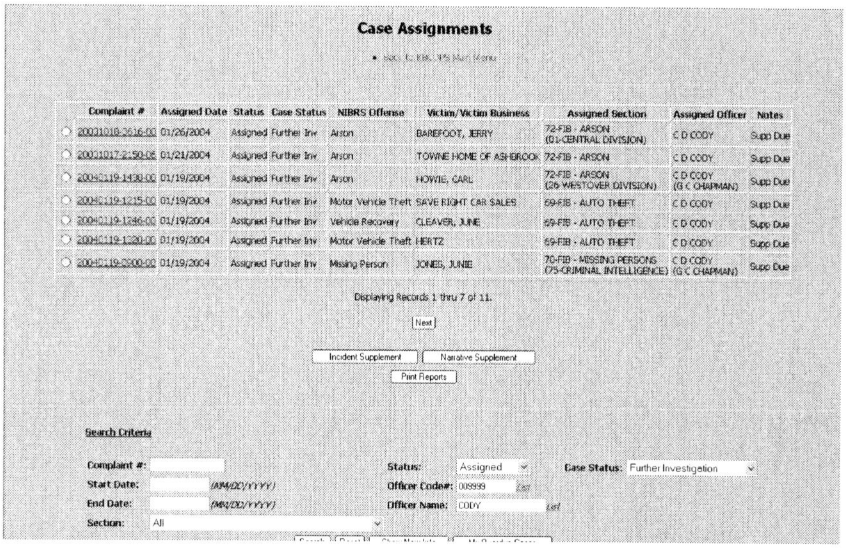

Figure 8. Vehicle Search — Illustrates a search for an orange cadillac

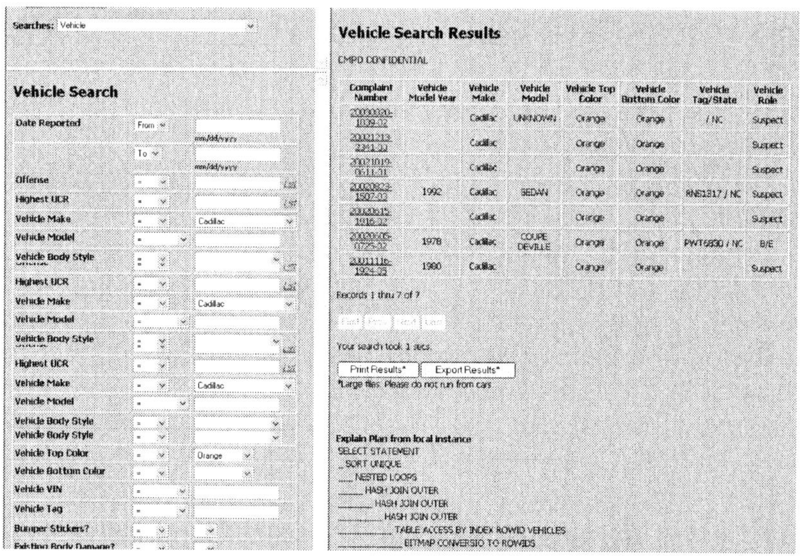

Figure 9. Suspect MO search — Illustrates a search for a black male, age 30-40, with dreadlocks and gold teeth who committed a robbery

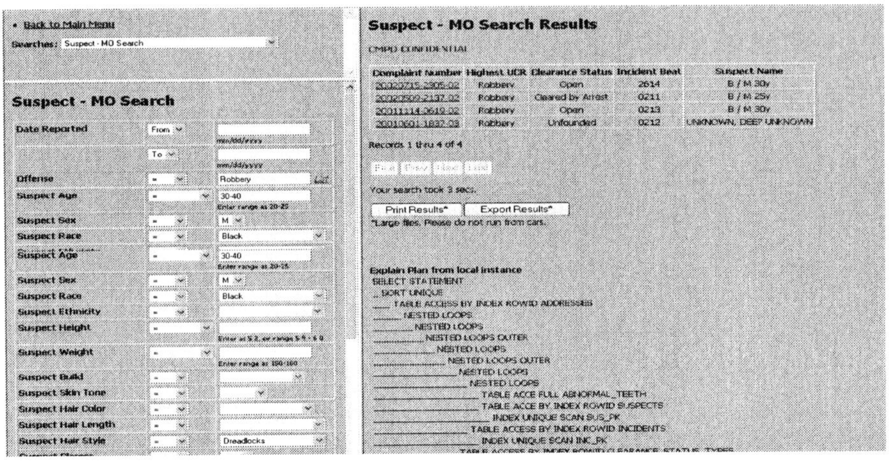

APPENDIX C

Multiple visits were made to CMPD to interview project participants. The first round of interviews was conducted in February 2001 during initial system rollout. The second round was conducted in November 2003. Participants in each round were purposively chosen to span diverse areas of functional and technical expertise.

Questions in the first round were directed primarily to developers. Questions were based on the Varshney, Vetter, and Kalakota (2000) mobile commerce framework and focused on identifying and understanding: (1) development methodologies, (2) infrastructure, (3) interface of mobile and land-based technologies, and (4) functionality of the application.

Questions in the second round focused on understanding implementation issues and user acceptance of the system. The following questions guided the second round of interviews:

1. At the time of our last visit, the Incident Reporting System was being rolled out. What other modules are now in place? What kind of roll out approach have you used?

2. What organizational difficulties have you encountered in implementing new modules?
3. In general, what is the level of acceptance of the system?
4. What are the "before" and "after" views of the users (police officers)?
5. To what extent have you integrated KBCOPS with external systems (hospitals, emergency services, federal and state law enforcement agencies, etc.)?
6. What technical difficulties have you encountered as the system has grown?
7. How do you train officers to use the system?
8. How do you support users in the field?
9. In what ways has the quality of policing improved since the implementation of KBCOPS?
10. Are other police departments following your lead and adopting similar systems?

To improve reliability, all interviews were conducted with two researchers present, each taking notes independently. These notes were later compared and synthesized to arrive at a clear and consistent interpretation of the verbal data.

Susan Rebstock Williams is professor and acting chair of the Department of Information Systems in the College of Information Technology at Georgia Southern University. Prior to earning a PhD at Oklahoma State University, she spent 13 years in the IT industry, where she worked as a programmer, systems analyst, and information systems manager. She has published three books on object-oriented software development as well as numerous articles addressing the impact of IT.

Cheryl Aasheim is assistant professor in IT in the College of Information Technology at Georgia Southern University. In 2002 she received her PhD in decision and information sciences from the University of Florida. Dr. Aasheim's publications include papers on research areas including information retrieval, text classification and the impact of IT.

This case was previously published in the *Journal of Cases on Information Technology*, 7(1), pp. 71-91, © 2005.

Chapter VI

Implementing Relational Database Systems: Implications for Administrative Cultures and Information Resource Management

Andreea M. Serban, Santa Barbara City College, USA

Gregory A. Malone, Cabrillo College, USA

EXECUTIVE SUMMARY

Traditionally, administrative computing has been the main, or often only, unit in a campus developing and maintaining the basic operating systems of an institution (McKinney et al., 1987). Information resources have been confined to an infrastructure, such as a mainframe computer or minicomputers, which processes registration, financial aid, and other services (Van Dusen, 1997). The advent of increasingly sophisticated software and hardware tools has challenged the centralization of the control and manipulation of information resources. Crow and Rariden

(1993) describe an ideal information resource management model as follows:

> *Powerful software tools are available that can essentially eliminate the technical expertise necessary to process either university-wide data or off-campus research databases. ... Students, faculty, and administrators will be able to ask and answer their own data-related questions from their desks without the assistance or intervention of a computer center's staff. (p. 467)*

To date, no institution has achieved this ideal (Van Dusen, 1997). However, colleges and universities are making progress toward it. This chapter describes the experiences of two institutions, University of Redlands and Cabrillo College, as they implement similar relational database systems. It describes the effects of the implementation process on the institutional administrative cultures, and the implications for information resource management.

CASE QUESTIONS

- What factors drive an institution to replace its existing administrative information system (AIS)?
- What are the elements and phases of the implementation process?
- What are the expected benefits of implementing a new AIS? What are the potential risks?
- When replacing an existing AIS, in what ways should an institution consider changing the organizational structure that was supported by the original system?

CASE NARRATIVE

Background

Founded in 1907, the University of Redlands (UOR) is a private institution, located 60 miles east of Los Angeles. The organizational structure of the University includes the board of trustees, the president and vice presidents for Finance and Administration, and Academic Affairs. The University has two colleges — the College of Arts and Sciences (CAS) and the Alfred North Whitehead College of Lifelong Learning (ANWC). CAS offers more than 25 majors in liberal arts and programs of study in professional and pre-professional fields to over 1,500 residential students. ANWC offers undergraduate and graduate programs to more than 2,200 students. The University has a main campus and five adult learning regional centers throughout Southern California. The structure and size of the University have fostered a climate of high-quality, personalized education for both traditional-aged students and adult learners.

Cabrillo College is one of the 107 California community colleges and enrolls almost 14,000 students on three campuses. The main campus conducts most of the classes and all of the administrative business. The organizational structure includes a Governing Board with decision-making authority over all site functions, the president, and vice presidents of Business Services, Instruction, and Student Services. The Cabrillo community college district is a supportive environment characterized by extensive collegiality in both instructional and administrative areas.

Cabrillo College is a union organization in both the academic and nonacademic domains. In this aspect, it differs sharply from most private institutions of higher education, including UOR. Whereas private schools generally allow and even encourage employees to contribute extra time, this is not an option for a unionized organization. Union employees are required to work no more than eight hours per day unless prior approval is granted. One result of this has been that there are often longer implementation times when urgent and intensive project efforts are required.

The operations of the two colleges share some commonalities. The registration, student billing, and financial aid processes are located in the main campuses. However, UOR's adult college is decentralized. Each regional center conducts recruitment and admissions, academic advisement, enrollment services, and degree audit and graduation checks. Additionally, Cabrillo has two small branches in nearby cities.

History

Both institutions have relied on traditional administrative computing environments with the Information Technology Services (ITS) at UOR and the Computing Resources (CR) at Cabrillo to manage the structure, processing, and reporting of institutional information through mainframe and minicomputer systems. In 1987, UOR acquired and installed the Information Associates' (IA) suite of administrative software to support most of its administrative information processing needs. The implementation of IA was completed in 1990. However, some offices never fully converted to IA and continued to maintain their own systems. The IA suite was an example of a "monolithic software model" (Mignerey, 1996, p. 40) in which applications were developed to support university-wide (as opposed to department-level) processes. This system required heavy-duty maintenance. Any change involved ITS staff rewriting Cobol programs or modifying data dictionaries. The system also required nightly batch maintenance. Similarly, Cabrillo's legacy Santa Rosa system required 18 months of data conversion and programming when an upgrade was loaded.

Prior to 1993, UOR's system was heavily modified to accommodate the operational needs and processes of the University. The level of modification was so extensive that upgrades to newer versions required extensive programming. Functional users had very limited input and access to the management of institutional information. The communication between functional users and the ITS staff was weak. This setting led to duplication of efforts among different offices. Reporting and data retrieval were difficult and the reliability of data questionable. Many routine tasks required manual operation due to the lack of integration among the existing systems. All these issues increased the frustration of functional users and hampered the effectiveness and efficiency of the University's operations.

Two other major factors contributed to the decision to convert to a new system at UOR. In 1993, Systems & Computing Technology (SCT) bought IA and announced that it would not support development of new IA versions. By 1993, UOR was aware of the need to address the year 2000 compliance of its systems and IA was not compliant. In early 1993, UOR's senior administrative management, under the leadership of the vice president for Finance and Administration, decided that it had to evaluate its administrative computing needs and address issues such as ITS structure and role, data ownership and management, and core administrative processes.

At Cabrillo, Hewlett-Packard declared the main information system in use at the time obsolete as of 1998. Support for the equipment ceased and it was announced that it would not be made year 2000 ready. In October 1996, Cabrillo's Technology Committee met for a retreat to study and evaluate the existing condition of the administrative information systems. This group included teachers, bargaining unit representatives, power users from departments, and the vice presidents of the college. Difficulties encountered with the existing information systems provided incentive to conduct a meeting to generate recommendations to solve these problems. The retreat resulted in the following recommendation:

> *Cabrillo College must implement a new Student Support/ Administrative Information System (SS/AIS) to overcome the paralysis caused by our current software and hardware. The schedule for replacing the current systems is being driven by software and hardware incompatibilities with the year 2000 and current system inability to provide comprehensive SS/AIS information to the College Community.* (Cabrillo College, 1997a)

Conversion Strategy

UOR's strategy was captured in the acronym that became associated with the evaluation process: ACORN — **A**dministrative **C**onversion: **O**perational

Redesign and INnovation. As in process reengineering models (e.g., Davenport, 1993), this process encompassed a strategic vision, organizational processes, people, and technology. Although the emphasis was on operational processes, a strategic focus guided the administrative conversion. The focus was multifold: to align operational processes with the University's strategic priorities; to restructure the ITS in order to meet the computing needs of the University and improve its efficiency and effectiveness; and to create an organizational culture of change.

From an organizational perspective, the conversion had several goals: to establish a service-oriented culture; to create an environment proactive and adaptable to technological changes; to adopt a cross-functional team approach in managing operational processes; to improve organizational processes through better use of technology; to improve communication and collaboration between ITS and functional users; and to change the role of ITS from the gatekeeper of information to the facilitator of information processing and management.

The planners of the conversion process recognized that the keys to a successful implementation and to organizational change are the individuals affected by the process. The process incorporated the goals to establish and support leadership of the functional users, to provide incentives and resources for learning, and to increase the ability of all level users to manage and utilize information.

On the technology side, several priorities guided the process: to select and implement a system that best meets the needs of the institution and has broad capabilities; to create an integrated information environment; to implement process automation; to provide easy access to authorized users; to allow real-time interaction of information from various administrative units; and to provide a comprehensive source for accurate and timely data reporting.

Cabrillo embraced a similar strategy. The mission of the implementation project was to improve Cabrillo's service to students, faculty, staff, and the college community through the implementation of integrated information systems for student support, curriculum, finance, and human resources, and the concurrent improvement of operational processes. The goals of the project included: elimination of duplicate efforts and redundant systems; automation of manual processes; increased employee effectiveness; and availability of timely, reliable information. Strategies to achieve those goals included: communicating frequently with those involved with and affected by the project; providing appropriate project information to those who need it; providing appropriate training and documentation to team members; identifying and allocating the resources required for success; taking advantage of each application's flexibility to eliminate the need for programming modifications to the software; adopting and following a project plan; and knowing when to change the plan.

Both institutions sought a single vendor that could provide an integrated information system that met the following requirements. It could be: implemented without vendor customization; accommodate site-specific modifications through non-programming solutions such as rules; be designed to retain local modifications as new software releases are implemented; and have the ability to support all core institutional operations.

Pre-Implementation

At UOR, the first step in the conversion process was the evaluation of the University's administrative computing needs. In February 1993, UOR selected the Higher Education Technology and Operations Practice of KPMG Peat Marwick to conduct this evaluation. Its purposes were to:

> *Determine which functions might be supported by an automated system; ... obtain from functional users information required of the system; establish a benchmark against which software packages can be qualified and initially evaluated; and provide the level of detail necessary to identify the software package(s) which most reasonably "fit" Redlands' needs.* (KPMG, 1993, p. 7)

The evaluation found that the existing systems met 35% of the administrative computing needs, partially met 24%, and did not meet 41%. The main reasons cited for the existence of the unmet needs were: poor implementation, planning, and execution of the IA; poor training; lack of functionality; and weak vendor and ITS support. The report concluded that the unmet needs negatively influenced UOR's administrative operations through an abundance of manual work, "work around" procedures, redundant maintenance of data, and strain on employees (KPMG, 1993). KPMG recommended that:

> *UOR should undertake a long-term administrative systems upgrade project to focus on: investigating and implementing client/server technology; fostering increased systems integration with off-the-shelf vendor applications; allowing fewer or no modifications to vendor-supplied software; and decentralizing certain computer support services.* (KPMG, 1993, p. 3)

UOR faced the clear need for converting to a new system but it had to determine which system best met its needs, how the conversion could best be conducted, by whom, and with what resources. For the next year, UOR studied and discussed the results of the evaluation in order to establish the most appropriate course of action. During the summer of 1994, UOR developed a request for proposals to acquire a new administrative information system.

Before engaging in vendor selection, UOR had to decide who would lead the conversion. Due to the weak relationship between the ITS and the user community at the time, UOR's senior management decided that the conversion

Table 1. Total costs of the UOR Conversion Project

Conversion Project Costs	Dollars	Percent
Personnel, Administrative and Consultant Costs	$1,441,683	46%
Training/Travel of ITS and Project Office Staff	77,367	3%
Software	760,380	25%
Equipment (workstations, printers, minicomputers)	793,959	26%
Total Conversion Project	**$3,073,389**	**100%**

process would be better coordinated and conducted by a group especially dedicated to this purpose. In February 1995, the President's Cabinet established the Project Office, composed of three employees of UOR, to coordinate all aspects of the conversion project. The President's Cabinet appointed the vice president for Finance and Administration as the senior manager (Program Sponsor) in charge of the conversion project to work directly with the Project Office. In order to ensure the continuity of the conversion process without disruptions due to possible turnover, UOR converted two of the Project Office positions from full-time employees to contract positions for the duration of the project.

UOR committed to acquire and provide the financial and human resources needed for the conversion process. In 1995, UOR applied for and obtained a bond issue which covered, along with some other major projects, most of the costs associated with the conversion: consulting, software, hardware, training, personnel, and administrative costs (see Table 1 for costs).

With the leadership of the project established and the financial resources secured, the next step was the selection of a vendor. The KPMG evaluation clarified the general requirements of a new system in terms of system integration, user control, usage, transaction and document processing, inquiry capabilities, correspondence control, query and reporting, security, and interface with other systems. In addition, the system had to address the major functional areas of the University: admissions, registration, financial aid, student housing, alumni development, human resources, and financial management.

The Project Office, in collaboration with the managers of the major functional areas and ITS, reviewed the vendor proposals. Narrowing down the qualified vendors was easy at the time, since there were not many choices available. The finalists were two major vendors: SCT with its product Banner, and Datatel with its products Colleague (student, financial, and core demographics systems) and Benefactor (alumni development system). During July and August 1995, the two companies conducted demonstrations of their products at

UOR. These demonstrations combined general overviews of the products with specific demonstrations developed in response to "business cases" developed by UOR and submitted to the two vendors in advance. The business cases exemplified some of the processes that UOR's functional users employed routinely. In addition, during the summer of 1995, the Project Office, functional area and ITS managers conducted visits to colleges and universities already using these products and to each company's corporate headquarters. UOR considered the potential of each of the prospective vendors as a business partner for at least five years. Consequently, UOR selected Datatel for all functional areas except for Human Resources. The perceived weakness of Datatel's human resource module led to the selection of a different vendor (ProBusiness) for human resources.

Cabrillo College staff approached the search for a new information system as a collaborative effort with meetings and on-site visits resulting in: multiple vendor demonstrations; advice of an outside consultant regarding major providers of SS/AIS appropriate for use in California community colleges; and reviews of current SS/AIS requirements and requests for proposals utilized at other community colleges in California.

Cabrillo's staff attended vendor demonstrations of SCT Banner, Datatel Colleague, and Buzzio. Additional meetings with the Higher Education and Technology Operations at KPMG Peat Marwick confirmed that the major SS/AIS packages available had been identified. Based upon responses to the requests for proposals, site visits, and positive customer feedback, Cabrillo selected Datatel's Colleague software. Several California community colleges had selected Colleague during the same period. The significance of this migration of multiple sites to the Colleague product resulted in Datatel producing some specific data modifications for California colleges. Such a notable modification is the "California Gold" version of the human resources module that deals with retirement programs unique to California.

During October 1997, Cabrillo College continued to evaluate Datatel Colleague to ensure a close fit with its needs. The College organized a four-day series of demonstrations to address the needs of the various departments, with half-day sessions provided for each department. Numerous representatives from Cabrillo and three other colleges attended these meetings. Cabrillo provided an additional full-day session to present information for instructional areas and to answer some of the concerns of the business services department. A representative from a neighboring college attended this session. Cabrillo staff met with Datatel representatives and discussed optional modules needed, number of concurrent user licenses necessary, and pricing structure. These sessions addressed most of the concerns of the College community and reinforced the impressions of the staff that this was a complete, flexible, and configurable solution.

Table 2. Estimated costs of the Cabrillo College Conversion Project (Cabrillo College, 1997b)

Conversion Project Costs	**Dollars**	**Percent**
Personnel, Administrative and Consultant Costs	$302,500	26%
Training/Travel of ITS and Project Office Staff	85,000	7%
Software	630,000	55%
Equipment (workstations, printers, minicomputers)	139,000	12%
Total Conversion Project	**$1,156,500**	**100%**

At the December 1, 1997, Governing Board meeting, the board adopted the action item for the vice president of Business Services to execute a contract to purchase Datatel's administrative information system. Cabrillo estimated the total cost of the project at $1,156,500 (see Table 2 for estimated costs). This estimate included the software, data conversion, travel expenses, training, consulting, utility software tools, hardware replacements, and hardware and software support.

On December 22, 1997, Cabrillo College purchased Datatel's Colleague to replace its legacy systems for financial management, human resources management, and student, faculty, and curriculum management. The College targeted the replacement of these systems and conversion of data from spring 1998 to summer 2000 (see Table 3 for implementation timetable). In 15 months, Cabrillo progressed from the realization that something needed to change to the purchase decision of the appropriate system.

Implementation

At UOR, the implementation of the new system lasted almost two years (September 1996-August 1998; see Table 4) and involved 75 individuals from various administrative units.

One of the most important aspects of the conversion process at UOR was the transfer of information ownership from ITS to the administrative units (for example, the Registrar's office became the owner of modules such as registration and degree audit/advisement). This resulted in a change in the role of the ITS from manager of the information to facilitator of data input, processing, and reporting. Such a transition meant addressing several critical issues:

- Establishing a system of continuous communication between ITS and administrative units, on one hand, and among administrative units, on the other.

Table 3. Cabrillo implementation timeline

System/Modules	Full Start Date
Core System	
Demographics	August 1998
Scheduling	August 1999
Facilities Profile, Communications Management	October 1999
Finance System	
General Ledger, Accounts Payable, Purchasing	August 1998
Budget Management	March 1999
Auxiliary Funds—General Ledger, Accounts Payable, Purchasing; Decentralized Account Management Lookup	July 1999
Human Resource System	
Personnel	May 1999
Student System	
Faculty Information, Curriculum Management	August 1999
Admission/Recruiting, Accounts Receivable, Registration, Academic Records, Degree Audit, Advising, Counseling (Education Plans)	October 1999
Financial Aid	March 2000
Web Registration	April 2000

- Rethinking the operations of computing services and their relationships with administrative units.
- Ensuring that operational processes are clearly defined and understood and the effects of the system integration on overlapping areas are continuously monitored and communicated between administrative units/functional areas.
- Training of an initial group of end users on both the use of the Datatel systems and personal computer software, who would then train users within their units.
- Defining and establishing levels of data access for various clients of the Datatel system.
- Establishing mechanisms for ensuring data integrity.
- Developing policies and procedures for access to and use of the information.
- Determining mechanisms of data manipulation, analysis, interpretation, and reporting.

In light of these principles, the implementation process evolved around several distinctive features. Individuals from all functional areas were involved

Table 4. ACORN chronology

1993	February: UOR hires KPMG Peat Marwick's Higher Education Division to evaluate the administrative computing needs. September: KPMG completes the evaluation of administrative computing needs.
1994	UOR develops request for proposals to acquire a new administrative system.
1995	February: Project Office established to conduct and oversee the conversion project. July-August: On-site demonstrations by Datatel and SCT and visits to colleges and universities using the products of the two companies. October: Contract with Datatel finalized. November: Equipment purchased.
1996	Installation of equipment and software. Initial training of selected functional users and contract employees of the Project Office. Functional analysis and implementation begin.
1997	Training of selected functional users, functional analysis and implementation continue. Units start full use: July: Finance (General Ledger and Accounts Payable/Purchasing). August: Benefactor. November: CAS Admissions. December: ANWC Admissions.
1998	Implementation continues. January: Human Resources (with a different vendor — ProBusiness). February: Financial Aid. April: Housing. July: Finance (Budget Management, Fixed Assets, Inventory, Physical Plant, Pooled Investment). August: Billing and Registration and Student Systems. September: Implementation completed, Project Office closed.

in the implementation process. Two functional user-based teams were formed at the outset of the implementation, the system implementation managers and the Implementation Team. The system implementation managers were the managers of the main functional areas: the controller for the Finance Area, the registrar for the Student Area, the director of Alumni Development for the Alumni/Development Area, and a human resources analyst for the Human Resource Area. The Implementation Team included, along with the system implementation managers, the designated module leaders. Each of the four major systems (student, finance, and alumni development with Datatel and human resources with ProBusiness) included a number of modules that reflect various processes within the major functional areas (see Table 5 for the structure of systems and modules within systems).

The two functional user teams were the champions of their systems and modules. The Project Office and functional user teams agreed that a technical group composed of ITS staff and two of the Project Office staff was also needed. This group would deal with the installation and testing of the new software systems and the conversion of the data from the old to the new systems.

Table 5. Structure of the integrated systems

System	Modules
Student (Datatel Colleague)	Financial Aid, Accounts Receivable, Communications Management, Registrar, Degree Audit/Advisement, Student Affairs/Housing, Demographics, Admissions
Alumni Development (Datatel Benefactor)	Major Prospects, Activities and Events, Individual Information, Organizational Information, Campaign Management, Correspondence Control, Gift and Pledge Processing
Human Resources (Pro Business and Datatel Colleague)	Personnel, Payroll
Core Demographics (Datatel Colleague)	Person Demographics, Corporation Demographics, Facilities, Correspondence Control, Parameter Definition

These four groups represented the driving forces throughout the implementation process.

Based on KPMG's recommendations, the UOR's Program Sponsor and implementation groups decided to engage in a functional analysis of all university processes concurrent with the implementation of the new systems.

> *Functional analysis is a holistic methodical approach to establishing a new vision for providing services and fully exploiting the functional capabilities of the new software. Functional analysis will result in processes designed to meet UOR's objectives and tasks defined to complete the conversion project.* (Caudle, 1996, p. 25)

The analysis was accomplished by creating work groups that focused on various processes. The work groups addressed specific and cross-functional processes, established communication between administrative units, and provided decision making for process streamlining to be more service oriented. A KPMG consultant acted as facilitator for each functional analysis meeting.

At both institutions, the implementation tasks were divided into three major phases to help organize the workflow and activities (Caudle, 1996). This was based on the design of the Datatel systems, which included the creation of three separate environments: the "education" environment where functional users could learn the systems; the "test" environment that contained the same data as the actual production database but where functional users could try various processes and procedures without the risk of corrupting the data; and the "live" environment that represents the actual production database. In the initial phase of the implementation, only the first two environments were available. The "live" accounts were created at the final stage of the implementation of each of the systems. The creation of the "live" environments meant the completion of the implementation for a particular system. The three phases represent the implementation sequence for each of the major systems:

- **Phase I — Planning, Analysis, and Learning. "Getting Understanding"**
  This phase included tasks performed in the "Education" account that allow the implementation team leaders to gain an understanding of their modules. Tasks associated with this phase included: analysis of current tasks and procedures; preparation for vendor training; module training for technical staff, decision makers, and internal trainers; design of code tables for the new system; test of reports; translation of current procedures to the new software; consultation with software vendor; planning data conversion; and conversion data mapping.
- **Phase II — Decision Making Phase. "Getting Crazy"**
  During this phase, the implementation team for each system and module formalized decisions and procedures. Tasks were performed in the "test" account. Tasks associated with this phase included: writing test plans; setting up codes and parameters in the test account; testing codes and parameters; creating test data manually; creating print programs for standard forms and/or order forms; writing and testing conversion programs; testing processes; determining and writing procedures; writing specifications for reports; and preparing manual or converted end-user training data in the "test" account.
- **Phase III — Going "Live." "Getting Real"**
  In the last phase, final decisions made in the test account were duplicated in the "live" account. Tasks associated with this phase included: document procedures; training end users; setting up security in live account; setting up codes and parameters in live account; testing reports; manually creating the live data files not being converted; duplicating reports from the "test" to the "live" account; running data conversion in the "live" account; cleaning up data; and going "live"!

During the implementation at UOR, there were multiple issues that the Project Office, functional user teams, and technical group had to address. They had to decide in what order the four systems and their modules should be implemented. The four groups decided to start the implementation with the easiest system — the Finance system. The assumptions driving this decision were twofold: the experience gained with the implementation of this system would facilitate an easier transition to the more complicated systems, and the first system had to be implemented successfully to increase the enthusiasm for and trust in the conversion. During the two-year scheduled implementation timeframe, the University experienced only a one-and-a-half-month delay that did not involve any major adverse consequence to the University operations (University of Redlands, 1998).

Cabrillo decided to implement each of the four major applications that comprise the Colleague software. The scope of this implementation, by design, did not include every module within each application. For example, Cabrillo did not implement the alumni development module (Benefactor) because the College's Foundation that conducts alumni development activities was using stand-alone software that did not require integration with the student and financial systems. As at UOR, Cabrillo organized the implementation into a number of teams and committees with responsibilities for implementing or overseeing a particular aspect of the project (see Table 6). The organization into teams was intended to make the process of implementation more manageable.

Table 6. Cabrillo College: Organization for implementation

Team	Responsibilities	Membership	Escalation
Steering Committee	General Implementation Guidelines & Policies — Final Adjudication of Unresolved Problems	President, Vice Presidents, Director Computing Resources	None
Implementation Oversight Committee	Data Standards Technical/Security Scheduling General Guidelines & Policies	Implementation Manager Application Team Leader Application System Administrators Technical Services Representatives	Steering Committee
Core Development Team	Shared Codes Team	Application Team Leaders Analysts Instruction	Implementation Oversight Committee
Teams: Colleague Applications	Finance Student Human Resources	Application Team Leader Application System Administrators Representatives from Each Module Area Technical Services Representative	Implementation Oversight Committee
Module Teams: One Per Module or Module Office	Various	Department Manager Decision Makers Selected Others	Application Team

At both institutions, the teams were not intended to be static, but instead to accommodate new conditions and events as they occurred. Compared to UOR, the senior management of Cabrillo was more directly involved in the implementation process. At UOR, the senior management oversaw the major decisions but left the details and management of the implementation to the Project Office.

At Cabrillo, the sequence of implementation of systems and their modules was similar to that at UOR. The Finance System was implemented first, live production being achieved in a record four months. As at UOR, the implementation sequence was driven by the degree of complexity of each of the systems. Furthermore, Cabrillo's project management benefited from the expertise gained by two of the UOR's Project Office members with the prior implementation of Datatel's products.

ANALYSIS

Both institutions recognized that the implementation of a new administrative system is a very complex task. From the President and the senior management to administrative departments, the project was viewed as a truly significant undertaking that would include pain and suffering in order to achieve potentially remarkable results. The implementation at both institutions demonstrated that this project was expensive, difficult, and required a great deal of effort on the part of employees who had to accept change and assume additional concurrent work tasks. A related effect has been the realization, across job roles, of the amount of information needed and work done by others. A positive synergy has resulted from this sharing of information about workflow.

Additional challenges presented by the implementation project included the balancing of the difficult conflicts between valuable change and historical process ("the old way"). The outcomes required compromise, rethinking, and reengineering of how business was conducted. In some cases, this required a change in process that improved service. The benefits of discarding isolated separate systems in favor of an integrated data system brought about a new thinking and a greater willingness to accept change.

The cumbersome interface of the Colleague system was one of the implementation challenges. If the software creates difficulty to the performance of the job or even makes itself felt as a challenge, then the software is not providing a reasonable service to the user.

> *Something as banal as printing a computer file can be a debilitating exercise that resembles voodoo more than respectable human behavior.* (Negroponte, 1995, p. 92)

It is not surprising to see a very powerful relational database system with an awkward front-end interface. Most information management systems have evolved from the data processing model based on mainframe computing that required finite programming to run the interface. Unfortunately, this has generated a credibility problem for users who expect to see the more popular graphical user interface as represented by the Microsoft Windows interface. Some assume that an interface that is awkward represents software that is not as capable as packages with graphical features. More importantly, the issue of navigation to specific screen locations is a critical issue. The ability to find the proper location and appropriate function for completing the task at hand is paramount to software productivity. The Datatel software combines these forces by providing a very rigid system as the interface while allowing users to define some elements such as "validation codes" as values represented by mnemonic codes and abbreviations.

At both institutions, the predominant theme of the implementation has been boundary crossing. The implementation of a relational database and its applications providing integrated data throughout the institutional infrastructure has led to cross-departmental discussions of workflow, shared decision making, and an increased understanding of how processes in one area affect and are affected by those in another. The implementation has been methodical due primarily to effective project management, and effective staff and team involvement and leadership. Further, by making sure the implementation was at the user level, it resulted in a higher degree of success.

Before the conversion, at UOR, there were 100 users of the mainframe-based systems. Currently, there are 230 users. Throughout the conversion process, the University purchased, installed and networked 250 personal computers and 21 printers, conducted a total of 1,800 hours of group discussions, and provided on-site training that covered system modules for all 230 users. The relational nature of the new system has increased the awareness of the various administrative units and system users of the necessity of updating and maintaining the data in an accurate and timely manner. The implementation of the new system has reduced organizational barriers by increasing communication between the various administrative units.

In spite of successful implementation processes at both institutions, the elimination of all "shadow" systems and discouragement of duplicate or add-on systems are still goals to be achieved. Another difficult task has been helping users understand the required changes due to the implementation of the new system. Long-range use of data and its effect on administrative units, data confidentiality, and storage requiring constant updating of system processes to take advantage of the newest technologies, and continuous training of users are just some examples of challenges that both institutions still need to tackle.

In spite of the differences in structure, size, and mission, the two institutions and their respective implementations of the Datatel software share significant similarities. This is in part a function of the software manufacturer's philosophy and in part due to recommendations of the consultants hired to facilitate the implementation. The software requires many user-defined values and codes leading to extensive input from the client. These values and codes "personalize" and customize the implementation at each site. Cooperative decision making is essentially built-in to the product due to the interaction and some overlap between the major systems and their modules.

The amount of work, time, and staff resources required always seems to be more than is available, yet somehow deadlines are met and progress is achieved. The initial efforts were crucial as they set the stage for all that followed. Progress tracking and adequate celebration of success were important to the continuity of the project. The project manager at Cabrillo and the Project Office at UOR provided critical information to the governing board and the president's cabinet, respectively. Their reports were instrumental in sustaining the effort and flow of project activity as well as providing benchmarks to those inside and outside the project implementation.

At both institutions, the projects could not have been accomplished without the expertise and assistance of the project consultants. As overall project manager and resource to all functional committees, a competent consultant provides direction, leadership, and technical expertise regarding a very sophisticated management information system and the requirements to successfully implement it. A senior manager at Cabrillo College stated that an important factor was bringing in outside help in the form of a skilled project manager, who was also one of the Project Office staff at UOR. The outside help brings "out-of-the-box" thinking to the project. Cabrillo College chose this path for its implementation. Although at UOR existing employees managed the implementation, the university benefited from the expertise of KPMG that facilitated the process through the initial evaluation of administrative computing needs and the functional analysis.

At both sites, the senior management provided support and encouragement as needed to facilitate workflow and meet deadlines. The involvement of executive management at Cabrillo College in all critical decision-making phases of the project was essential and supportive. At UOR, the Project Sponsor and Project Office informed the President's Cabinet of all steps taken and decisions made in collaboration with the implementation teams.

Cabrillo reached its vendor selection decision in a shorter period than UOR mainly because of the interaction it had with numerous similar institutions in California that had already decided to implement the same system. There was also an existing contract between the Community College District and Datatel. UOR, on the other hand, had to make this decision from the perspective of its unique needs.

The two institutions had similar implementation teams. The organization of the implementation teams was a consequence of the structure of the software and of the main functional areas that exist in most higher education institutions, regardless of size and mission.

There are also important differences between the two sites in terms of goals and costs of the projects. UOR used the conversion to the new system as an opportunity to thoroughly analyze all operational processes of the University by engaging in a functional analysis and redefining the role and structure of its ITS staff. The former endeavor led to higher project costs and much more time invested in cross-functional meetings and discussions. The latter goal increased the complexity and scope of the project.

Without a doubt, the most important achievement of the implementation for both institutions was the synergy created between the administrative units and the significant progress made towards transforming the organizational cultures to embrace change as a normal and permanent process.

CONCLUSION

As Mignerey (1996) suggests:

> *For all of its problems, there is little if any doubt that distributed computing is the computing environment of the future. As solutions are found to some very difficult technological problems, more and more traditional computing applications will migrate to the distributed client/server model.* (p. 45)

Cabrillo and UOR have confirmed Mignerey's prediction. Although information technology is advancing rapidly, the market of integrated information systems for higher education has remained fairly stable in terms of major vendors and systems available. The choices available in 1999 are not much different from those available in 1995. The difference is mainly in the quality and sophistication of the products rather than in their number. Thus, it is safe to assume that had the two institutions engaged in the selection process in 1999, it is likely that their final choices would be similar to those they decided upon in 1995 and 1997, respectively.

The experience of Cabrillo College and University of Redlands with the implementation of the Datatel products suggests the following factors and steps be considered by institutions planning for or contemplating similar projects:

1. Evaluate the need for change to a new system.
2. Determine the goals of change.
3. Analyze resources — are there sufficient budget, staffing, and time resources available?

4. Make a careful determination of the match between 1, 2, and 3 and resolve differences.
5. Do not try to do it all yourself — outside consultants are valuable for many reasons (objective point of view; "outside the box" thinking; expertise from similar sites; not a long-term expense).
6. Choose consultants who have expertise and support local "capacity-building," not dependency.
7. Dedicate some personnel exclusively for the implementation project.
8. Factor at least 30% over initial budget.
9. Ensure very broad user input to conversion and design processes.
10. Emphasize service orientation and campus-wide communication and collaboration.
11. Involve executive management to lend credibility and support to the efforts needed.
12. Have a clear decision-making strategy for all aspects of the project.
13. Network heavily with other schools, especially those with the same implementation projects, which are showing success.
14. Be flexible — allow timelines to shift.
15. Obtain everything in writing from the vendor. Vague promises or statements will not suffice.
16. Place a priority on training and preparation of staff.
17. Collaboratively solve problems and seek solutions. Communicate with all those involved.
18. Celebrate successes.

The implementation of such projects is not an endeavor to approach casually. It is a major series of significant events requiring a great deal of preparation to accomplish successfully. Decision makers at institutions faced with a project of this magnitude are advised to collect as much information as possible about the nature of the process before implementation.

DISCUSSION QUESTIONS

1. How does an institution determine the magnitude of change required by the conversion to a new administrative information system (AIS)?
2. What are some of the critical factors in successfully implementing an AIS?
3. How does an institution address resistance to change?
4. How does an institution evaluate the outcomes of implementing an AIS?
5. In what ways was the implementation in this case successful?
6. What was the role of senior leadership in the process?

ACKNOWLEDGMENTS

The authors would like to thank the following individuals for their invaluable insights and support that enabled the completion of this project:

- **From University of Redlands:** Mr. Philip Doolittle, Vice President for Finance and Administration; Ms. Georgianne Carlson, Associate Vice President for Finance and Administration; Ms. Patricia Caudle, Controller; Mr. Hamid Etesamnia, Director of Integrated Technology; Mr. Cory Nomura, Director of Administrative Services; Ms. Betty Porter, Senior Software Analyst; Mr. Steve Garcia, Senior Software Analyst; Mr. Matthew Riley, System Manager; Ms. Nancy Svenson, Associate Dean of Admissions for Operations.
- **From Cabrillo College:** Ms. Pegi Ard, Vice President for Business Services; Ms. Tess Hunt, Manager Business Services; Ms. Marcy Wieland, Technology Computer Systems Coordinator; Cabrillo Project Consultant and Project Manager Mr. Darren Rose of Rose & Tuck, LLD.; Sue Hass, Manager, Computing Resources; Project Consultant and former member of the Project Office at University of Redlands: Mr. Mark Tuck, also of Rose & Tuck, LLD.

REFERENCES

Cabrillo College. (1997a, October 6). Presentation to the board of trustees.

Cabrillo College. (1997b, December 1). Presentation to the board of trustees.

Caudle, P. (1996, January 11). *Administrative system conversion implementation plan*. University of Redlands.

Crow, G. B., & Rariden, R. L. (1993). Advancing the academic information infrastructure. *Journal of Research on Computing in Education, 25*(4), 464-72.

Davenport, T. H. (1993). *Process innovation: Reengineering work through information technology*. Cambridge, MA: Harvard Business School Press.

KPMG Peat Marwick. (1993). *Evaluation of administrative computing needs*. University of Redlands. September.

McKinney, R. L., Schott, J. S., Teeter, D. J., & Mannering, L. W. (1987). Data administration and management. In E. M. Staman (Ed.), *Managing information in higher education: New Directions for institutional research* (No. 55). San Francisco: Jossey-Bass Publishers.

Mignerey, L. J. (1996). Client/server conversions: Balancing benefits and risks. *CAUSE/EFFECT, 19*(3), 40-45.

Negroponte, N. P. (1995). *Being digital.* New York: Alfred A. Knopf, Inc.

University of Redlands. (1998, September 8). Presentation to the board of trustees.

Van Dusen, G. C. (1997). The virtual campus — Technology and reform in higher education. *ASHE-ERIC Higher Education Report, 25*(5). Washington, DC: The George Washington University, Graduate School of Education and Human Development.

ADDITIONAL RESOURCES

There are numerous publications and useful Web resources that can provide further insights into similar projects undertaken by other higher education institutions. Listed below are just a few:

- *CAUSE/EFFECT* is a practitioner's journal for college and university managers and users of information resources — information, technology, and services — published quarterly by EDUCAUSE: http://www.educause.edu/pub/ce/cause-effect.html.
- A site of resources related to managing computer technology in higher education: http://www.temple.edu/admin/other.htm
- *Technology Tools for Today's Campuses*, James L. Morrison (Ed.): http://horizon.unc.edu/projects/monograph/CD/
- On the Horizon: http://horizon.unc.edu/horizon/

This case was previously published in L. A. Petrides (Ed.), *Cases on Information Technology in Higher Education: Implications for Policy and Practice*, pp. 102-117, © 2000.

Chapter VII

Public Sector Data Management in a Developing Economy

Wai K. Law, University of Guam, Guam

EXECUTIVE SUMMARY

An island state government agency responsible for publishing monthly import/export data had problems meeting the monthly publication schedule. It took the group more than three months to process data from a single month. A new director for the unit was under pressure to publish the import/export data at least quarterly. An initial investigation reviewed problems of inefficiency, poor technical support, downsizing under budget reduction, and confusing data standards. The data processing staffs had minimal technical skill with some approaching retirement. There were increasing expectations for the unit to provide enriched and customized data, which could strain the capability and resources of the unit. A general deficiency in computer and information literacy gave little hope for internal information resource development. On the other hand, concerns for information privacy, shrinking budget, and control over data resources limited potential assistance from outside groups.

BACKGROUND

A small island state has emerged as a prime tourism destination since the eighties. A combination of financial assistance, foreign investments, and bank loans modernized the local facilities, with proud showcases of a modern airport, luxury hotels, amusement parks, and major retail chain stores. The island has attracted over a million tourists annually for luxury goods shopping, relaxation, and for its numerous world-class golf courses. In the '80s, the local government organized a Commerce Division to compile local economic data to satisfy financial sponsors. The same published data provided critical support for favorable financial credit rating, local infrastructure planning, and for attracting new investor groups. The Import/Export Unit in the Commerce Division was tasked to publish monthly import/export reports. The Commerce Division also compiled other data series such as the census report, consumer price index, and had access to all public data to support its data compilation efforts. The director of the Commerce Division was an appointed position that typically changes every four years with each new governor of the island. Staff positions were censored by a Civil Service Commission, which was slow in recognizing emerging technology-related job descriptions. Until recently, a high school diploma was not required for many civil service positions. Once employed, it was rare to dismiss a civil servant even for poor performance. It was especially difficult to enforce performance standards when majorities of the population were blood relatives. The local culture discouraged negative comments towards relatives and close friends. It was a taboo to contradict statements of elders and local leaders, even when the statement was based on incomplete or inaccurate data. A strong sense of pride rejected practices that could not be easily integrated into local culture and traditions.

SETTING THE STAGE

Initially, the harmonized system for commodity classification was adopted in January 1, 1988, as the direct basis for the collection of import and export data. The harmonized system represented a global standard for commodity classification codes on invoices, bills of lading, and airway bills. The full implementation of the harmonized system would simplify data collection, and allow the eventual development of automated data collection through an electronic data interchange system. The standard also would allow easy comparison of economy activities on a global basis. However, local business owners were reluctant to invest in information systems to comply with the harmonized system coding standards.

The developing island state was struggling with the limited supply of physical resources. Although there was an ample supply of water, the island imported most of its food, fuel, materials, and dry goods. Prices of goods were high and with limited supplies. The local government was eager to provide incentives to attract business investments to lower the cost of goods. Quality information was not considered a high priority, and data collection was mainly for the purpose of compliance rather than as a valuable resource. A decision was made by the local government to relax the information reporting requirements by accepting a simplified classification system. The new system tracks 233 items instead of 1,500 items in the harmonized system. Importers and exporters were encouraged to adopt the harmonized system classification codes in invoices, bills of lading, and airway bills, but few complied. New government leadership adopted a political view to data management, and ceased to enforce the scheduled publication of economic data. At times, the administration allowed directors of divisions to ignore information requests, in contrary to a local Sunshine Law ensuring open access to public information. Under a culture where loyalty was valued over performance, data-driven decision making by the division heads was a rare practice.

The simplified classification system required a staff to manually code all items on import and export documents to reflect the 233 new grouping identities. PC Trade, a donated database software, was adopted as the data processing software. PC Trade supported verification of the harmonized classification code and provided checksum as the assigned item codes were entered into the computer. The staffs were glad to have a computer system to help capture the massive volume of data. However, none of the staff members had any detail knowledge of the software system. It was not clear who made the decision to adopt PC Trade, and who initially installed the software. It was not clear how data was stored, even though the staffs faithfully saved data files to a floppy disk at the end of each day.

CASE DESCRIPTION

Recently, the Import/Export Unit began to publish the import/export report on a quarterly basis instead of monthly. Moreover, the quarterly reports were several months late, to the point that the community ceased to expect the publication of import/export data. Tara, a new director of the Commerce Division, felt the pressure to publish the import/export data in a timely manner. A consulting team was invited to interview the Import/Export Data Unit, to seek solutions to improve the reporting capabilities of the Import/Export Unit. The consultants were required to be officially sworn in to protect information privacy prior to meeting members of the unit.

The primary information source originated from shipping documents attached to custom declaration forms. Since the Customer Unit was part of the Commerce Division, access to the custom documents was never a problem. In

1994 a new local legislature separated the Custom Unit as an independent government division, and assigned it as the sole custodian of all information collected by the Custom Division. The reorganization severely limited the capabilities of the Import/Export Unit to manage data quality. Although the Import/Export Unit has been given the authority to request data from any other government agencies, the form, timing, and frequency of data transfer between agencies was at best a negotiated arrangement between individual directors. It was even more difficult to influence the data collection procedure and data standards.

Under the new organizational structure, the Custom Division still regularly supplied data to the Import/Export Unit. However, it was not obligated to support the collection of specific data elements such as commodity classification codes. It became increasingly difficult to implement a standardized coding system to improve data processing efficiency. The irony was that the harmonized system was partially designed to simplify and speed up custom clearing. Many governments had successfully utilized an electronic data interchange system to clear cargoes through customs before the arrival of transportation vessels. The new arrangement provided the Import/Export Unit limited access to custom documents. A monthly batch of custom reports was delivered to the Import/Export Unit, and needed to be returned to the Custom Division after data processing. The Import/Export Unit staffs extracted all the data from the monthly lot of custom reports before the delivery of the next lot.

A batch of custom reports came in boxes. The total number of documents varied with economic activities. The bills of lading from the ocean port were kept separated from the airway bills from the airport. Although standardized custom declaration forms were used, there was no standard in filling out the form, and supporting invoices were prepared in every imaginable format. Judy has been a long-time worker and was responsible in assigning one of the 233 simplified classification codes to each item on every invoice attached to the bills of lading. Judy was an efficient worker, and she had committed the coding list to memory. Judy was so good at her task that on the days she was absent from the office, workflow slowed down. The office supervisor Kurt was very concerned about losing Judy, especially since Judy had been thinking about retirement in the next couple years. Kurt wished that the legislature had not cut back half of his staff. He could not afford to assign another worker to learn from Judy in sorting out the item classifications scheme. Kurt pulled out several sheets of worn paper listing the simplified classification codes. The item classifications were complex, but it was even more perplexing how Judy could quickly assign the thousands of items into the correct item groups. Occasionally, items included in invoices were to be excluded from the statistics. This included shipments for special user groups and transshipments. Judy identified these exempted items and refrained from assigning a classification code to them.

Tom worked part time at the office to add up the total values of item groups identified by Judy. When Tom was not in the office, any worker with a light workload would perform his task. Kurt helped with the task frequently between his other responsibilities. Kurt considered the manual calculation of group values an important step in data processing, but could not explain the purpose of this laborious and error-prone activity. The processed documents were forwarded for data entry.

There was only one computer assigned for data entry. Kurt worried that the computer might not last for too much longer. There was no budget for computer equipment, and the software currently used was a free gift from a New Zealand trade association. Kurt made sure that the daily data inputs were saved on a floppy disk. That way, if the computer malfunctioned, they could take the floppy disk and continue data entry in the second computer owned by the unit. Kurt kept copies of all published import/export reports, and he was more concerned about the failure of the computer before he could finalize the monthly data summary.

Betty was the data entry clerk. She complained about eye problems from typing long hours. Betty was quiet, and was delighted to show off the computer software she used. PC Trade was customized, fast, and provided quick search capability for harmonized classification codes. The software was a customized Microsoft Access Application. However, no one in the division had any knowledge about relational database. As a matter of fact, no one in the Custom Division realized that the software was a customized Access database. Betty was curious about the many other features in the command menu. However, no one had ever found out about the full capability of the software. It was not clear who to contact for technical support. Betty was careful to compare the group subtotals on the computer screen with the calculated values. She would ask Kurt to investigate and resolve any conflict between the values. Betty had developed a good habit of saving the data file, but she really had no experience in any software besides PC Trade.

Kurt had worked in the unit since graduation from high school. He had been promoted to the rank of Statistician II, as the supervisor of the unit through his many years of service. He remembered the time period when the unit faithfully published monthly data reports. Recently, it took his staff two to three months to complete processing of each monthly batch of data. He was glad that the local economy was slowing down, because he knew it would take his staff longer to process the documents with a robust economy. He believed that the unit could use better computer equipment. He found himself frequently filling in for Judy, Tom, and Betty. He considered his most important responsibility was in resolving all data entry conflicts, and reclassified items to ensure consistency with historical data. Kurt was committed to ensuring that the published data would not fluctuate between reports. He carefully compared monthly data summary with previous reports, ensuring that the import volume for item groups remained very consistent throughout the years. From time to time, Kurt found it necessary to reclassify item groupings to control the data quality.

Kurt was greatly puzzled by questions concerning data flow, data definition, and data processing procedures. He assured his boss and the consultants that every member of his unit was willing and able to help each other out to resolve problems. As far as he could remember, the sole responsibility of the unit was to generate the import/export report in a predefined layout. He indicated that the unit had received many requests for data not included in the import/export reports. His staffs would manually research the data, although he admitted that such requests slowed down the regular data processing activities. He recognized that the data processed by his group had great commercial value to user groups. Kurt was highly confident of the ethical standard of the group, and they would never disclose any private information to individual user groups. For the same reason, neither part-time workers nor volunteers were allowed to work for the unit. Kurt was receptive to any new instruction from his boss. He was more interested in keeping the group intact before his retirement.

CURRENT CHALLENGES/PROBLEMS FACING THE ORGANIZATION

Tara, the new director of the Commerce Division, changed the monthly import/export report to a quarterly publication. She cited the decision on the basis of budget reduction, and the inability of the Import/Export Unit staff members to complete their tasks. She believed that by extrapolating data from several key months of the year, there would not be significant loss of information on the quarterly reports. Data from the first month of each quarter would be used for the quarterly reports as quarterly data. Tara believed that a timely publication of the quarterly import/export reports would be a more valuable service than trying to capture all available data. She was eagerly seeking a low-cost approach to verify the accuracy of the quarterly reports. Tara recently heard about a full database for agricultural imports and she wondered how she might be able to request a copy of the data, and use the data to support her approach of selective data compilation.

Tara was pleased with the recent acquisition of some color printers that allowed the production of the first batch of colored data reports. The director believed that a new multi-color import/export data report could demonstrate the technical capabilities of the division. However, it might be necessary to charge a fee to cover the much higher production cost of the color reports. Tara had great confidence in her technical staff. Dan could present data in spreadsheet tables, even though he had some difficulty in aligning the numbers. George could duplicate data CD and perform software installation. Tara was confident that her staff could handle the technical development within the division. She proudly showed off a couple of new personal computer systems with 31-inch monitors and a plan for a Web site for the division. She believed that a Web page would help to improve the image for the division. The only obstacle was that the division was not allowed to contract its own Internet service provider. Tara believed that she could leverage technical expertise within the division to resolve problems associated with the Import/Export Unit. However, she was still concerned about the short timeframe she had for implementing changes, and the pending retirements of Kurt and Judy.

Tara began to turn to Sonia for leadership in the Import/Export Unit. Sonia was a supervisor in charge of export data. Sonia and her assistant had faithfully completed their tasks in a timely fashion. Sonia reported to Kurt, but she worked independently most of the time. There were not many export activities, and when Sonia ran out of tasks to do, she would take a box of import documents and process the data. Sonia was very organized, but she still needed the simplified classification code sheets to assign item codes. When all the import documents were processed, Sonia would combine her data summary with the data summary from Kurt. The combined data would be written on a sheet of paper, and hand-delivered to Dan to create the data tables for the reports.

Sonia wished that she could receive training to prepare the data tables and charts without the help from Dan. Sonia had kept all the floppy disks from the years she processed data in the unit. However, she was not sure who kept the rest of the data. Sonia was also concerned that she could no longer retrieve data from disks created before the last version upgrade of PC Trade three years before. She was confident that the floppy disks were still functioning; however, no one knew how to retrieve data from the old disks, and no one seemed to have a copy of the older software version. As a matter of fact, it was not certain who installed the current version of PC Trade.

Tara was surprised to learn that all the data were kept on floppy disks, but she assured the consultants that printed copies of all past data reports were on file. Kurt also kept printed copies of data from previous years, even though he could not figure out any value for the collection of computer printouts. Tara heard that businesses were willing to pay for data, and she wondered how she could start charging for the data reports. She began to give strict instructions that all inquiries for data must be routed through her office. There was rumor that the legislature was unhappy with the performance of her division and was considering disbanding her staff into other divisions. Tara was receptive to any recommendation to speed up data processing in the Import/Export Unit with the current staff.

THEORETICAL BACKGROUND

Before 1980, data management was centralized and operated mainly by information specialists who designed, controlled, and maintained computing equipment, databases, and the development of application software. The introduction of microcomputers and generic application software gradually shifted the data management responsibilities to end users. End users referred to non-technical personnel that used information systems to accomplish tasks. In the early days, end users would explain their requirements to DP/MIS personnel, who created systems to provide data to the users. The DP/MIS staffs provided full support to protect the integrity and security of the organizational data (Regan & O'Connor, 1994).

However, with increasingly powerful microcomputer and user-friendly application software, many end users eventually assumed the full responsibility of selecting information systems, specifying data processing procedures, and managing the full spectrum of information processing responsibilities. The trend has been accelerated through the widespread availability of application service providers, who could be contracted to provide various information services (O'Brien, 2002). Fluctuating budget cycles severely affected the undisrupted availability of services from the application service providers. The absence of internal DP/MIS expertise created a vacuum on the continuous protection for the enterprise information assets.

With a formal information system development cycle through DP/MIS personnel, some of the valuable by-products included data-flow diagrams, flow charts, data dictionaries, and schematic diagrams for the computing equipment (McLeod, 1998). These provided valuable information, also known as metadata, for the maintenance and adaptation of the information system to changing user requirements (Bischoff & Alexander, 1997). In a pure end-user environment, especially in the absence of technical support from the DP/MIS personnel, much of the data management practices would be neglected (Raman & Watson, 1997). This often resulted in the tainted integrity of the database system, severely affecting the quality of the enterprise information assets.

A primary objective of data management was to provide quality data. Data quality was frequently confused with the presentation quality of reports, or the information content of reports. The primary data must be accurate, well sorted, consistent, timely, clearly defined, complete, and easy to use to meet needs. Filtering processes could then be applied to create data derivatives valuable to various users. Some organizations chose to manage the data derivatives such as published reports to improve efficiency of distributing the documents. These activities should never replace the critical role of data management (Bradley, 1998). Cultural influence tends to shift the priority and definition of information quality (Hofstede, 1980; Shea & Lewis, 1996).

Metadata, or documentation, was important in data management. Data management would be difficult without the elaborate supporting information on data definitions, design specifications, physical data sources, data representations, software and hardware supports, and acceptable domains. There should be a single definition for each data item, rather than on-the-fly interpretative definitions (Bischoff & Alexander, 1997). As such, data usage should be tightly integrated with the designed data definitions, which must be published and widely distributed in a form easily understandable by end users. The absence of metadata was a major challenge in the end-user computing environment.

The relative importance of the data management function was closely related to the decision-making style of leaders (Rocheleau, 1999). In cultural settings where a political view was adopted for decision making, there would be low expectation on the availability of data, and hence little attention would be given to the compilation of quality data (Hill & Jones, 2001; Davenport, 1997). The traditional DP/MIS approach to data management assumed rational decision making supported by a highly organized data center. Unless the DP/MIS function could be established as an independent data center, frequent leader changes would greatly affect the data management practices in a public organization (Duncan, 1999).

REFERENCES

Bischoff, J., & Alexander, T. (1997). *Data warehouse: Practical advice from the expert.* Upper Saddle River, NJ: Prentice-Hall.

Bradley, L. C. (Ed.). (1998). *Handbook of data center management.* Boca Raton, FL: Auerbach Publications.

Davenport, T. (1997). *Information ecology: Mastering the information and knowledge environment.* New York: Oxford University Press.

Duncan, G. T. (1999). Managing information privacy and information access in the public sector. In G. D. Garson (Ed.), *Information technology and computer applications in public administration: Issues and trends* (pp. 99-117). Hershey, PA: Idea Group Publishing.

Hill, C. W., & Jones, G. R. (2001). *Strategic management: An integrated approach.* Boston: Houghton Mifflin Company.

Hofstede, G. (1980). *Culture's consequences: International differences in work-related values.* Beverly Hills, CA: Sage Publications.

McLeod, R. M., Jr. (1998). *Management information systems* (7th ed.). Englewood Cliffs, NJ: Prentice-Hall.

O'Brien, J. A. (2002). *Management information systems: Managing information technology in the e-business enterprise.* New York: McGraw-Hill.

Raman, K. S., & Watson, R. T. (1997). National culture, information systems, and organizational implications. In P. C. Deans, & K. R. Karwan (Eds.), *Global information systems and technology: Focus on the organization and its functional areas* (pp. 493-513). Hershey, PA: Idea Group Publishing.

Regan, E. A., & O'Connor, B. N. (1994). *End-user information systems: Perspectives for managers and information systems professionals.* New York: Macmillan.

Rocheleau, B. (1999). The political dimensions of information systems in public administration. In G. D. Garson (Ed.), *Information technology and computer applications in public administration: Issues and trends* (pp. 23-40). Hershey, PA: Idea Group Publishing.

Shea, T., & Lewis, D. (1996). The influence of national culture on management practices and information use in developing countries. In E. Szewczak, & M. Khosrow-Pour (Eds.), *The human side of information technology management* (pp. 254-273). Hershey, PA: Idea Group Publishing.

Wai K. Law is an associate professor at the School of Business and Public Administration, University of Guam. He earned his PhD in strategy & policy and MS in computer science, both from Michigan State University. His research interests are in the areas of strategy information systems, pubic sector information management, information resource development and information technology education.

This case was previously published in the *Annals of Cases on Information Technology,* Volume 6/2004, pp. 584-591, © 2004.

Chapter VIII

The Benefits of Data Warehousing at Whirlpool

Barbara J. Haley, University of Virginia, USA

Hugh J. Watson, University of Georgia, USA

Dale L. Goodhue, University of Georgia, USA

EXECUTIVE SUMMARY

In today's competitive, high-velocity business environment, companies are focusing their attention on several key areas, including:

- *Incremental continuous quality improvement;*
- *More radical redesign of business processes;*
- *Supply chain management;*
- *Improved customer orientation; and*
- *Globalization of business operations.*

At Whirlpool, data warehousing is providing important support in all of these critical areas (see Table 1). To illustrate, Whirlpool's data warehouse enables quality engineers to easily track the performance of component parts. This allows the engineers to assess new components that are being field tested, to quickly detect problems with particular parts, and to identify the high and low quality suppliers. From a different perspective, suppliers can check on the performance of the parts they supply and, consequently, can manage proactively the quality provided to Whirlpool. Purchasing managers have parts information from around the world so that they can find the lowest-cost, highest quality part available on a global basis. This case study briefly describes Whirlpool, the business need that suggested a data warehouse, the approval process, and the data warehouse that was built. It describes how the data warehouse is accessed, how users are trained and supported, and the major applications and benefits. The lessons learned also are described to benefit those companies that are implementing or thinking about implementing data warehousing. Like most companies, Whirlpool is continually changing. This case study describes Whirlpool and its data warehousing initiative through the end of 1997.

THE WHIRLPOOL CORPORATION

Whirlpool Corporation is the world's leading manufacturer and marketer of home appliances. The Whirlpool family consists of over 45,000 people who manufacture fine appliances in 12 countries and market them under 11 major brand names. The company is based in Benton Harbor, Michigan and reaches out to approximately 140 countries around the world. It is the only major home appliance company with a leadership position in North America, Europe, and Latin America, plus a growing presence in Asia.

Whirlpool began as a small family-owned business in 1911, and it now ranks 159 in the Fortune 500. The corporate vision for the company fosters growth and progress: *Whirlpool, in its chosen lines of business, will grow with new opportunities and be the leader in an ever-changing global market.* This vision is manifested in Whirlpool's Worldwide Excellence System (WES), its

Table 1. Key strategic areas for Whirlpool

- incremental continuous quality improvement
- more radical design of business processes
- supply chain management
- improved customer orientation
- globalization of business operations

blueprint for approaching quality, customers, and continuous improvement. Initiated in 1991, WES incorporates the best of all Whirlpool quality programs, worldwide, with Malcolm Baldrige Award and International Standards Organization criteria to establish a common approach to quality, one that dedicates the company to the pursuit of excellence and total customer satisfaction.

Whirlpool is an information-intensive business. In North America, it has three or four thousand products that it sells at any point in time. Every one of the products has hundreds or thousands of components that are assembled every day in 12 major factories. The products are stored in 28 places. Over 16 million appliances are sold a year and they are tracked throughout their lifetime.

THE BUSINESS NEED FOR DATA WAREHOUSING

One of the keys to thriving in this information-intensive environment is the ability to effectively coordinate and control its myriad processes and activities. This can be challenging from an information systems perspective. Business units need a complete understanding of the processes for which they are responsible, and the diversity and heterogeneity among systems make it difficult for them to get the information they need and to manipulate it in a useful, timely manner.

In the early '90s, several business units identified a variety of specific information needs. For example, Quality wanted to create an application (later called Customer Quality Information System [CQIS]) that would proactively identify quality problems based on customer complaints. Data existed in several places, including Whirlpool's OneCall System that allowed any customer to take care of any necessary business, be it services, product information, or complaints with one phone call. CQIS was to provide an environment in which the data could be queried and analyzed.

These applications had obvious value to the business, and senior management understood that the information systems infrastructure was inadequate to effectively support the various initiatives. In fact, around that timeframe an expensive executive information system initiative had just been discontinued after several years of trying to combine data from multiple data sources and manipulating the data in a meaningful way for its users.

It was apparent that an infrastructure had to be put in place at Whirlpool to support the numerous decision support initiatives that its business units had identified and were expected to demand in the near future. At that time, the marketplace was promoting data warehousing as a viable alternative to organizations that wanted to create a decision support infrastructure. Data warehousing is the process of creating, maintaining, and using quality data for decision support purposes, and its technology had become cost effective and mature enough for organizations to implement. In the spring of 1993, the first efforts to use data warehousing at Whirlpool were approved, and CQIS was the first application to utilize the new infrastructure. It was expected that data warehousing would allow IS to provide business units with their applications quickly, with less cost, and with a greater likelihood of meeting their needs.

Many business initiatives, which rely on data warehousing, have emerged since 1993. Currently, the data warehouse contains 14 specific collections of data (i.e., subject areas) that describe important facets of Whirlpool's business, like competitors, business partners, and facilities (see Table 2). Table 3 presents a listing of the 10 primary applications that use information from the subject areas along with the sponsors of the applications and the business needs that they address. With enhancements and alterations, the data warehouse has effectively evolved to support each of the applications.

DATA WAREHOUSING APPROVAL PROCESS

The business needs for Whirlpool's data warehouse and its applications were examined and assessed throughout their approval processes. Whirlpool gives approval for systems initiatives through a unique process called value oriented systems planning (VOSP). The idea of VOSP is to identify the value of an initiative to the company and the funds necessary to provide that value. The VOSP document has two parts. The first part is owned by the customer and identifies the functionality that is needed to meet some business need. The second part is completed by IS and describes the specific actions that IS will take to address the specified business needs and the funding required to accomplish this. The executive committee then ranks the VOSPs and decides whether or not to fund each one. A blanket IS VOSP is approved for significant hardware upgrades. The VOSP process continues after a system or application is in place; a post-implementation audit is conducted to ensure that the stated business needs are met.

Because data warehousing is an infrastructure investment, with benefits typically coming from subsequent applications, it was included under the blanket IS VOSP. Therefore, data warehousing per se has not received a post-implementation audit. However, individual VOSPs were created for each data warehousing business application. In keeping with the VOSP approach, each of these applications was reviewed for its value after its implementation. The successful audits of these dependent applications show data warehousing's importance. In addition, it is thought that the benefits from the data warehousing applications are much greater than the post-implementation audits demonstrate. (Interestingly, business units admit to downplaying benefits for fear of a negative impact on budget levels or future funding).

Table 2. Subject areas represented in Whirlpool's data warehouse

BUSINESS PARTNER	Information about an organization or individual with whom Whirlpool has a business relationship (e.g., customers and vendors).
BUSINESS TRANSACTION	Information about the transaction of business between Whirlpool and a business partner (customer, supplier, etc.) such as sales, purchases or shipments; and the documentation of those transactions (e.g., orders, invoices, bills, manifests, etc.).
COMPETITOR	Individuals or organizations that presently offer, or may in a future offer, competitive products and services to Whirlpool's customers.
CONSUMER	A person who owns and/or uses a unit of any brand of product sold by Whirlpool.
EQUIPMENT	All the fixed assets other than land and buildings of a business enterprise. This includes machines used with tools in the factory.
FACILITY	Information about property and plants owned or used by Whirlpool Corporation. Includes location, size, cost, value, depreciation, usage, classification, etc.
FINANCIAL	Information about the assets and liabilities of the Corporation, the internal and external reporting and management thereof. Includes general ledger and sub-ledger information, income and expense, taxes on profits, information about currency, and all financial reports.
GEOGRAPHIC AREA	An area of jurisdiction; may be state, province, county, township, city, etc.
HUMAN RESOURCE	Information about rewards and services provided by Whirlpool for its employees.
MANAGEMENT SUPPORT	Information about the mechanisms used by management to perform day-to-day activities. Includes communication, computer systems and related components, messages, projects, records, reports and surveys.
MANUFACTURING	Information about the procurement of parts and materials, and assembly of parts and materials into other parts, assemblies or finished products.
ORGANIZATION	Information about the structure of the company. Includes business components, organizational units, branches, divisions, parts distribution centers, and departments.
SERVICE	Information about the provision of product diagnostic and repair services to the customer or consumer.
PRODUCT	A standard group of items that is, or has been in the past, manufactured or purchased by Whirlpool and competitors for distribution and sale.

Table 3. Data warehousing applications and the business needs that they satisfy

Application	Sponsor	Business Need
Consumer Quality Information System (CQIS)	Product Quality	Early warning system for product quality issues
Customer and Model Profit Analysis (CAMPA)	Sales	Analyze profitability by specific dimensions
Global Procurement (GPDW)	Global Procurement	Identify lowest cost part available globally
Logistics Information for Everyone (LIFE)	Logistics	Provide availability analysis, inventory analysis, inventory turn analysis, and analyze overall cost of delivery
Online Waste Elimination Network (OWEN)	Manufacturing	Identify and eliminate inefficient processes through scrap analysis
Product Cost Analysis System (PCAS)	Manufacturing	Analyze costs associated with production by design changes and production mix
Super Efficient Refrigeration Program (SERP)	Sales	Track sales and customers of the high efficiency refrigerator in order to qualify for rebates from the SERP association
Marketing (DIALS)	Marketing	Analyze external market information on price points and demographics
SEARS POS	Sales	Analyze Sears Point of Sale Information
Service Management Analysis and Reporting Tool (SMART)	Consumer Service	Analyze cost and quality of service
Parts and Accessory Information System (PAID)	Consumer Service	Analyze profitability of part and accessory business by specific parts and customers

CONSTRUCTION OF THE DATA WAREHOUSE

Before data warehousing, Whirlpool traditionally relied on IBM mainframe systems running DB2 for major systems initiatives. When data from these operational systems were needed, Whirlpool used IBM's QMF as the data access tool. However, Whirlpool's new business needs created data access requirements that were not achievable on operational data stores that included data in raw form, in inconsistent formats, and without the ability to support queries, reports, and historical requests. Whirlpool needed to handle large amounts of data, support batch loads, and perform hundreds of complex, often ad hoc, queries from large numbers of users.

NCR was selected to provide Whirlpool with a total data warehousing solution that included hardware and software. A careful review of multiple data warehouse solutions and technology alternatives led to the best solution for Whirlpool. This decision was based on several points:

- The ability to handle complex, ad hoc, multi-table queries against data stored in third normal form;
- Ease of data warehousing administration;
- Low cost of database management (e.g., database administration resources over a long period of time);
- Superior mainframe integration for data loading, archiving, and user access;
- The ability to integrate a multidimensional dependent data mart (Pilot Analysis Server) into the same data warehouse hardware and software environment; and
- A proven data warehousing methodology and expertise in implementing successful data warehousing environments.

The decision has been reexamined a number of times since NCR was first introduced, and each time NCR was found to be the most cost-effective solution and one that best meets Whirlpool's business needs.

Whirlpool's production data warehouse platform in North America is the NCR WorldMark 5100MPP system configured with three 8-way SMP nodes running the Teradata relational data base management system (RDBMS) and one 4-way SMP node running Pilot Analysis Server. The 5100M is directly channel connected to Whirlpool's MVS mainframe and LAN connected to the corporate and remote LAN sites. This configuration provides over 200 gigabytes of usable storage to Whirlpool whose current levels of raw data exceed 90 gigabytes. For development, Whirlpool uses an NCR 4500 4-way SMP server also running the Teradata RDBMS, Pilot Analysis Server, and a development Web server that provides limited browser access to the data warehouse. The 4500 supports 40 gigabytes of RAID-protected disk storage.

Until 1994, data warehousing activity was limited to North America; however, global initiatives prompted the creation of a second regional data warehouse in Italy to support European information requirements. Ultimately, Whirlpool hopes to integrate regional data warehouses to meet global information needs. The North American data warehousing team members were instrumental in communicating the existing data warehousing methodology, practices, and technology choices to their European counterparts. However, to date the two warehouses remain segregated. One global application (i.e., Global Procurement) is running on the North American data warehouse, and is accessed by procurement users from all regions.

Figure 1 illustrates Whirlpool's data warehousing environment. Currently, the North American data warehouse is fed by at least six external data sources (e.g., data for appliance newspaper advertisements; POS information from appliance retailers) and over one hundred mainframe sources. Additionally, the warehouse provides data to dependent data marts that support marketing, logistics, manufacturing, and procurement applications. Overall, 1,700 users (from logistics, sales, quality, engineering, etc.) have access to warehouse applications, and 400 to 600 unique users access the applications each month

Figure 1. Whirlpool's data warehousing environment

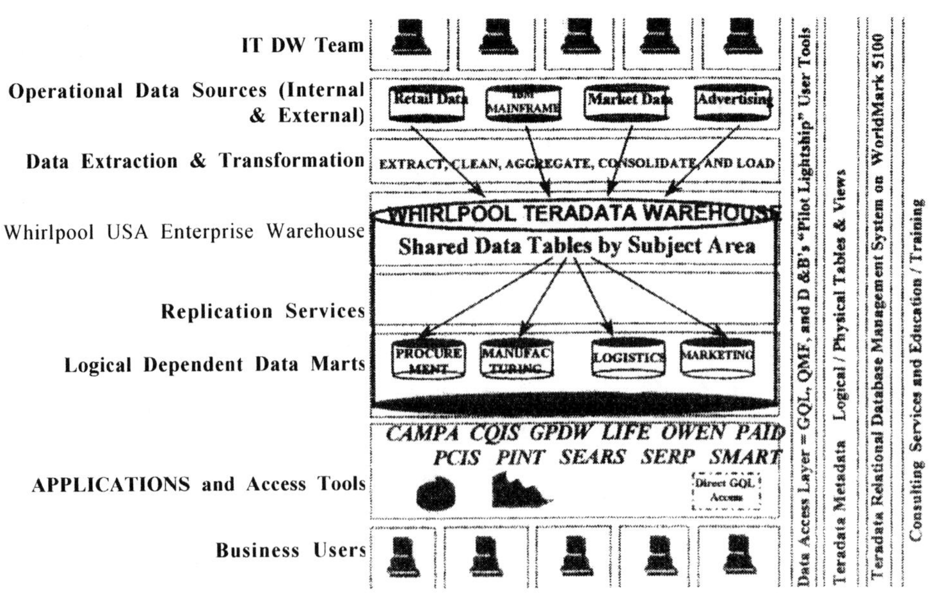

Table 4. Use of the data warehouse as of final quarter 1997

Total users	1,700
Active users per month	400-600
Queries per month	>40,000
Views	500

(see Table 4). The volume of queries has risen to 40,000 in one month, and this figure continues to grow. Six full-time Whirlpool employees comprise the team that supports all of the North American data warehousing initiatives. This includes the team that designs the applications, develops the designs, loads the data, manages the Teradata RDBMS, provides security to the data warehouse, and assists the business users with their queries and future requirements.

USE OF THE DATA WAREHOUSE

Accessing Data

Three primary access tools are used to access Whirlpool's data warehouse. Originally, QMF emulation was used because QMF already existed at Whirlpool. However, QMF has a number of limitations, including its unwieldy user interface and its requirement for advanced knowledge of structured query language (SQL). In 1992, a Windows-based managed query environment called GQL from Andyne Computing was introduced to serve as a generic access tool for all applications that were supported by the data warehouse. The tool has become accepted as the ad hoc access tool of choice because it has an improved graphical user interface, and it supports flexible, ad hoc queries. However, users still need to know the data well before they can execute effective queries. Recently, Pilot Corporation's Decision Support Suite (desktop software) and Analysis Server (a multi-dimensional database) were implemented to complement GQL, and these will be used for predefined queries. Pilot Decision Support Suite does not require users to be quite as skilled in order to access data.

Whirlpool's Marketing Department has taken a different approach than other organizational units in terms of how warehouse data are accessed. First, most marketing users access data marts instead of the warehouse. They cite two reasons for this — better response time and less data complexity. But, data in the data mart are updated only monthly; consequently, marketing users still must turn to the data warehouse for the most current data. The big difference between marketing and other areas lies in the user interface tool. For standard marketing applications, PowerBuilder has been employed to develop simple interfaces.

This approach has evolved because of a highly skilled and respected application developer within Marketing who has learned to create intuitive marketing applications using PowerBuilder.

Educating Users

The data warehousing education provided to Whirlpool users varies greatly depending on the area within the company. In the Washers area, all new employees get an overview of CQIS as a part of orientation. However, one manager explained that in Quality, "*there are engineers that don't have the foggiest idea of what the data warehouse is about. So we haven't communicated that it exists and what its contents and potential benefits are.*"

Overall, there are three approaches to warehousing education at Whirlpool:

- No education;
- Education during employee orientation; and
- Classes available for employees to sign-up on an as-needed basis.

A combination of the two latter approaches has the best results. Education allows employees to understand the ways in which data warehousing can support their jobs and to understand how to use the data warehouse tools effectively. Mary Schmidke, decision support analyst, performs warehousing training:

> *I find that if I get one or two people from a department that is not using the data warehouse to come to training — all of a sudden I have a massive entourage of the whole department coming and wanting to find out how to use the warehouse that same day.*

Education improves users' understanding of how data warehousing can meet business needs, and educated users have great enthusiasm for using the data warehouse to do their jobs.

Supporting Users

A six-member group exists within IS to support warehousing and to help with future initiatives. But, in terms of supporting users, the most effective support has been found to come from the business units. Several business units have identified a functional person or persons to help in the use of the warehouse. The profile of such a person includes functional knowledge, technical know-how, and the ability to communicate with the users. This approach works well. The CAMPA application has a business analyst appointed to be its decision support analyst. Former data warehousing manager Laura Sager explains: "*She is in the business, she does all of the training for the CAMPA application, and she is the center of CAMPA's data warehousing support.*"

Informal power users have sprung up for areas that do not have formalized data warehousing support in place. For example, in Washer Engineering, quite a few people try to access the warehouse. A power user in this group states:

> *Once they make mistakes then I end up running all of the queries for them. They come to me and I write them. They know that I am the expert at it and I can do it better. Now I'm a product engineer, and I do very little product engineering because I'm doing this.*

Whirlpool is working to minimize this situation. For example, Sager has made concerted efforts to identify business areas that heavily use the data warehouse and to encourage them to formally assign business users to data warehouse support roles.

THE BENEFITS FROM DATA WAREHOUSING APPLICATIONS

The benefits from data warehousing can be considered in a variety of ways. Figure 2 provides a generic framework that is used to organize the discussion of the data warehousing benefits at Whirlpool.

Time Savings

> *Now you can access a whole division in a matter of seconds. Now you can do just about anything you want to do to analyze the production for that plant in a matter of minutes; whereas, somebody would have keyed in for hours to provide that to you before we had the warehouse.* (Jason Denman, Financial Analyst)

Figure 2. Benefits from data warehousing

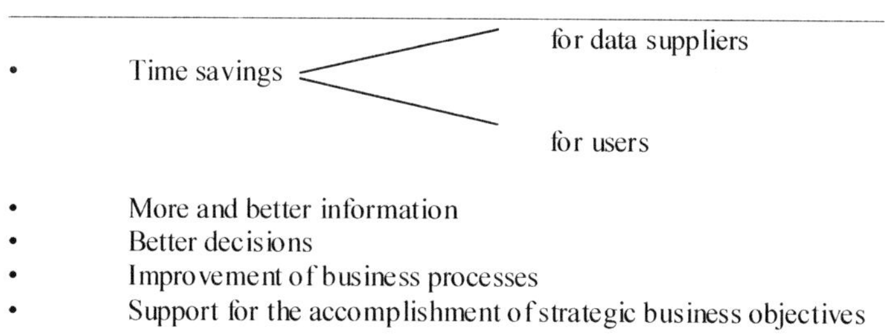

Time savings can occur for two groups: data suppliers and end users. While developing a data warehouse is time consuming for IS, once it is in place, there should be less time spent responding to ad hoc requests for data because users can help themselves. More importantly, data warehousing creates the decision support infrastructure upon which future applications are built. If data warehousing is conducted effectively, the start-up costs associated with new decision-support initiatives are dramatically reduced. On the users' side, business analysts spend less time accessing data, processing it, and putting it in a format appropriate for their needs.

Before the data warehouse was in place, IS and functional area personnel were often called upon to make data available. This required a combination of downloading files, re-keying data, and creating extract files. These time-consuming tasks are no longer required because of the existence of the data warehouse.

Jerry Briney is a former manager in Quality, and he uses CQIS to investigate quality problems. Before CQIS, Briney would read upwards of twenty thousand service call tickets a month looking for and investigating problems. Tickets had to be (1) sorted by product and brand, (2) sorted by defect, (3) manually counted, and (4) read thoroughly. This was a mind-numbing task, as Jerry explains, "*After a while you don't know what you are reading. You would read a ticket and not pay any attention to it.*" With CQIS, Briney can specify a problem of interest and access all of the service tickets that report that problem. About 30 to 40 times as many service tickets can be checked using the data warehouse. Briney explains how this translates to the bottom line:

> *We produce 17,000 washing machines each day. If we find a problem as small as a .1% service incident rate (SIR), we save 17 service calls per day (17,000 * .001). Each call is $75 which results in $1,275 saved in service calls per day and in a $38,250 savings per month.*

More and Better Information

> *The data warehouse gives us backorder information so that we can expedite what we need to expedite. There was no backorder report in the company before the data warehouse.* (Bill Friend, Logistics Manager)

A data warehouse lets users get at data that were previously locked away in legacy systems or that did not exist. Through cleansing, aggregating, and possibly augmenting (e.g., external data) processes, warehouse data are used to create better information than was previously available. John Doyle is a manager in Procurement Quality. He helps insure that parts received from suppliers conform to standards. The data warehouse makes it feasible for him to access and use data in new ways. Previously, Doyle had difficulties getting information that required aggregation. As he describes it:

> *I couldn't really use or summarize information without manually going through all the data. It was very difficult and cumbersome to do that. With the data warehouse, I can tell it what I want to see. I want to see an alphabetical listing of all the suppliers, and I want to know how many receipts that we have had from them, how many rejects we have, and what their PPM (parts per million) value is.*

With this information, Doyle is able to track the performance of individual suppliers. Only suppliers who meet expected performance levels are given additional business. Prior to the warehouse, Doyle had to write complex queries to a mainframe, and even then could not access the information that he receives today.

Warehouse data make it possible to think about, ask questions, and explore issues in ways that were not previously possible. Sue Bailey describes her experience with the warehouse in the following way:

> *In the past, you asked standard questions that were related to the reports that you got. Now we are able to think about our business differently. I can get information in response to very specific questions. If I see a problem, I can ask a series of questions to get a much better understanding of the dynamics of what is going on.*

For example, using the data warehouse, Bailey and colleagues obtained actual sales and margin impacts by contract segmentation for a contract strategy study. The actual margin was obtainable rather than estimates based on samples. The savings in manual effort plus the actual data provided insights that would have been missed using small sample sizes. Additionally, they could change segmentation codes within the data warehouse and observe the impact on the prior year sales. Bailey explains that "*in essence, the data warehouse allowed us to test an approach prior to implementation.*"

Better Decisions

> *Our analyst really doesn't spend less time analyzing. The data warehouse is providing for a much more thorough analysis and a much better understanding of what is happening in our business.*

> *Our top-level analysts are no longer just cranking data.* (Jason Denman, Financial Analyst)

The fact that employees now access more and better information impacts the quality and process of decision making. People can ask questions that they could never ask before, rely on facts instead of intuition, and understand situations at a much lower level of detail. Sue Bailey explains that the data warehouse has made people at Whirlpool "*rethink the way we solve problems.*"

Whirlpool is continually looking for ways to produce a higher quality, lower cost product. A major way to do this is through the component parts used in its appliances. When a potentially better component is identified, it is placed in a test run (possibly 100,000) of appliances, and then monitored using CQIS. Before the warehouse, it took up to a year to learn about its performance. Now it is possible to more quickly decide whether to put it into all of the appliances. As Jerry Briney describes it:

> *You want either a quality improvement or a cost improvement. Either one, you want to get it as fast as possible, and it (CQIS) makes it much faster to do this. If you don't see any failures for six months in that 100,000, you say "let's put it in four million per year."*

The CAMPA application supported hard dollar benefits through improved decision making. Bailey describes the process:

> *Analysis of floor planning costs compared to sales of those floor planned models provided hard data to support change in flooring policy. This was one area that the field operations managers actually tracked hard costs reductions of over $1.0 M in the first year to the change in policy.*

Improvement in Business Processes

> *We have realized that now with these tools we can detect a hazard that was not recalled two years before, versus two years after, it was out in the field.* (Larry Latack, Product Safety Manager)

Many of the biggest returns from the use of IT is when it is used in the redesign of business processes. This redesign can take place at the individual worker level. Before the warehouse, most of the quality data were based on 3 months of rolling data. Averages computed over the 3-month horizon tended to hide important developments. With the warehouse, monthly data became available for control chart purposes. According to John Doyle:

> *When you get into actually charting the monthly data, you can see the swings in the data. When something "pops" on the control chart, you can take immediate action and find out what is going on with that particular activity.*

When Doyle sees that a part is out of control, he is able to drill down into the data warehouse to see whether the problem is occurring in a particular plant or is due to a particular supplier. The ability to quickly identify and correct the problem source results in tremendous savings. Before the warehouse, problems were slow to detect and difficult to correct.

Some business processes are being changed to include a broadening of the organizational boundary. As mentioned earlier, parts suppliers can access quality information by querying data from the warehouse and analyzing it using GQL. This allows suppliers to see the entire history of a part failure from the initial customer call to the final resolution by a service technician. In addition to studying a single part incident, suppliers can look at the performance for all parts of a single type in order to gain a higher-level perspective on parts performance.

Supplier access to the warehouse has also affected the cost recovery process for failed parts. Because supplier and Whirlpool personnel have access to the same parts failure data, it is easier to determine and agree upon the reason for a failure; decide who is responsible for it; and if it is the supplier, decide upon the suppliers' share of the warranty cost payment.

Support for Strategic Business Objectives

The most significant impact of IT is when it becomes an integral part of corporate strategy. At Whirlpool, senior management recognizes the need to align IT with business needs and corporate strategy (as identified earlier in Table 1). Like many companies, Whirlpool's systems were developed separately and in an unintegrated manner, which limits Whirlpool's ability to operate. Even though Whirlpool is in the early stages, senior management feels that the warehouse will ultimately allow the company to function more effectively as a "global, customer-oriented" company.

Whirlpool is beginning to work toward making IT and the data warehouse important parts of its corporate strategy. There are several reasons that make this a challenging undertaking: multiple production and business processes that frequently differ from facility to facility (i.e., plant or warehouse), different data definitions, and a variety of computing platforms and databases. For example, it is a challenge to develop performance metrics for various processes (since they differ) and then compute the associated performance measures (since the data are not easily accessed). The data warehouse is a partial solution to this problem since it intended to provide a single source of clean, consistent data to support decision making and planning and controlling activities.

INSIGHTS ABOUT DATA WAREHOUSING

Other companies' experiences are helpful to organizations that are involved in similar activities. Through the evolution of data warehousing at Whirlpool, ideas surfaced and practices were put in place that have made the data warehouse more effective. For companies that are planning to build a data warehouse, the insights gained at Whirlpool can help guide their efforts.

End Users Are Heterogeneous

End users differ in ways that should be considered when designing a data warehouse. Some users, for example, need narrow slices of detailed data that they manipulate further using a spreadsheet. For them, a dependent data mart and copy and paste capability may be the best solution. Other users may have broad data needs that are best served by a comprehensive "enterprise data warehouse" that provides a cross-organizational and cross-functional view of Whirlpool information. Users also differ in their computer skills, how often they need data in the warehouse, and their willingness and ability to be power users. At one extreme are users who simply want to click on a button to receive a report based on predefined queries. Power users, on the other hand, are more willing to deal with complexity in order to be able to access and analyze data in flexible ways.

Carefully Understand Users' Information Needs

Like any systems analysis and design effort, the starting point is to understand the existing system and the requirements of the new one. This is done through individual and group interviews with future users. There are several requirements for doing this well. Designers should understand that users and their needs are heterogeneous. Designers must also have the ability and willingness to communicate using the users' mental models and terminology. Users have little understanding and interest in the data models, relational tables, and primary and foreign keys that are so important to the world of database professionals. Users will not be able to articulate all of their data needs initially; many needs will surface only after they have used the data warehouse for awhile.

Provide Appropriate User Interfaces

Because users and their data needs differ, it should be expected that different interfaces (and the associated underlying software) will be needed. Managed query environment software, such as GQL, provides a friendlier interface than using straight SQL, but it is still perceived by many users to be difficult to use correctly. The result may be that either the data warehouse is not used or someone emerges (either formally or informally) who prepares the queries for their technically challenged colleagues. From an IS perspective, it is tempting to blame users for being unwilling and unable to master what is believed to be easy-to-use data access software, while from the users' perspective, they find the software difficult and time consuming to learn. For many users, the simple point-and-click access to information that is associated with executive information systems is a better solution when their information needs can be well defined.

Metadata for Users is Important

Being computer literate and able to use data access tools are necessary but not sufficient conditions for successful data warehousing. Users must also understand the data that they are accessing, including the data definitions, the source systems used, when the data were last updated, and peculiarities (e.g., the result of merging two data sources). Most data access tools provide a semantic layer that shields users from having to know cryptic database table and attribute names, but they do not eliminate completely the need to understand the database. Users without this understanding either refrain from using the warehouse, spend inordinate amounts of time developing and testing queries, or ask someone more skilled to write the queries. Well-developed metadata can address these inefficiencies by giving users a helpful tool that explains the relevant pieces of the data warehousing environment. This should be viewed as an important task, and personnel who provide the metadata must be end user oriented, knowledgeable about the subject area databases, and willing to actively involve users in the development process.

Business Units Need to Support Their Data Warehousing Applications

A skilled data warehousing team is critical to provide effective technical solutions that meet users needs; however, it is the business unit that understands the full potential of the data warehouse for its members. A data warehouse will best meet the business needs through the involvement of the business area during all phases of data warehousing, including the post-implementation phases. Too often the assumption is made that technology can meet needs without much effort. Instead the business units need to devote resources to continuous education and internal marketing so that warehousing can support the necessary business objectives. In fact, business users should be assigned permanent roles that support data warehousing efforts.

Benefits from Time Savings, More Information, and Better Decisions Are Easy to Realize

Virtually everyone who has access to a data warehouse can give examples of these benefits being realized. These benefits are intertwined. Because data can be more quickly and easily accessed, it is possible to do a more thorough analysis, which results in higher quality decisions. Whirlpool's data warehouse has delivered significant benefits on this front.

Benefits from Changing Business Processes and Support for Strategic Objectives Are More Difficult to Actualize

The benefits from the improvement of business processes and support for the accomplishment of strategic business objectives are more difficult to realize. At the individual level, a warehouse affects how workers perform their jobs. It's more difficult to affect changes, however, at the organizational level. Changes require a clear vision of what should be done, a champion, commitment, groups to work together, the handling of political resistance, as well as the data and technical infrastructure required to support the change. The potential benefits are great, however.

CONCLUSION

The evolution of data warehousing at Whirlpool reflects significant growth in data warehouse usage, support for an increasing number of business needs, a variety of benefits to the company, and valuable learnings. As mentioned earlier, nearly 600 business users access data from the data warehouse each month, and this number should continue to grow. The data warehouse supports many business applications, and interest in these applications deepens with training and internal marketing efforts.

Most importantly, Whirlpool has experienced numerous benefits from data warehousing at the operational and strategic levels, in both quantifiable and intangible forms. An in-depth, exhaustive analysis of these benefits has not been conducted, per se, primarily because the analysis would be time-consuming and expensive. The identified benefits and high satisfaction with the data warehouse make this investment unnecessary. Instead, assessments of benefits are conducted during the post-audit process on an application-by-application basis.

There are opportunities for Whirlpool to increase the return on investment from data warehousing by focusing on the high-level benefits derived from changing business processes and alignment with corporate strategy. In this way, Whirlpool can move forward with its business objectives supported by a sound and responsive information infrastructure.

Barbara J. Haley is an assistant professor of commerce at the University of Virginia's McIntire School of Commerce. She is an associate editor for the Journal of Data Warehousing, *has published in journals that include* Information Systems Research, Communications of the ACM, Journal of Data Warehousing, *and* Information Systems Management, *and has presented her work at national and international conferences.*

Hugh J. Watson is a professor of MIS and a holder of a C. Herman and Mary Virginia Terry Chair of Business Administration at the Terry College of Business, University of Georgia. He is the author of more than 100 articles and 22 books.

Dale L. Goodhue is an associate professor of MIS at the University of Georgia's Terry College of Business. He has published in Management Science, MIS Quarterly, Decision Sciences, Sloan Management Review, *and other journals.*

This case was previously published in the *Annals of Cases on Information Technology and Management in Organizations*, Volume 1/1999, pp. 14-25, © 1999.

Chapter IX

Developing a Homegrown Course Management System: Community/ Course Action/Interaction Management System (CAMS©)

Brian G. Mackie, Northern Illinois University, USA

Norbert L. Ziemer, Northern Illinois University, USA

Nancy L. Russo, Northern Illinois University, USA

Wayne E. Mackie, Saginaw Valley State University, USA

EXECUTIVE SUMMARY

This case describes the development of a unique, student-centered, online course management systems (OCMS). The system grew from a fairly straightforward grade reporting system into a full-blown collaborative system within a short — in traditional information systems development terms — timeframe of approximately one year. The Community/course Action/interaction Management System, known as CAMS©, was developed iteratively with specifications derived from faculty and students working together to address the limitations of existing OCMS and to identify new functions and features that would contribute to the value of the educational experience. To address the most critical issue identified — limited interactive functionality — the participant became the focus of the development process. This case describes the evolution of CAMS© from both a product and a process perspective. Changes made to the system and the factors motivating the changes are discussed, as are challenges faced before, during, and after the development process.

BACKGROUND

Midwest University is a large state-funded university located in the central portion of the U.S. At every level, the organization was experiencing high demand for limited resources. The post-9/11 economic situation affected state budgets and mandated belt tightening at state funded institutions. Facing limited resources, the organization's ability and willingness to support change dramatically decreased.

The university was beginning the process of carving out a strategy to integrate Web technology into standard classes, called Web enhanced or hybrid courses, which involved primarily a face-to-face environment with some online interaction (Ko & Rossen, 2002), and into online classes with little or no face-to-face interaction. In spite of the economic situation and without additional funding, the university had mandated that *all* courses have a Web presence within the academic year 2001-2002.

Within the Information Systems academic department in the School of Business, this mandate was seen as critical to maintaining credibility as a technology-focused department. During the previous year, the department had designed and implemented an innovative online presence implemented with Active Server Pages (ASP) as the front end and a database as the back end. All faculty members in the IS Department had been encouraged to provide some type of Web-based support for their classes, and in an attempt to force this, the department announced that syllabi would no longer be printed for each student. In the fall semester of 2001, 85% of the IS faculty had developed course Web sites.

Also at this time, the School of Business selected Blackboard™ as its product of choice in supporting Web-enhanced, hybrid, and online courses. (See Table 1 for a description of Blackboard™ and related products and terms). Faculty were encouraged to put their new course materials on Blackboard™ and to move course Web sites over to the Blackboard™ environment. Departments were publicly compared on percentage of faculty/courses using Blackboard™.

The University IT staff was heavily burdened with many high priority projects. One of their major endeavors was to develop and implement the IT

Table 1. Definitions and background information for the case

*An **Online Grade Book (OGB)** allows the student to login to an application across the intranet/ Internet to monitor their course progress at any time, which is frequently stated as "24/7" (24 hours a day, 7 days a week). This could be in the form of numeric scores as well as feedback such as subjective comments.*

*An **Online Course Management System (OCMS)** integrates various course components into an application that the participant (facilitator/instructor or student) can access online. Some of these components are:*

- *Syllabus*
- *Schedule*
- *Assignments*
- *Notes*
- *Grade book*

***Blackboard™** is a prominent OCMS. It allows a central login to access all courses taken using Blackboard. Once logged in the student can select a specific course to work on. Once in the course the student can access any of the modules implemented for that course. These modules include:*

- *Course Announcements*
- *Course Information*
- *Staff Information*
- *Course Documents*
- *Assignments*
- *Communication*
- *Virtual Classroom*
- *Discussion/Groups*

***WebCT™**, another prominent OCMS, essentially has a similar structure to Blackboard. Many state that the largest difference is that Blackboard is more pre-formatted and structured than WebCT. This enables the seasoned online facilitator increased flexibility to customize the virtual learning environment.*

***Community/Course Action/Interaction Management System (CAMS©)** is another OCMS. It has many of the features of Blackboard and WebCT. It differs, though, in that it focuses on the participant. It allows the participant to be both a major supplier and user of information in the system. It allows the participant to interact with other participants and facilitators frequently and easily. The system is designed to be dynamic and intuitive to operate.*

infrastructure for a new Business School building. This was occurring in parallel with the ongoing updates to the university's Blackboard™ application and the addition of many new users to the system. (In fact, the number of new users to the Blackboard™ environment overwhelmed the system in the fall of 2001, and a new server was required). This realistically exhausted the majority of IT resources at all levels of the organization.

The School of Business, with approximately 4,000 students and over 150 faculty and support staff, had its own IT Department consisting of six people. In addition to responsibility for identifying the technology requirements for the new building, the director of IT for the School of Business was also responsible for facility design, furniture and fixture selection, and moving logistics and deployment for the new Business School building. The remaining staff dealt with on-going hardware and software support issues, installation of hardware and software in the new building, including the programming of information kiosks and message screens, and training faculty and staff in new and existing technology.

SETTING THE STAGE

By the end of 2001, approximately 85% of the classes in the Business School had an online presence. Business students were familiar with Blackboard™ and other types of Web course support, and were introduced to Web page design, including HTML, in the introductory management information systems course. Within the IS Department, students could elect to take courses in which they learned to use additional Web design tools such as ASP and XML.

Although the Web enhancements to courses were generally met with favor, students and faculty were finding many limitations within their class Web presences (Blackboard™ other applications and faculty developed Web sites). These limitations included:

- Minimal access to other students
- Poor response time
- Not user friendly (large number of screens to navigate through to access a desired feature)
- Lack of a personal feel
- Minimal personal customization
- Very low user interactivity

Two faculty members in the IS Department, a tenure-track professor, Dr. Green, and an instructor, Mr. Lewis, were interested in doing something to improve the situation. Both faculty members had been teaching in the department for three years or more. Dr. Green was teaching two or three classes each semester, all of which were Web-enhanced. Most students in these classes were very Internet literate and the classes ranged in size from 20 to 45. Mr. Lewis was teaching three classes per semester, with class sizes ranging from eighty to two hundred and fifty. He provided some Web support for all of his classes, and most of his students were Internet literate. Mr. Lewis' initial interest in the project came from his desire to have a system that would provide 24/7 grade access to his students.

Dr. Green was using a "homegrown" OCMS with online access to grades and a unique approach that allowed peer-to-peer interaction (see www.cob.niu.edu/cams/casestudy/green.html). He had previously taught at St. John's University, a small university, where the normal class size was 15 and the organization's ability to embrace change was high. Dr. Green had a range of experience with and exposure to various course management applications. Dr. Green had previously set up, used and administered a Webs™ application for St. John's University in 1998. This was when WebCT™ had just been introduced and the integration of online course management systems (OCMS) into educational institution use was still in its fledgling state. Dr. Green also had a stated interest in and passion for the collaborative aspects of information systems. These factors were what helped to give birth to the vision for CAMS© and to carve out a direction for the development process.

However, before the notion of CAMS© was even visualized, Dr. Green and Mr. Lewis realized the need for a highly functional online grade book that would accommodate multiple faculty, students and classes. Dr. Green had a highly functional online grade book that granted his students 24/7 access to their scores. He agreed to rewrite his application to allow for multiple student, multiple class, multiple faculty and weighted scores. The initial application, which included restricted login and a complete online grade book module, was developed and launched. This will be referred to as OGB (see www.cob.niu.edu/cams/casestudy/ogb.html) for online grade book. Several faculty members expressed interest in using OGB for their classes, because the 24/7 access to grades translated into time savings for faculty members in that they would no longer need to generate paper progress reports.

The faculty members who requested OGB (and their teaching assistants) were quickly brought up to speed on how to use the OGB application within their courses. During the first semester of use, the faculty members, teaching assistants and students were asked to relay input regarding capabilities that needed to be added, deleted or modified from OGB. Using the feedback from faculty, teaching assistants and students, the developers (Dr. Green and Mr. Lewis) determined the following:

- Students were very satisfied with their grade displays and liked the ability to view their scores and determine course standing at any time.
- The display of weighted grades was confusing for students.
- Faculty and teaching assistants were having difficulty in setting up the backend application (for grade entry) at multiple sites in different environments due to inconsistent desktop software configurations. Any time the system was modified, problems would reoccur.

At this point, the developers revisited the whole issue including the initial OGB project objectives, the incremental development to date, and, in particular, the limitations of the developed OGB solution. The faculty side of the grading program had been implemented using Microsoft's Access DBMS as a front end to communicate with a SQL Server database across the Internet. The student side was implemented using Active Server Page (ASP) technology, and only required the student to use an Internet browser to interact with the database.

Microsoft Access was a limiting feature because of software configuration problems. Each time OGB was altered, several additional alterations were required to allow the system to work on most machines. The developers determined at this point that the cost in labor to rewrite the faculty portion of the grading program using the same ASP technology as in the student side would be minimal compared to the time spent continually correcting software configuration issues.

CASE DESCRIPTION: DEVELOPING CAMS

As was stated earlier, Midwest University was in the process of defining a Web presence for both online and standard face-to-face courses. This push toward more online education and online support for traditional education environments accelerated the need for software to manage and facilitate these courses. Even though Blackboard™ was already being promoted for all courses, Dr. Green and Mr. Lewis wanted to at least evaluate alternate options. They found that a number of commercially available course management systems including Blackboard™ and WebCT™ were deficient in both sociological and technical aspects.

Therefore Dr. Green proposed an OCMS application. This application would be unique in that it would focus on the participant/student and his or her needs. This focus would be fundamental from the earliest stages of development. Thus, the OCMS would be truly student centric. Student centric features would include but would not be limited to community orientation, user friendliness and an emphasis on peer-to-peer interaction. In addition, the OCMS would need to be extremely functionally robust and readily adaptable.

The overall best practices of departmental faculty — in building and fostering interaction, teamwork and community within the scope of the standard or online classroom — provided a solid foundation upon which the developers could build. By including and emphasizing the end users, the CAMS development approach was iterative, evolutionary and participative. Both faculty and students (participants) contributed enormously to the design, implementation and testing of CAMS©. The level of involvement of the end users was of what Franz (1985) called "type A." In this type, context represents the sharing of development responsibilities between users and developers. Users were primarily involved in analysis and design, whereas developers (who in fact were also users) conducted the physical construction of the system.

The system was named Community/course Action/interaction Management System to reflect the goal of using the system to create a sense of community and collaboration among the students and faculty using CAMS©. In addition it was viewed that the system should not be limited to supporting classes but should be able to support complete communities, such as professional organizations, student groups, alumni groups and others.

Stages of Development

Development of CAMS© Prototype 1

At this point, Dr. Green envisioned using ASP technology to meld the OGB and his Web presence approach to produce an innovative OCMS. His current Web site already included many unique features, such as photographs and links for fostering community within a class online presence (Salmon, 2002; Stephenson, 2001). He had previously developed a Web site template that allowed easy access to his students and easy access provided to his students for both course materials and for contact with other students. His class Web presence (see www.cob.niu.edu/cams/casestudy/green.html) was designed with the following layout:

- A class-page with rows of:
    - Students' photos
    - Phonetic spelling of students' names
    - Students' e-mail addresses
    - URLs for students' Web sites (including assignments for this class)
- Notes (topical notes)
    - An example could be a set of notes on installing Oracle
- Daily notes (class notes)
- Assignments (description)
- Grades (student could check grades)

Dr. Green spent four or more hours designing the class Web site each semester for classes ranging from 20 to 45 students in size. In addition, he spent approximately another hour reformatting the class-page layout every time a student was either added to or dropped from the course. This was required in order to maintain alphabetical order. Therefore, these community-rich features came at a high price in terms of faculty time invested.

Dr. Green determined that the modular approach used in developing the student side of OGB could be used to rewrite the faculty portion of the system. He also believed that once the system was rewritten, the time investment required to produce the initial Web site for a given class would decrease significantly. This notion of easy replication of the Web site including all the above-mentioned features far outweighed the labor cost of rewriting the faculty grading portion of the application.

The information system development literature generally agrees on the benefit of active involvement of participants (users) in the development process (Magal & Snead, 1993; Gasson, 1999). For this reason, Dr. Green sought input from several stakeholders (end users) rather than developing CAMS© immediately. Each of these stakeholders had already created their class Web presence and was using the OGB as an additional component. He asked each of them to make a list of the features that would be important to have in an OCMS and reasons for these features.

The participation of end users in specifying requirements and assisting in the design of the information system is known to contribute to the success of an information system (Li, 1997). Employing this concept, Dr. Green assigned a project to his master's level students. They were organized by Dr. Green into eleven groups of size four. He shared his vision for the future of online student faculty class interaction with the students. He explained his vision of an OCMS and how his "homegrown" OCMS aligned with that vision. He emphasized both the good and bad points of this OCMS. The students were then asked to develop a proposal for the new and improved OCMS. This would be an OCMS that could meet the needs of a community composed of students and faculty. To this end the students were asked to evaluate:

- OCMS systems they were familiar with
- Dr. Green's Web presence
- Other faculty members' class Web pages

After performing a thorough evaluation, the students were to write a proposal for this innovative OCMS. This allowed for a more deliberate consideration of the end users' needs from both a course management perspective and from a collaborative perspective. Effectively the students were the equivalent of both "developer" and "end user" simultaneously.

Making use of the student and faculty recommendations in addition to his own ideas, Dr. Green totally reworked the original system emphasizing reuse of developmental modules to create CAMS©. The system was developed and those classes that were using the OGB were moved to CAMS©. The nominal time investment required to create a Web site with 50 users was the time it took to rework the class-list into a file and upload it to CAMS©. This procedure of translating the class-list required approximately 15 minutes, compared to four hours when producing a class Web site without CAMS©. Once the Web presence for a class had been established, it was a trivial task to add or remove a student from the Web presence. The length of time to complete this task was approximately 20 seconds per student, whereas without CAMS©, it required about one hour to complete.

The basic system included the following features:

- A secure login
- HomePage with
    - Each student's picture
        - Picture linked to information about the student
    - Phonetic spelling of name
    - E-mail address
    - Link to student Web presence
    - Link to student class Web presence
    - Ability to edit all of the above information
- Assignments page
- Notes page
- Discussion
- Bookmarks
    - Students can create and update
- Chat (students highly recommended)
    - Each message includes the photo of the student sending the message
    - Searchable archives
- Online grade book

Implementation and Evaluation of CAMS© Prototype 1

This advanced the project to the initial beta-testing stage of development. Within four months of the initial concept, a prototype version of CAMS© was used for an online course in June 2002 (see www.cob.niu.edu/cams/casestudy/

proto1.html). The students in Mr. Lewis's course in particular made use of the new Chat feature. In fact, Mr. Lewis held his interactive office hours for the online class using Chat. Anyone not present during the session was able to search Chat and benefit from the discourse that had occurred. The students appreciated being able to see photos of their classmates online, particularly since some of the students had not met the others. The presence of photos helped them feel like a community. In addition, several of Mr. Lewis's students indicated that it was very easy to navigate through the CAMS© interface. Dr. Green and Mr. Lewis believed that this ease of navigation is helpful in fostering a positive online learning experience. If a student cannot find what they need they tend to become disenchanted.

The system was found to be stable, easy to use, easy to facilitate and engaging. Now that the basic system was complete and operating well, the next step would be to expand the collaborative nature of CAMS©.

Development of CAMS© Prototype 2 (Started July 2002)

During the summer of 2002, Dr. Green assembled a project team of four highly motivated students to elevate CAMS© to the next level. The students using CAMS© in Spring 2002 had been asked to evaluate CAMS©. Using this feedback, the summer team prioritized those features and/or capabilities that could be improved upon or added to the system.

Due to the rapid development approach in CAMS© Prototype 1, function had taken precedence over form and aesthetic appeal. Therefore, in this stage of the development, the project group determined that the first priority would be an aesthetic facelift to the menu system. The group determined via user feedback that in addition to the aesthetic facelift, two features should added. These two features were an online book exchange and an online calendar. The last feature that was deemed important to add was a HELP system.

The group evaluated several different potential solutions to accomplish the aesthetic facelift. They finally settled on using the look and feel of the search engine Web site, www.google.com. This was selected because most students would already be familiar with GOOGLE's layout.

It was recognized that CAMS© participants would benefit from the system's ability to allow seamless integration of additional tools. These tools could be developed from within or externally. The first tool to be incorporated was a proprietary forum developed by a Canadian firm. Participant feedback once again initiated the re-organization of course content layout. The re-organization made course content more accessible to the participants.

Dr. Green worked with the group to maintain code consistency. The group implemented the features and capabilities by July 2002. This allowed the new version of CAMS© to be tested and operational for fall 2002.

Implementation and Evaluation of CAMS© Prototype 2

The next stage in the development process was to deploy CAMS© in a larger setting. This entailed launching 10 classes employing CAMS©. The logistics of introducing multiple complete classes exposed the need for automated procedures to handle uploading of both class lists and photos. Upon gathering faculty feedback, it was determined that a class score file upload/download capability was also needed. This feature would allow faculty to upload a set of test scores into the appropriate class or to download all scores for the class into a spreadsheet for further manipulation.

In an effort to streamline administration of incoming student information, a plan was proposed and approved to automatically populate CAMS© from the university database through the Registrar's Office. The uploading of participant photos would be processed in a similar manner. University Card Services agreed to provide photos of all new students each semester in a common format.

Development of CAMS© Prototype 3 (Started November 2002)

Due to the large number of students and classes run through CAMS© more feedback was obtained. This feedback pointed toward several new features:

- Groups
- Group Chat
- Instant Messaging
- FAQ
- Full Help: totally revised for efficient use
- Highly customizable interface

These features would serve to drastically increase the collaborative feel within an online community. The ability for the facilitator to customize the interface to give it a more community-oriented environment was very useful, since by this time five communities (in addition to the academic classes) were currently using CAMS©. These features have now been integrated into CAMS© (see www.cob.niu.edu/cams/casestudy/proto3.html).

Implementation of CAMS Prototype 3

The development of the project is now in the growth stage. Additional classes and communities are adopting CAMS© daily. While CAMS© appears to be very stable at this point, it has the flexibility to be modified or enlarged at any time as new tools become available or new functionality is required. Feedback is on-going regarding the functionality of the technology, the usability of the interface, and the impact of the system on the learning community. The results captured within this feedback are then readily applied to the system. Refer to www.cob.niu.edu/cams/casestudy/ to track the evolution of CAMS©.

Summary

CAMS© has evolved considerably since its inception, and continues to evolve. A chronology of the evolution of CAMS© is shown in Table 2.

The CAMS© user base also continues to grow. The value of a constantly growing set of users is that new users bring fresh objectivity to the project. This has already resulted in generation of ideas for improvements or modified features. For example, one user asked that a feature be included to allow every participant to add links to their own Web presence. She felt that with these links added, CAMS© would become her portal — she wouldn't have to go anywhere else. In most instances, such requested changes were implemented very quickly since there are not layers of red tape required to make a change. Another factor that has allowed for the rapid incorporation of new or altered features has been reusable code.

The development process followed in the CAMS© project can provide a model for similar development projects. The focus was on the users; users participated as analysts, as designers, and as developers and evaluators of the system. Not only did this help to ensure that users got what they wanted, but it also increased user acceptance of the system. The use of evolutionary prototypes allowed the system to grow and change as new requirements were identified and better methods of presenting data were found.

However, it should be noted that this type of approach is not as likely to be valid in all development contexts. In this case, the original target user group was very small and within one department. The initial version of CAMS© was freestanding and was not expected to integrate with other systems. And the developers had in-depth knowledge of the development environment and the application context. This approach provided a useful learning experience for all participants as well as a popular, useful system.

CURRENT CHALLENGES/PROBLEMS FACING THE ORGANIZATION

The impetus for the development of this system originated with a small group of faculty members. This effort was undertaken independently from the central IT Department, the School of Business administration, and the School of Business IT Department, although it was supported by the IS Department chair.

One area of tension was the fact that the university had already selected a standard OCMS, Blackboard™ to be used across the board. Although there had been serious technical problems with the Blackboard™ installation, primarily related to insufficient capacity, the University *had* made an investment and *was* holding to that decision. The School of Business, which would logically be best-equipped as the incubator for an improved OCMS platform, also remained firmly

Table 2. Project milestones in the systems development of CAMS©

Version	Timeline	Project Event
Dr. Green's Original Web Presence	Aug. 2001	• Single-class web presence including online grade book, student pictures, names and phonetic spelling • Common course content
Grade Book Idea	Nov. 2001	• OGB was conceptualized from existing single-class grade book and course web interface for students
Pre-CAMS "OGB"	Feb. 2002	• Multi-user, multi-class, multi-faculty grade book implemented across the Internet
Participant Focused Community Idea	Mar. 2002	• Concept of community including pictures and student empowerment
Initial CAMS Shell	May 2002	• CAMS© shell including assignments, notes, Chat, threaded discussion and the ability to update information
CAMS© Prototype 1 Production Stage	June 2002	• Launched online course using CAMS©
CAMS© Prototype 2	July 2002	• Extreme aesthetic facelift with multi-line tabular menu, bookmarks, calendar, book exchange, upload/ download of course and student data, simple help system
CAMS© Prototype 2 Production Stage	Aug. 2002	• Launched 10 production courses, with pictures taken by faculty
Additions to CAMS© Prototype 2	Sept. 2002	• Forum link and schedule added, content layout re-organized, simple help system implemented
Student Information Transfer in Production Mode	Oct. 2002	• Uploaded all 4,000 students from Midwest's School of Business to the system • Administration time reduced to minimal (i.e., 30 minutes a week) • Three communities started
CAMS© Prototype 3	Nov. 2002	• Groups, Group chat, pictures supplied by outside vendor
CAMS© Prototype 3 With New Features Added	Dec. 2002	• IM & FAQ added, full help system implemented; • Ability to create course with content (notes, assignments, bookmarks) imported from previous course
Sharing CAMS© Within the Organization	Dec. 2002	• Conducted CAMS© info-workshops • Resulted in several classes/communities adopting CAMS© for use in Spring 2003
Project Reflection and Follow-Up	Dec. 2002	• Revisited and addressed the concept of Class and Community • Acknowledged that system had gone beyond just a class management system • CAMS© now functioning as a *community* management system

committed to the decision for Blackboard™ Blackboard™ was to be the standard interface for students and faculty.

The introduction of CAMS©, a new OCMS, did not fit into this agenda. Some administrators at various levels of the university had a misperception of the CAMS© project. Many questioned why the project was necessary or even viable, since the university "already had Blackboard™." These administrators quite likely perceived CAMS© as an internal organizational threat to the Blackboard™ directive. In addition, many faculty members showed little interest at the early stages of the CAMS© development.

The CAMS© application has weathered the skepticism and proven itself through successful use in two academic terms. The Spring 2003 term has more faculty members requesting that their classes be loaded into the system. Whereas some of these faculty members do recognize the virtues of this innovative platform and wish to leverage the capabilities CAMS© offers, others have initially signed on primarily for the benefits of being able to associate a student's name with his/her face. These faculty members seek to know their students' names because they know how much this means to their students. As Dale Carnegie (1936, p. 79) wrote many years ago: "Remember that a person's name is to that person the sweetest and most important sound in any language."

The CAMS© development project is undergoing other challenges on the operational and administrative level. As the demand for access to the system increases significantly, the ability to process the creation of additional classes becomes a new challenge.

The developers, who were given no release from regular duties to work on CAMS©, have been kept very busy in constructing and modifying code as well as supervising the graduate students who contributed to the development efforts. Maintenance and support of CAMS© is ongoing. Because it was not an officially sanctioned product, CAMS© was initially running off a borrowed server, which was unstable and unsupported. Although it has since been moved to a server administered by the centralized IT Department, capacity and maintenance issues will be of concern as use of the system grows.

Even though the CAMS© administrative functions are not complex, certain functions like resetting passwords and adding new students are only to be expected, and require time. New faculty members do receive training to highlight system features and functions. This training can be conducted quickly, but it does represent an additional time requirement for Dr. Green. Another pitfall discovered was that as new features are added to CAMS©, there is no mechanism for notifying all faculty users. Due to the fast turnover of versions, errors were sometimes not discovered until the new version was in use. With such a small, unpaid support staff for CAMS©, these difficulties are likely to increase.

Whereas the initial users of the system were all within one department in the School of Business, now there are users in all departments of the School, as well as in other departments of the university. This has raised a resource issue. The head of IT for the School of Business has made the decision that no users outside the School of Business can access CAMS© from any server in the School. Therefore it cannot be shared freely with outside users unless it is moved to a commercial hosting service. It is not clear who would bear the financial burden of this.

CAMS© is also undergoing growth with respect to the intended target user group. This has prompted the developers to examine the notion of creating customized CAMS© platforms tailored specifically for specific user groups. Whereas most of the user testing of CAMS© has occurred at the university level, at four different universities, it is being expanded to other markets.

A beta version of CAMS© has been tested at a high school. CAMS© has the potential to serve high schools very effectively. The high school version would contain all the same features as the higher education version, and include additional capabilities. The proposed high school version could be employed to track students (e.g., hall passes, library visits and more), and to allow parents to be up-to-date on their child's attendance, grades and assignments.

Another group which has shown an interest in CAMS© are various types of organizations. The potential organizational users could include professional organizations, student groups, sororities and fraternities, to name just a few of the possibilities.

The challenge for the CAMS© developers is to maintain the functionality of the system while meeting the needs of diverse groups. While the developers' commitment to CAMS© grows, so do their full-time teaching duties. Therefore it is essential that they find a way to keep the system running and evolving while minimizing their own time commitment.

REFERENCES

Carnegie, D. (1936). *How to win friends and influence people.* New York: Simon and Schuster.

Gasson, S. (1999). The reality of user-centered design. *Journal of End User Computing, 11*(4), 5-15.

Ko, S., & Rossen, S. (2002). *Teaching online: A practical guide*. New York: Houghton Mifflin.

Li, E. Y. (1997). Perceived importance of information system success factors: A meta analysis of group differences. *Information & Management, 32*, 15-28.

Magal, S. R., & Snead, K. S. (1993). The role of causal attributions in explaining the link between user participation and information systems success. *Information Resources Management Journal, 6*(3), 8-19.

Salmon, G. (2000). *E-moderating: The key to teaching and learning online*. London: Kogan Page Limited.

Stephenson, J. (2001). *Teaching and learning online: New pedagogies for new technologies*. Sterling, VA: Stylus Publishing, LLC.

FURTHER READING

CAMS© evolution. (2003). Retrieved May 30, 2003, from http://www.cob.niu.edu/cams/casestudy/

Collins, M. (2003). Not just another pretty course Web site. *Syllabus*, *16*(7), 28-31.

Field, M. H. (2002). Who is driving and other players: An integrated approach and the educational planner. *Forum*, *17*, 21-50.

Franklin, C. (2001, October 8). Are face-to-face interactions crucial? *InternetWeek*, 20.

Gundling, E. (1999). How to communicate globally. *Training & Development*, *53*(6), 28-31.

Marjanovic, O. (1999). Learning and teaching in a synchronous collaborative environment. *Journal of Computer Assisted Learning*, *15*(2), 129-138.

Brian G. Mackie earned a PhD in management information systems from the University of Iowa (1999). Since 2000, he has been a member of the Operations Management and Information Systems Department at Northern Illinois University (USA). He has published more than 12 conference papers. Dr. Mackie is leading a group of researchers in developing collaboration techniques within online communities.

Norbert L. Ziemer earned his MS in managerial leadership from National-Louis University (1999). He has been an instructor in the Operations Management and Information Systems Department at Northern Illinois University (USA) for four years, teaching both information systems and statistics courses. He entered academia after several years as a development engineer in the auto industry and continues his involvement with Z Tech, a consulting firm specializing in project management.

Nancy L. Russo earned her PhD in management information systems from Georgia State University (1993). Since 1991, she has been a member of the Operations Management and Information Systems Department at Northern

Illinois University (USA), where she is currently the chair. Her work has appeared in Information Systems Journal, Journal of Information Technology, Information Technology & People, Communications of the ACM, *and other journals. She has published two books and more than 25 conference papers. Dr. Russo was recently elected secretary of the International Federation of Information Processing Working Group 8.2 on Information Systems and Organizations.*

Wayne E. Mackie earned a PhD in finance from Michigan State University (1986). Since 1977, he has been a member of the Department of Law and Finance at Saginaw Valley State University (USA), where he is currently chairperson. Dr. Mackie is involved in expanding the use of online and collaborative techniques within the finance curriculum.

This case was previously published in the *Annals of Cases on Information Technology,* Volume 6/2004, pp. 278-292, © 2004.

Chapter X

Deliberate and Emergent Changes on a Way Toward Document Management

Tero Päivärinta, University of Jyväskylä, Finland

Airi Salminen, University of Waterloo, Canada

EXECUTIVE SUMMARY

A unit of Fortum Service Ltd. operates and maintains the Rauhalahti power plant in Central Finland. In 1996-97, the unit launched a project pursuing coordinated organization-wide electronic document management (EDM). This case follows deliberate and emergent changes related to document management in the organization since the initiation of the project until February 2000. New information technologies were adopted, and responsibilities for continuous improvement of EDM were assigned. The continuous improvement was implemented as an extension of the ISO 9002 quality system earlier adopted for process improvement. The case shows that a shift from the paper-based era towards organization-wide EDM is a comprehensive change both affecting and affected by several components in the organization. EDM development in the organization was part of organization recursive dynamics where the quality system supported both planning for deliberate changes and reacting to emergent changes.

BACKGROUND

The Rauhalahti power plant in Jyväskylä, Central Finland, is the chief supplier of district heat (140 MW, 1996) for an area of some 80 000 people. This middle-sized, peat-, wood-, and coal-fired plant also produces steam (65 MW, 1996) for local paper industry and electricity (87 MW, 1996) for the grid. The plant started energy production in 1985. A unit of Fortum Service Ltd. (IVO Generation Services Ltd. until 1998) operates and maintains the plant with c. 80 employees. The unit, our target organization, also remotely operates and maintains several small-scale power and heating plants in the area. In total, the unit looks after 755 MW power generating capacity (Virkkunen, 2000). Local energy suppliers and other industrial companies own the capacity of Rauhalahti and the other plants operated by the target unit.

A middle-sized power plant is an immense and complex construction that includes several interrelated technological components, for instance, varying mechanical machinery, physical and chemical processes, automation, and electrical systems. The routine operations of the Rauhalahti plant (as well as the small-scale plants in the area) can be remotely controlled from one control room where tens of monitors show the status of numerous automated processes: for receiving fuel, changing it into energy, supplying heated water and steam to regional pipe systems and electricity to the grid, etc. The routine maintenance processes, rare (but still possible) technical breakdowns, and yearly revisions of the equipment, however, require working also in several stations physically located around the plant(s) in separate buildings and floors. In addition to the technical operation and maintenance processes, several administrative and managerial activities are naturally needed in running the plant.

A great amount and different kinds of documents play a crucial role in the technical and administrative processes of the target organization, as in contemporary organizations in general. Since the plant started 1985, numerous advances in information technology (IT) related to documents and document management have occurred, as well as changes in the business environment and organization structures of our target organization. Hence the case represents an interesting opportunity for investigating the shift from the paper-based era towards organization-wide electronic document management (EDM) from several viewpoints.

For this case description, we collected data from multiple sources between January 1996 and February 2000:

- Two researchers' participant observation for five months between January and May 1996 in a development project, which was launched as the first step towards coordinated improvement of EDM,
- Documented material describing the target organization and its document management (e.g., Aro, 1993; Repo, 1996; Rauhalahti 1, 2, & 3),

- Several discussions and 19 structured interviews (aiming at a requirements definition for an EDM system) during the development project with the employees representing different work roles in the organization, and
- Two follow-up interviews with the representatives of management, document management, and IT development in June 1997 and February 2000.

SETTING THE STAGE

Document Management in the Organization

At the turn of the 1990s, document management had not been generally identified as carrying great importance in the organization. Documents were archived in paper and other non-digital forms, although a great number of them already was produced by computerized office applications. A separate IT intermediary was responsible for acquiring and updating IT applications according to occasional needs of the employees. No coordinated cooperation existed between document management and the management of IT applications. The attitude towards document management among the personnel, including the management, was described as follows (translated from Finnish by the authors, like the subsequent quotations):

> *As long as our plant is running and producing energy everything else [e.g., document management] is irrelevant.* (Aro, 1993, p. 48)

An archivist was responsible for the most critical — mainly legal and technical — documents. No documented guidelines existed for organization-wide document management. The technical documentation was, however, organized according to the standardized document categorization offered by the plant vendor. The original, official versions of technical documents (describing the plant equipment) were archived by the vendor in a centralized archive at another site. The reference data for the most critical documents were stored in a mainframe database originating from the plant vendor. The archivist was the only user of the database in the target organization. The mainframe application together with manual archives was not an effective solution in supporting document utilization. Hence the employees had many personal, unofficial documents (printouts and personal files) on which they relied at work. In 1992 and 1993 two major renewals of the plant equipment took place. In connection to these renewals, a significant part of technical documentation (about the revised equipment) became available in digital form from the plant vendors.

Establishing a Quality System

Because secure, reliable, pro-environmental, and efficient production of energy is a necessity in the current Finnish power market, high quality is self-evidently required at Rauhalahti. In 1992, the organization started an initiative aiming at a certified *quality system*, and reached the ISO 9002 quality certificate in 1994 as the first power plant maintenance unit in Finland. The ISO 9000 series of standards offers a well-known model to demonstrate the quality of products or services (e.g., ISO 9001, 1994; ISO 9002, 1988). ISO 9000 standards have, however, been criticized for their limitations (Braa & Øgrim, 1994; Reimann & Hertz, 1993). In some companies the external auditing of quality has been the most important motivation for the implementation of ISO 9000 standards. Quality award criteria (e.g., Malcom Baldrige Award Criteria, 1995) instead explicitly address customer focus, benchmarking, organizational learning and continuous improvement and require organizations to be able to prove that they actually use specific methods for these purposes. The management in the target organization saw the fulfillment of the ISO 9002 requirements as a starting point towards the continuous improvement of processes, where the minimum quality assurance activities required by ISO 9000 standards are augmented by activities typical in quality award criteria. The following means of process improvement were implemented in the quality system:

- Defining responsibilities for process improvement.
- Conducting systematic analysis and description of the processes and gathering suggestions for future development needs.
- Setting up of development groups to resolve organizational problems and to promote new initiatives, for example, to adopt new technologies, to benchmark best practices of other organizations, or to implement new ways to organize work.
- Creating of a feedback system in which every employee can identify problems or development initiatives and report them to the persons responsible for the area. Ideally, the identified problems must be reacted to and resolved immediately, but where this is not possible, the managers may set up a development group for the purpose.
- Explicating criteria and metrics to analyze the performance of processes.
- Documenting guidelines for processes.

Improvements in Document Management

From the beginning of the implementation of the quality system in 1992, improvements in document management were regarded as an essential aspect of efforts to achieve quality. An effort was taken to collect and organize important paper documents from personal bookshelves to central archives.

Logical documentation structures were clarified; documentation categories comprised technical documentation, administrative documentation, quality documentation, and the plant library. The first version of the document management manual was created together with the main quality manual. It covered the management of non-digitally archived documents. The official version of any document was supposed to be archived and distributed in paper form. Responsibilities and means for EDM improvement were not determined in the first version of the document management manual.

Organization Assessment

In Klempa (2000) a set of four-position typologies is introduced to be used for analyzing IT acquisition and organization change. The typologies are described for the organization culture, organizational learning, organization frame of reference, and IT-enabling. *Organization culture* refers to the ideologies, beliefs, values, and norms of people in the organization. The four ideal types recognized by many researchers in organizational culture are hierarchical, consensual, rational, and developmental. *Organizational learning* occurs when an organization is able to achieve its goals, capable to recognize the mismatch between its goals and achievements, and also capable to correct the mismatch (Argyris, 1995). The ideal types for organizational learning are bureaucratic learning, participative learning, information-seeking learning, and experimental learning. *Organization frame of reference* includes assumptions the people in the organization make about acquiring and using information. The four ideal types are bureaucratic, political, pragmatic, and prospectic. Finally, *IT-enabling* refers to the organization change impacted by IT acquisition and utilization. The ideal types recognized are incremental change, modular change, architectural change, and radical change.

In the target organization, information technology was utilized by incremental refinements both on the core business as well as on work processes, the organization thus resembling most *incremental* IT-enabling. The quality system was implemented as a reflection to the demands of the clients. On the other hand, from the begin of the case study it became clear to the investigators that the quality of the product, i.e., production of energy, and the maintenance of quality, were taken as part of the organizational culture and frame of reference. The implementation of the quality system was a means for organizational learning, supporting both the *information-seeking* and *participative* type of learning. The implementation caused a shift from hierarchical towards *developmental* organization culture and from pragmatic to *prospective* organization frame of reference.

From the beginning, the quality system was considered a success (Aro, 1993; Repo, 1996). The resource savings gained from process optimization were redirected to new business instead of shedding personnel. The changes in

Figure 1. Organization/individual change curve from Klempa (2000, p. 79)

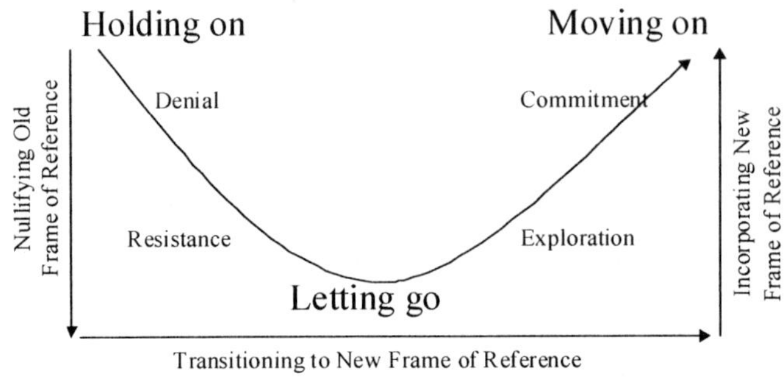

working brought about by the quality system were, excluding two or three dissenting opinions, widely accepted among the personnel. Considering the change curve of Klempa (2000) shown in Figure 1, individuals were more moving on than holding on. There were some influential change agents who can be positioned in the change curve at the commitment state but there were also individuals who regarded the quality system too bureaucratic and showed either resistance or indifference.

The changes affecting document management before the quality system initiative can be regarded as emergent, i.e., not consciously coordinated at the managerial or organizational level:

> *...our document management was rather primitive ... we had paper copies but not any system or systematic guidance.*

The collection of paper-based documents mentioned earlier represented the first deliberate — i.e., purposeful and planned — development initiative on organization-wide document management. In 1995, the mainframe application for the reference data was regarded as obsolete, and transfer to organization-wide electronic document management was suggested; e.g., in the feedback provided by the employees and collected within the quality system. Because the managers had to explicitly respond to the feedback, it was decided to set up an EDM project. Two researchers were invited to participate in the first phases of the project as outside facilitators.

CASE DESCRIPTION

Our case description follows the deliberate and emergent changes concerning EDM at the Rauhalahti unit of the Fortum Service Ltd. from the beginning

Figure 2. Changes related to EDM at the Rauhalahti Unit of the Fortum Service Ltd.

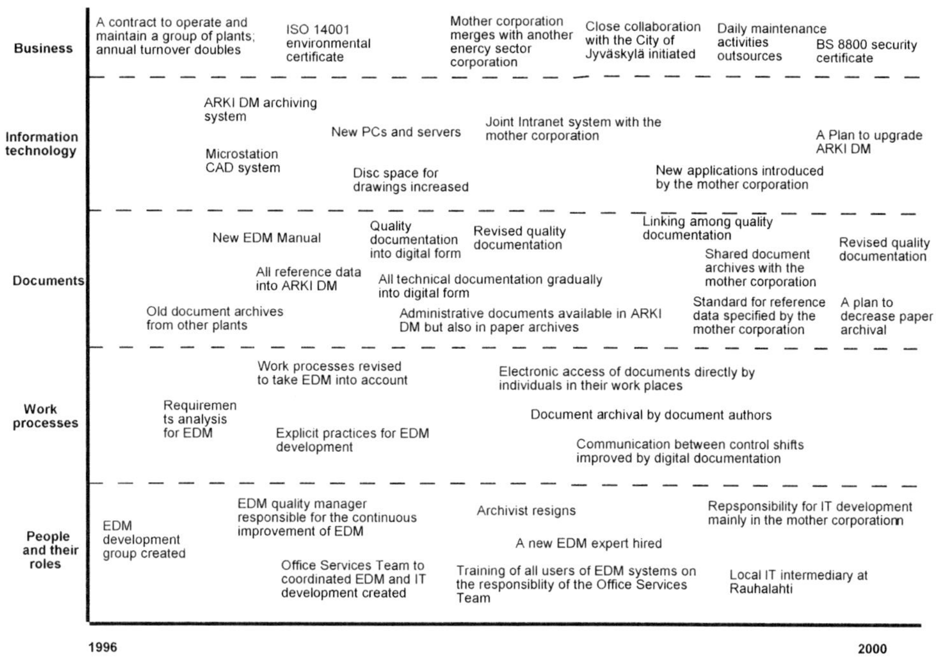

of the EDM project in 1996 until February 2000. It demonstrates that EDM development is part of organization recursive dynamics where both a quality system and information technology can serve as enablers in a continuing process of deliberate and emergent changes (Orlikowski, 1996; Klempa, 2000). The transformation during the time at the Rauhalahti unit is depicted in Figure 2.

Planning for Organization-Wide EDM

The planning for organization-wide EDM was participated in by two authors between January and May 1996. This phase took place in three phases:

- Creation of the EDM development group
- Identification of the actors with interests in EDM
- Requirements analysis

Creation of the EDM Development Group

Creation of a council representing different interest groups has been found important in EDM development (Sprague, 1995; Salminen, Kauppinen, &

Lehtovaara, 1997). In the target organization, the use of development groups was initially regarded as an important means for obtaining continuous process improvement. Hence launching a development initiative by a development group was a familiar approach. In addition to the members from the organization, two researchers participated in the group as outside facilitators.

Identification of the Actors with Interests in EDM

To identify EDM-related needs, problems, and ideas, the group determined who the relevant types of actors were. Document *users* were prioritized as the most important actor type and defined as "persons who need documents in their work". The users were classified further into 19 different user roles according to the contemporary organization chart. The main emphasis of EDM development was placed on analyzing and fulfilling user needs. Other actors with interests in EDM were identified as follows: *managers of the organization* (concerned with EDM costs and security), the *parent company* IVO Generation Services Ltd. (concerned with the generalizability of the new solutions), and *quality system auditors* (concerned with the quality system and its conformity with ISO 9002 specifications).

Requirements Analysis

In the quality system approach, explicit quality criteria are an important means of improvement (Juran, 1988). Here, the requirement analysis was regarded essentially as a two-step definition of the EDM quality criteria. First, the problems, needs and ideas of document users were studied and reported. Second, the development group transformed the observed user needs to commonly agreed criteria, which were then prioritized. The second step added the requirements of the actors that were not in the group of document users to the user needs.

To determine user needs, the development group selected 19 interviewees representing the range of user roles. The researchers performed the interviews as structured conversations. The interviewees seemed mostly motivated to contribute to EDM development; only two or three showed some suspiciousness in the beginning of the interviews. The researchers wrote a report for the development group describing the use cases, document types used, and problems and needs observed in the interviews. The problems, ideas and development needs were classified into 21 organization-level preliminary criteria.

The second step included the formulation and prioritization of the EDM quality criteria. The development group, including one researcher, participated in a computer supported (GroupSystems™) meeting where they discussed the preliminary criteria, defined each criterion more precisely, and prioritized the criteria. The specified criteria were immediately utilized to define the requirements for an electronic archiving system. The list of requirements was attached to an invitation for bids.

Organizing Continuous Improvement of EDM

The development group identified EDM as an important area of continuous improvement. Document management was no longer regarded as the responsibility of the archivist as earlier, but the responsibility of every actor working in their different roles of producing and utilizing documents as well as developing EDM systems and practices and collaborating together. An important basis for operational collaboration was the new EDM manual, revised and restructured from the old document management manual. The new manual was made available to all users in electronic form. New document categories were defined and document types in each category were named and listed. The manual stated the document management systems to be used for each category, and the instructions for use of the systems in processing documents in that category. Especially for the categories technical and quality documentation, the roles and responsibilities of different users were made explicit.

The development group assigned an EDM quality manager to be responsible for the continuous improvement of EDM. The tasks of the EDM quality manager included updating the EDM manual, active analysis of user needs, and yearly collection of feedback and suggestions from other "process owners" regarding new EDM initiatives.

Changes During the Implementation of New Systems

The implementation of the plans in the EDM project caused deliberate changes in four components of EDM: information technology, documents, work processes, and roles of human actors in the processes. In addition to deliberate improvements, several events in the organization caused emergent changes in EDM during the implementation phase. Below, the changes will be briefly discussed.

Information Technology

ARKI DM™ was installed for electronic archiving to replace the earlier mainframe application (DOKU) containing reference data of paper documents. Microstation™ was chosen for the new CAD system and it was installed for the engineers and integrated with the archiving system. Necessary servers were acquired and additional disk space was installed for storing technical drawings and other documentation into electronic form. The systems were gradually adapted to everyday use in 1997. New (25-30) personal computers were provided for workplaces on the shopfloor. Previously personal computers had been only in the offices of administrative personnel, managers and engineers. With IT-enabled information management becoming more important at the corporate level, the technology at Rauhalahti became constrained by the policy of the mother corporation. The new systems had to fulfill the guidelines of the mother corporation.

Documents

Organization-wide documentation categories were clarified and a new documentation category was defined for the plant's project documentation (i.e., business projects outside the plant and significant projects concerning the renewals of plant equipment). Guidelines for documentation were expressed in the EDM manual and access rights were specified. While the development of norms and guidelines in some other IT acquisition and utilization cases occur as emergent changes (e.g., in the case of the Zeta corporation described in Orlikowski, 1996), in our case the development of norms was planned and changes were made deliberately.

The quality documents were digitized and most of the technical, previously paper-based, documents were gradually transformed into a CAD-compatible digital form. The reference data for all archived documents, digital as well as paper, was stored in the new archiving system. The practice to store the most important incoming paper documents in digital form after scanning was initiated. The amount of digital documentation in personal document archives and the use of paper were clearly reducing soon after the implementation of the new solutions started. As the plant manager put it:

> *At least I do not hoard up information any more because I know the information generally is available and within a reasonable time.*

A new document collection emerged as a result of business extension. In 1996, a contract was made to operate and maintain a smaller power plant, a back-up steam boiler, and 10 peak-load heating plants in the region in addition to the Rauhalahti plant. Archives were inherited and received from the additional plants. These archives were in paper form, incomplete, and not organized according to any systematic way. Extra effort was required to organize and archive those documents systematically.

Work Processes

Work processes were deliberately improved and guidelined to utilize the opportunities of the new archiving and CAD systems. In the EDM manual especially the guidelines concerning technical, legal and quality documentation had been redefined to support document handling in digital form instead of the paper form used earlier. For example, the inspection and approval of updates in quality documents or technical drawings no longer required the manual circulation of papers and collection of signatures.

Electronic searching and access of documents needed in the course of day-to-day work became possible without the help of the archivist. Instead of walking to the archive room to take copies or maintaining unofficial sets of copies, engineers and operators, for example, were able to access the documents they needed on-demand directly from their own workstations in their regular work place. One of the most evident changes in work processes thus was the reduction of paper document distribution. The EDM manual was considered as an important means to ensure appropriate common practices to archive and retrieve documents.

In control activities an improvement in turning work shifts emerged. Communication between control shifts (the plant naturally requires round-a-clock control) was enhanced via shared digital documentation about the shifts. Also plant projects involving several organizations became more efficient because the electronic archiving system was utilized in the processing and distribution of the project documents.

In the development work, the managers realized that the organization had proceeded from a plain trial-and-error approach towards more deliberate and holistic improvement in EDM. As the EDM quality manager observed:

> *It was precisely that improvement aspect, ... we had not debated it in our minds [before the project], we had done everything [concerning document management] in the same way for 10 years.*

This indicates that the organizational learning in the issues concerning document management had proceeded from single-loop learning to double-loop learning (Argyris, 1995).

People and Their Roles

The EDM quality manager and the team for integrated coordination of EDM and IT development were defined as new actor roles in the organization. During 1996-97, their responsibilities were gradually clarified and elaborated further. A team for office services (aimed at promoting EDM in practice) was created. The team took responsibility for maintaining the paper archives, administrating the archiving system, training the system to the end users, and putting the existing archives into the system. The system vendor trained the administrators. The vendor however was considered too technologically oriented and thus rather incapable of providing support for actual tailoring of the system for the organizational needs:

> *The vendor support in the beginning was really lousy. There was a support person who was an expert of that system but not an expert of document management.*

In 1997, all employees were trained to use the new systems and to utilize documents in electronic form. Every worker received an intensive and personal training in which a trainer from the office services team stood beside the worker when he or she used the archiving system in actual work situations.

Similarly to some other IT acquisition and utilization cases (e.g., Orlikowski, 1996; Klempa, 2000; Salminen, Lyytikäinen, Tiitinen, & Mustajärvi, 2000), redistribution of work from individual to shared responsibility was clear. In this case the redistribution concerned especially document archival and access. The role of the archivist disappeared, but not as a consequence of the changes in EDM but as an unexpected consequence of the resignation of the person for family reasons in 1996. The archivist had also acted as a drafter of paper-based drawings. A member of the office services team had to take a responsibility for manual drawings and their drafting for the period before the new systems were implemented. A new person with previous experience of EDM and the similar archiving application was recruited from another power plant of the mother company, as an opportunity for this suddenly emerged.

Changes on EDM After the Implementation of the New Systems

There has not been any clear end of the EDM project unless the implementation of the new systems in 1997 is taken as the end. EDM has been under continuous redevelopment. Since the implementation, several changes affecting EDM have occurred. A major organizational change took place at the corporation level. In 1998 the mother corporation (IVO Group) merged with another energy-sector corporation. In 1999 the name of the mother corporation was changed to Fortum Service Oy. The daily maintenance activities of the Rauhalahti unit and 20 people who had taken care of the activities were shifted to a new subunit of the new mother corporation. A bit earlier, a new collaboration had started with the City of Jyväskylä and 24 people had moved from the City to the Rauhalahti unit. Considering the whole analysis period, the number of people in the Rauhalahti unit thus has remained about the same, whereas, the revenue has at least doubled. Below the changes after 1997 on EDM will be discussed.

Information Technology

Rauhalahti joined to the intranet system of the mother corporation. A new system for managing personnel information was introduced by the mother organization but at Rauhalahti it was considered to be too much oriented plainly for the needs of the mother. A plan was made to acquire the new version of the ARKI DM™ system. With the new version a size constraint concerning electronic cabinets emerged; this will cause extra work at Rauhalahti. However, the user interface of the new version was considered user-friendlier by the office services team.

Documents

Electronic links between quality documents have been created to great satisfaction of users:

> *... from process descriptions through links you can directly access instructions and that is really wonderful!*

The ARKI DM system and EDM guidelines clearly improved version management. Improvements in version management increased the commitment and satisfaction towards the change:

> *It was very positively accepted because there are no more divergent versions. That was the problem earlier.*

Although almost all documents could be found at the end of the analysis period in electronic archives, a major part of documents (except quality documentation) was still archived and stored parallel in paper form. The motivations for keeping the paper archives were not quite clear and explicit:

> *... we are a little afraid of ... and we have thought about these auditing situations, we are able to give paper folders for the situations ...*

A decision has been made to gradually decrease the archival of paper documents where considered possible. Some people also have unofficial personal archives "just for the case to write one's memoirs after retirement." The mother corporation insists a number of shared documentation folders in the corporate intranet that causes redundancy of information, uncertainty of versioning, and extra work.

The Rauhalahti unit received both environmental (ISO 14001) and security (BS 8800) certificates. Hence, the quality system documentation was fundamentally restructured two times alongside with the new certificate requirements, and related process development initiatives. The mother corporation introduced a standardized form of reference data for documents. The office services team considered this as a mistake:

> *We were against it. It was planned from the viewpoint of administration, not engineering.*

Work Processes

Distribution of paper-based documents for the purposes of communication in work processes has crucially, if not totally, diminished. People who need documents in their work use the archiving (and CAD) system actively. The administration, support, and coordination of electronic document management has become a routine-like set of activities of the office services team, which now actively interacts with process owners of the organization with regard to new development initiatives. The archiving system has been considered extremely useful in generating automatically several kinds of reports for the management and for supporting information retrieval in general. Some groups of people still use e-mail for distributing documents although the archiving system could as well be used for these purposes.

Along with the corporate intranet system the problem of uncontrolled document distribution has emerged:

> *The information overflow is huge, no coordination, only sent, there should be an informant to acquire adequate information for adequate receivers.*

The incompatibilities between different CAD systems of the target organization and its vendor organizations have caused troubles in receiving and reusing documents from the vendors. Manual work for converting those documents is needed.

People and Their Work Roles

Archiving of documents is increasingly transformed into the responsibility of end users. At first, the employees had expressed several negative comments about the new system but after a while, according to the EDM quality manager:

> *Folks do not want to go back to the old systems and practices any more; for instance, to the circulation of quality documentation in paper form.*

Document management has become a responsibility of every employee who needs documents at work. Despite the specified archiving rights, some difficulties still exist in the practices to archive documents properly. Sometimes, people forget to store important documents received via e-mail into the archiving system.

Local IT development and document management have somehow "separated" again into two different stakeholders keeping not much contact with each other. The local IT intermediary looks after the PCs, servers, back-up practices, etc. The IT development staff of the mother organization has introduced new solutions that have not satisfied the local document management staff; a potential conflict between roles of these stakeholders exists.

At the end of the analysis period the changes in EDM were widely accepted among the personnel; nevertheless, there were also obvious problems. Individuals were more moving on than holding on as was the case after the implementation of the quality system (see Figure 1). According to persons of the office services team, there are however clear differences among individuals. Especially managers, people needing documents regularly in their work, and young people were committed to the IT utilization. In respect to the use of the archival system, engineers were holding on more than other groups. Interestingly this was noticed also in the case of Sterkoder, Ltd. (Klempa, 2000).

CURRENT CHALLENGES FACING THE ORGANIZATION

The organization will face several new challenges concerning EDM. Many of them are related to the situation where two different organization cultures and information management practices have been merged in the new mother corporation. The coordination of EDM and IT issues between the mother corporation and the local target unit is a major challenge. Redundancy has occurred both in the contemporary applications (some documents have been archived in both local and corporate systems) and in the development and adoption of new ones (the responsibilities between local and corporate-level development of EDM and other IT applications have not been always clear).

At the Rauhalahti unit, cooperation between the developers of EDM and "other IT" has not been totally unproblematic. Especially, the persons having their background in the discipline of archiving expressed difficulties in finding a "common language" to discuss IT-related issues with the persons responsible for the plant's IT in general. Interestingly, after the EDM project, the coordination between the development of EDM and IT in general has again decreased.

The business environment of the Rauhalahti unit will become ever more demanding as a consequence of the opening of the European energy markets. The current trends set demands for more effective interorganizational cooperation and thereby for document exchange and management in business projects. Some kind of standardization of document formats to be shared across organizational borders most probably has to take place in the future.

An important challenge concerns the continuously advancing IT in general. Evolving Web-based technologies provide new opportunities to share and implement EDM within the company and among its collaborative organizations. The new opportunities have to be carefully considered and reflected on the existing systems. Novel technologies (for instance, digital photographing and image processing) have also been under consideration as possible means for providing improved information capture and access in the demanding maintenance processes.

Considering the development efforts illustrated above and the future challenges emerging in the target organization, we can argue that our case organization clearly represents an emergent organization facing a constant need to change and continuously adapting to its shifting environment (Truex, Baskerville, & Klein, 1999). The case demonstrates that in an emergent organization, one should not try to fix an organization-wide "EDM system" to a "perfect condition" by one deliberate and technologically oriented development effort, but rather gradually integrate and elaborate different aspects of EDM (information technology, documents, work processes, and the roles of human actors) in a coordinated way along time. Several changes in organizational environment and various technological opportunities will affect EDM along time. Hence, the continuous improvement of EDM cannot be idealistically deliberate all the time. However, if the organization would be plainly drifting along with emergent impulses and opportunities from outside the organization without any responsibilities specified for coordinating the change, the situation would not lead to effective EDM. The Rauhalahti unit seems well prepared to meet the known and unknown future challenges using its quality system approach, which includes development practices and guidelines both for planning deliberate changes and for reacting to emergent changes.

ACKNOWLEDGMENTS

This study was financed partially by TEKES (the Finnish Technology Development Center). Tuomo Peltola played a significant role during the first phase of this research. The authors wish to thank also Jarkko Ahtikari, Airi Hannula, and Kari Kotirinta for their invaluable support.

REFERENCES

Aro, M. (1993). *Toiminnankehittämisprojektin hallinta voimalaitoksessa* (Managing an organizational development project in a power plant, in Finnish). Unpublished master's thesis on engineering. Tampere: Tampereen teknillinen korkeakoulu, Teollisuustalouden laitos.

Rauhalahti 1. Version 1. (1996, January). *Päälaatukäsikirja* (Quality system manual, in Finnish). IVO Generation Services Ltd, Rauhalahti power plant.

Rauhalahti 2. Version 1. (1996, January). *Hallinnolliset ohjeet, asiakirjahallinto* (Document management manual, in Finnish). IVO Generation Services Ltd, Rauhalahti power plant.

Rauhalahti 3. Version 10. (1997, June). *Hallinnolliset ohjeet, asiakirjahallinto* (Document management manual, in Finnish). IVO Generation Services Ltd, Rauhalahti power plant.

Repo, A. (1996). Successful quality campaign at Rauhalahti. *IVO Review* (Customer Magazine of IVO Group), (1), 22-23.

Virkkunen, H. (2000). Puuhake pöllysi pitkin Nisulan pihoja. *Sähköviesti* (Customer magazine of the local energy supplier — Jyväskylän Energia Ltd.), *61*(2), 2-3.

FURTHER READING

Argyris, C. (1995). *On organizational learning*. Cambridge, MA: Blackwell.

Braa, K., & Øgrim, L. (1994). Critical view of the application of the ISO standard for quality assurance. *Information Systems Journal, 5*, 253-269.

ISO 9001. (1994). *International standard, quality systems. Model for quality assurance in design, development, production, installation and servicing* (2nd ed.). ISO.

ISO 9002. (1988). *International standard, quality systems. Model for quality assurance in production and installation*. Suomen standardoimisliitto.

Juran, J. M. (1988). *Juran on planning for quality*. New York: The Free Press.

Klempa, M. J. (2000). Managing Web technologies acquisition, utilization and organization change: Understanding sociocognitive processual dynamics. In M. Khosrow-Pour (Ed.), *Managing Web-enabled technologies in organizations: A global perspective* (pp. 54-102). Hershey, PA: Idea Group Publishing.

Malcom Baldrige Award Criteria. (1995). Gaithersburg: National Institute of Standards and Technology. Retrieved June 1996, from http://www.nist.gov/quality_program/doc/95_Criteria/1995_AWARD_CRITERIA.html

Orlikowski, W. J. (1996). Improvising organizational transformation over time: A situated change perspective. *Information Systems Research, 7*(1), 63-92.

Reimann, C. W., & Hertz, H. S. (1993). *The Malcom Baldridge National Quality Awards and ISO 9000 registration: Understanding their many important differences*. Gaithersburg: National Institute of Standards and Technology. Retrieved June 19, 1996, from http://www.nist.gov/

Salminen, A., Kauppinen, K., & Lehtovaara, M. (1997). Towards a methodology for document analysis. *Journal of the American Society for Information Science, 48*(7), 644-655.

Salminen, A., Lyytikäinen, V., Tiitinen, P., & Mustajärvi, O. (2000). SGML for e-Governance: The case of the Finnish Parliament. In A. M. Tjoa, R. R. Wagner, & A. Al-Zobaidie (Eds.), *Proceedings of the 11th International Workshop on Database and Expert Systems Applications* (pp. 345-353). Los Alamitos, CA: IEEE Computer Society Press.

Sprague, R.H. (1995). Electronic document management: Challenges and opportunities for information systems managers. *MIS Quarterly, 19*(1), 29-50.

Truex, D. P., Baskerville, R., & Klein, H. (1999). Growing systems in emergent organizations. *Communications of the ACM, 42*(8), 117-123.

Tero Päivärinta earned his PhLic (econ.) in information systems from the University of Jyväskylä, Finland (2000) (MSc, 1996). He is a senior assistant in digital media at the Department of Computer Science and Information Systems, University of Jyväskylä. His research interests include enterprise document management, genre theory, method engineering, and critical perspectives on information systems development. Concerning these topics, his work history includes several research and development projects in collaboration with industrial companies and the public sector, and related publications in information systems conferences.

Airi Salminen is a visiting professor at the University of Waterloo, Department of Computer Science, Canada, while on leave from the University of Jyväskylä, Finland. She earned her PhD in computer science from the University of Tampere (1989). She was responsible for planning a new master's program in digital media at the University of Jyväskylä and headed the program from its beginning in 1995. She has been the leader of several projects where research has been tied to document management development efforts in major Finnish companies or public sector organizations. Her current research interests include document management, structured documents, XML, user interfaces, and software environments.

This case was previously published in the *Annals of Cases on Information Technology Applications and Management in Organizations,* Volume 3/2001, pp. 320-333, © 2001.

Chapter XI

Implementing a Data Mining Solution for an Automobile Insurance Company: Reconciling Theoretical Benefits with Practical Considerations

Ai Cheo Yeo, Monash University, Australia

Kate A. Smith, Monash University, Australia

EXECUTIVE SUMMARY

The insurance company in this case study operates in a highly competitive environment. In recent years it has explored data mining as a means of extracting valuable information from its huge databases in order to improve decision making and capitalise on the investment in business data. This case study describes an investigation into the benefits of data mining for an anonymous Australian automobile insurance company.[1] *Although the investigation was able to demonstrate quantitative benefits of adopting a data mining approach, there are many practical issues that need to be resolved before the data mining approach can be implemented.*

BACKGROUND

Melbourne Automobile Insurers (MAI) is a leading car insurer in Australia. It was established in the early 1970s. Today it has more than 40 branches and has nearly 2 million policy holders with an underwriting profit of over $50 million.

MAI, like all insurance companies, operates in a highly competitive environment. In recent years, there has been a proliferation of non-traditional retailers of car insurance that has caused great concern for MAI. Banks and finance companies are now joined by manufacturers and distributors of cars in the marketing of car insurance. Many of MAI's competitors have been intent on maintaining their market share and have kept premium rises to a minimum, thereby discouraging their policy holders from shopping around for a better price. The competitive environment extends beyond premium pricing issues to include a range of value-added products and incentives such as "liftetime rating 1" and discounts on multiple policies.

The Australian general insurance market went through a turbulent year in 2000. General business issues such as Y2K, the implementation of a new tax system, including the introduction of a goods and services tax, and corporate law reform program (CLERP) consumed a great deal of non-productive time and resources.

SETTING THE STAGE

In 1999, MAI established a SAS data warehouse. Periodically, data was extracted from their operational system and deposited into the data warehouse. The variables extracted included:

- Policy holders' characteristics such as age, gender.
- Vehicle characteristics such as age, category, area in which vehicle was garaged.
- Policy details such as sum insured, premium, rating, number of years policy held, excess.

The Information System Department is responsible for maintaining the data warehouse. The Business Analysis Department extract data from the data warehouse for periodic reporting and as well as statistical analysis. The statistical analysis is done using Excel spreadsheets and online analytical processing (OLAP).

MAI realised that their current method of premium pricing has its limitations. With increased competition, MAI knew that they needed better tools to analyse data in their data warehouse to gain competitive advantage. They hoped to obtain a greater leverage on their investment in the data warehouse.

In the meantime, Jack Pragg, the account manager of SAS, had been trying to convince MAI that the next logical step to take is to embark on data mining and that the SAS data mining suite Enterprise Miner was the most appropriate tool for them. According to SAS "the Enterprise Miner is the first and only data mining solution that addresses the entire data mining process — all through an intuitive point-and-click graphical user interface (GUI). Combined with SAS data warehousing and OLAP technologies, it creates a synergistic, end-to-end solution that addresses the full spectrum of knowledge discovery."

MAI did not have data mining expertise and wanted an independent opinion before they invested in the SAS Enterprise Miner. The CEO of MAI, Ron Taylor, approached his former university lecturer, Professor Rob Willis, for help. Rob was at the time the Head of School of Business Systems at Monash University. Monash University has a Data Mining Group Research Group headed by Dr. Kate Smith. The aims of the group are to provide advanced research and training in data mining for business, government and industry.

Rob together with Kate conducted a proof-of-concept study to determine whether there was scope for data mining. In determining the optimal pricing of policies there was a need to find a balance between profitability and growth and retention. The study looked at the sub-problems of customer retention classification and claim cost modelling. A neural network was developed to predict the likelihood of a policy being renewed or terminated and clustering was able to identify groups with high cost ratios. The initial study demonstrated the potential of data mining.

The case that follows describes the subsequent three-year project: its aims, outcomes, and the implementation issues currently facing the organisation. The main players in the case, and their respective roles, are summarised in Table 1.

CASE DESCRIPTION

MAI decided to engage Monash University in a three-year extended study which aimed to produce quantitative evidence of the benefits of data mining. Kate had a prospective PhD student, Angie Young, who was interested in data

Table 1. Main players and their roles in the case

Organization	Players	Role
Monash University	Dr. Kate Smith	Supervior of PhD Student
	Angie Young	PhD Student
Melbourne Automobile Insurers	Mark Brown	Business Analyst Manager
	Sophie Green	Business Analyst
	Andrew Boyd	Business Analyst
	Charles Long	System Analyst
	Ryan Lee	Pricing Manager

mining and was looking for sponsorship. MAI agreed to provide a scholarship for Angie to carry out the data mining research at MAI under the supervision of Kate.

Mark Brown, the Business Analysis manager, was in charge of co-ordinating the data mining project. He had worked in the company for more than twenty years and he knew the business very well. He was also familiar with the data and had knowledge of the processes behind the data collection. He was able to determine useful questions for analysis and select potentially relevant data to answer these questions.

MAI is driven by two main concerns: the need to return a profit to their shareholders and investors, and the need to achieve market growth and retain a certain level of market share. These two goals are seen as imperatives to success, but are often conflicting. Premiums play a critical role in enabling MAI to find a balance between these two goals. The challenge is to set premiums so that expected claims are covered and a certain profitability is achieved, yet not to set premiums so high that market share is jeopardised as consumers exercise their right to choose their insurer. In other words, MAI has to balance profitability and market share when setting premiums. This involves combining the results of three main tasks: risk classification, prediction of claim cost and price sensitivity analysis (see Figure 1). The initial study showed that data mining could be of benefit to premium setting, but the three-year extended study needed to show the quantitative benefits of the approach.

In the automobile insurance industry, companies adopt "class ratings" to determine premiums. Policy holders are assigned to various risk groups based on factors which are considered predictors of claim cost and premiums are charged based on the risk group to which they belong. An insurance company has to discriminate between good and bad risks so that they can engage in selective marketing, otherwise they may end up losing good customers due to uncompetitive premiums that are inadequate to compensate for the risks of customers of dubious quality. "Bad risks drive out good risks," when the same premium is charged (van Gelder, 1982). Another reason for discriminating between good and bad risks is so that premiums can be set equitably. The premium should be fair in the sense that each policy holder, or group of policy holders, should be charged a rate which reflects the policy holder's expectation of loss (Athearn, 1969; Denenberg, 1974).

Having classified policy holders into various risk groups, an insurance company has to decide on an appropriate method for predicting claim costs within each group. Currently MAI uses a point system. Each rating factor is scaled such that the higher the risk, the higher the points. For each risk factor, the policy holder will be assigned points. These points are aggregated for all factors and premium is charged accordingly. The higher the aggregated points, the higher the premium. The points system has some limitations however, and these will be

Figure 1. Balancing profitability and market share

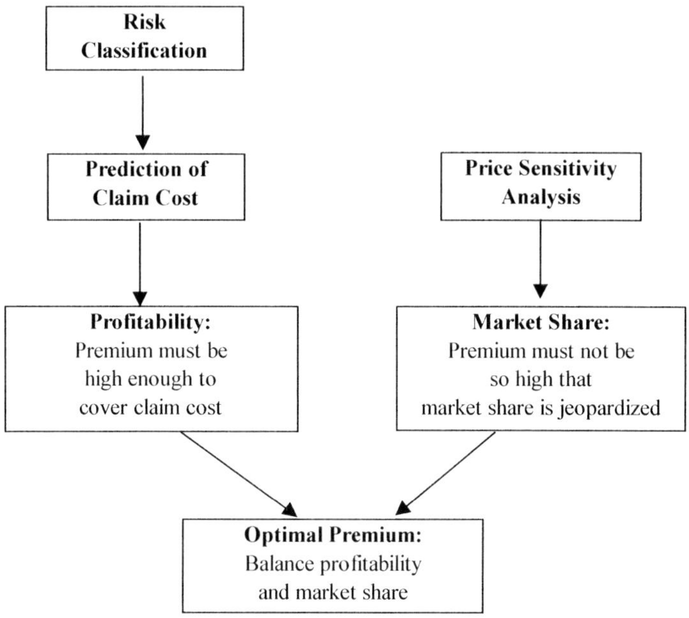

illustrated with an example. For simplicity, we assume that points are assigned to policy holders based on only two factors: the policy holder's age and vehicle age (see Table 2). The aggregated points for the various risk groups are shown in Table 3. Continuing the illustrative example, Table 4 shows an example of what the cost ratio (claim cost/premium) matrix may look like for the various risk groups (claim cost and premium information have been intentionally omitted for brevity).

Suppose the company is not happy with the cost ratio of 94% (policy holder age group D and vehicle age group E) and would like to increase the premium to cover the high claim cost of the risk group. Since the premium is calculated based on points, the company would have to either increase the points of policy holder age group D or vehicle age group E. However, this would this would increase the points for other cells in the row or column even though the company may be satisfied with their cost ratio. Ideally, premium should be charged based on a reflection of actual risk. We could change the points for that particular cell in isolation, but if many variables are considered this point system becomes very large and complicated

In determining optimal premiums, MAI has to be mindful of the effect of changes in premiums on retention rates. In a competitive environment, setting the premium at too high a level can lead to a loss in market share. The broad framework shown in Figure 1 was used in the initial study to guide the data mining tasks, and now became the basis of the three-year investigation.

A business analyst, Sophie Green, was recruited to carry out data mining. Sophie's background was in statistics and she was not familiar with data mining tools. Although she attended an introductory course in data mining run by Monash University shortly after she joined MAI, she found it difficult to use the Enterprise Miner. She did not know which tools were appropriate for analysis. She found herself going back to statistical analysis she was familiar with using an Excel spreadsheet.

Angie was not familiar with many of the terms of the insurance industry. She had to learn about the business before she could begin any data mining. She spent

Table 2. Points for risk factors

Policy Holder Age Group	Points	Vehicle Age Group	Points
A	50	A	0
B	40	B	1
C	35	C	2
D	30	D	3
E	25	E	4

Table 3. Aggregated points of risk groups

	Policy Holder Age Group				
Vehicle Age Group	**A**	**B**	**C**	**D**	**E**
A	50	40	35	30	25
B	51	41	36	31	26
C	52	42	37	32	27
D	53	43	38	33	28
E	54	44	39	34	29

Table 4. Cost ratio of risk groups

	Policy Holder Age Group				
Vehicle Age Group	**A**	**B**	**C**	**D**	**E**
A	57%	65%	74%	75%	72%
B	54%	57%	70%	78%	71%
C	58%	48%	71%	75%	76%
D	66%	62%	72%	83%	79%
E	72%	72%	83%	94%	70%

a substantial amount of time understanding the business. Mark was a great help in this respect. She also required the help of Mark to interpret intermediate results of the analysis. At times they found that the results indicated that there were problems with the data used for analysis and it was back to the drawing board.

Charles Long, a system analyst, was asked to extract data sets from the data warehouse. He knew what data was available, exactly where the data could be found and how different sources could be combined. Charles extracted two data sets (training and test sets) consisting of 29 variables and 12 months of comprehensive motor insurance policies of one of the Australian states, New South Wales. The training set consisted of 146,326 policies with due dates from January 1 to December 31, 1998 while the test set consisted of 186,658 policies with due dates from July 1, 1998 to June 30, 1999. Restricted by the availability of data at the time of collection, the period of overlap was to enable comparison of exposure and retention rates over a one-year period and to ensure that sample sizes are sufficiently large. Forty percent of the policies in the test set were new policies. The training set was used to train the models while the test set was used to evaluate the results.

Charles had to convert some of the variables into a format required for data mining. For example, age of policy holders and vehicles were computed based on date of birth and year of manufacture respectively. While Angie was obtaining some descriptive statistics of the data sets to familiarise herself with the data, she discovered some errors. For example, a few of the policy holders had an age of 999. She removed records with errors from the data sets. She also noticed that there were several types of excess and she aggregated the various amounts.

Nine months after the project began, Sophie resigned. Andrew Boyd was recruited to take her place but also resigned after a month. Angie found herself carrying out the project on her own. Although it was agreed that Angie was to make monthly presentations to the management of MAI on the progress of her research, it turned out that during her three years she only managed four presentations. It was difficult for the MAI management team (some based in Melbourne and others in Sydney) to find a common time slot for the presentations.

Angie met with Kate weekly to report on the progress of her research. With the help of Kate she was able to decide which data mining algorithm or tool was most suited to address the various research questions and interpret the results. At the end of her three-year research at MAI, Angie proposed a detailed data mining framework (see Figure 2) to determine the premiums to charge automobile insurance policy holders in order to arrive at an optimal portfolio.

The framework, which is a holistic approach, consists of three main components:

- The first component involves identifying risk classifications and predicting claim costs using clustering. The total premiums charged must be sufficient to cover all claims made against the policies and return a desired level of profit.
- The second component involves price sensitivity analysis using neural networks. Premiums cannot be set at too high a level as customers may terminate their policies thus affecting market share.
- The third component combines the results of the first two components to provide information on the impact of premiums on profitability and market share. The optimal mix of premiums to achieve a pre-specified termination rate while maximising profit is determined by integer programming.

The first component of the data mining framework involves identifying risk classifications and predicting claim costs. In designing a risk classification structure, insurance companies attempt to maximise homogeneity within each risk group and heterogeneity between the risk groups. This can be achieved through clustering. The k-means clustering model was used to classify polices. The k-means clustering model performs disjoint cluster analysis on the basis of Euclidean distances computed from variables and seeds that are generated and updated by k-means algorithm (Anderberg, 1973; MacQueen, 1967). Least squares is the clustering criterion used to measure the distance between data

Figure 2. Data mining framework for determining optimal premiums

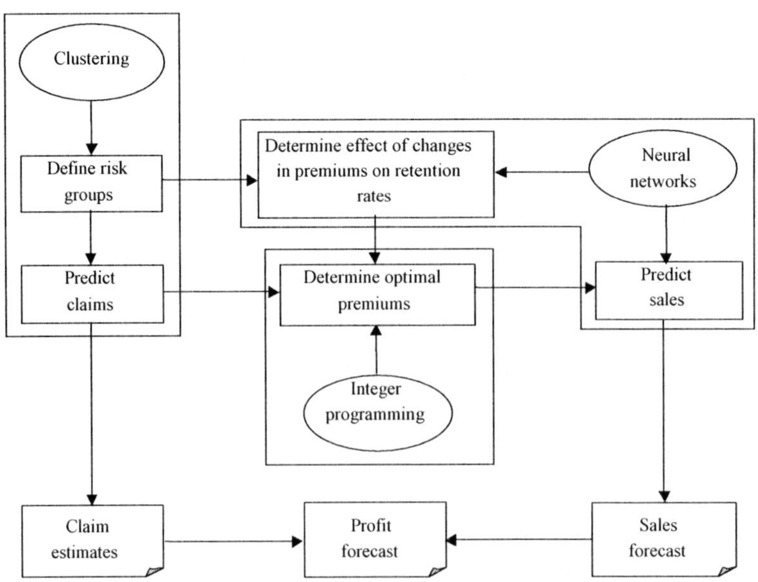

observations and seeds. Using the least squares clustering criterion, the sum of the squared distances of observations to the cluster means is minimised. Thirteen variables were used for clustering. They were:

- Policy holder's age
- Policy holder's gender
- Area in which the vehicle was garaged
- Rating of policy holder
- Years on current rating
- Years on rating one
- Number of years policy held
- Category of vehicle
- Sum insured
- Total excess
- Vehicle use
- Vehicle age
- Whether or not the vehicle is under finance

Having classified the policy holders into risk groups, the price sensitivity within each cluster was examined; the second component of the data mining framework. Neural networks were trained to classify policy holders into those who are likely to terminate their policies and those who are likely to renew. Neural networks are ideal tools for solving this problem due to their proven ability to learn to distinguish between classes, and to generalise their learning to unseen data (Bigus, 1996; Han & Kamber, 2001; Smith, 1999). A multilayered feedforward neural network was constructed for each of the clusters with 25 inputs, 20 hidden neurons and one output neuron (whether the policy holder renews or terminates to contract). The inputs consist of the 13 variables used for risk classification plus the following premium and sum insured variables:

- "Old" premium (premium paid in the previous period)
- "New" premium (premium indicated in renewal notice)
- "Old" sum insured (sum insured in the previous period) which was also included as input in the clustering model
- "New" sum insured (sum insured indicated in renewal notice)
- Change in premium ("new" premium — "old" premium)
- Change in sum insured ("new" sum insured — "old" sum insured)
- Percentage change in premium
- Percentage change in sum insured
- Ratio of "old" premium to "old" sum insured

- Ratio of "new" premium to "new" sum insured
- Whether there is a change in rating
- Whether there is a change in postcode
- Whether there is a change in vehicle

Sensitivity analysis was then performed on the neural networks to determine the effect of premium changes on termination rate of each cluster. Separate data sets were created from each cluster with all variables remaining unchanged except for new premium and related variables. These data sets were scored against the trained neural networks to determine the predicted termination rates under variations of premium.

The third component of the data mining framework combines the results of the first two components to provide information on the impact of premiums on profitability and market share. The problem of determining optimal premium is akin to portfolio optimisation where an investor strives to find a balance between risk and return across their portfolio of investments (Markowitz, 1952). In portfolio theory, an asset has a given rate of return and risk. In the insurance optimisation problem, the termination rate and the profit earned from each cluster depend on the premium that is charged. Integer programming was proposed to determine the premium to charge for each cluster to maximise total profit for a given overall termination rate. The termination rates of individual clusters may vary to maximise the profit but the overall termination rate for the portfolio will be constrained by a user-defined parameter (Yeo et al., 2002)

The optimisation problem was solved for varying termination rates. The results are shown in Figure 3. The curve is similar to the efficient frontier of portfolio optimisation. It is a smooth non-decreasing curve that gives the best possible trade-off between profit and termination rate. If MAI selects an

Figure 3. Optimal profit for varying termination rates

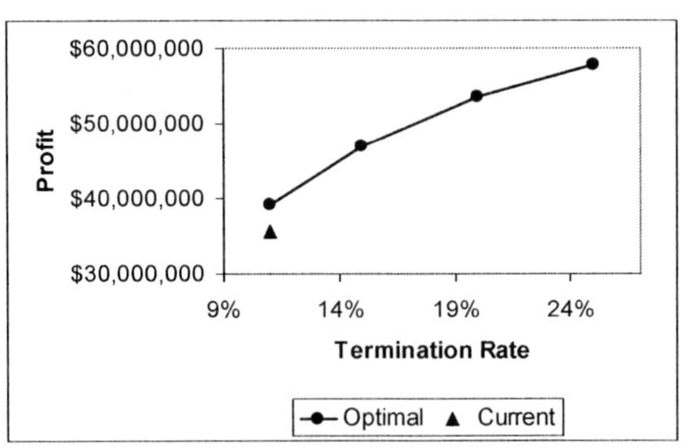

acceptable termination rate, the model will then determine a portfolio (mix of premiums to charge various risk groups) that maximises profit. If MAI were to maintain its current termination rate of 11%, profits could be increased by changing the mix of premiums.

Thus Angie was able to provide MAI with clear evidence of the quantitative benefits of adopting a data mining approach to premium pricing.

CURRENT CHALLENGES/PROBLEMS FACING THE ORGANISATION

MAI were quite excited about the outcome of Angie's research. The MAI management was in the process of reviewing their current point system of premium pricing and they agreed that it needed to be revamped. Angie's results had shown that strong quantitative benefits were theoretically possible if the proposed data mining solution was adopted.

However there were several issues that needed to be resolved before MAI could begin to implement the data mining approach. Firstly the approach needs to be validated; for the various Australian states. The research was based on only one of the Australian states and there were differences in the premium pricing for the various states. Should the approach be validated using real cases or historical data? Also, the data mining framework does not model the effect of competition. Can the approach be implemented if it has only considered the dynamics of MAI in isolation from their competitors? How can competition be factored into the framework? If it is mathematically too difficult to consider the effect of competition, how should MAI proceed?

MAI do not have any data mining expertise and none of the MAI staff were very involved in the Angie's research project. It is therefore difficult to transfer the skills and knowledge acquired during the project to MAI staff to carry out the validation and implementation. MAI realise that data mining is more than just acquiring the software. Data mining expertise is required to decide which algorithm is most suited for a problem and to interpret the results. Should they recruit people with the data mining skills or should they train the current business analysts to do future data mining work?

Implementing the proposed data mining framework will also require significant business process re-engineering. How will staff react to the changes? How can resistance to change be managed? How are they going to integrate data mining into the existing information system infrastructures?

Since the data mining approach is "modular", the pricing manager, Ryan Lee, suggested implementing the data mining approach in phases. They could use the MAI's existing risk groups to replace the clustering stage of component one, and use neural networks to model the price sensitivity of these risk groups. If the neural networks proved to be successful, they could then look at implementing the integer programming for determining the optimal premium to charge for each risk group. The final phase would be to look at implementing the clustering method of risk classification.

Clearly there are many practical considerations that MAI need to resolve before the proposed data mining approach can be adopted. Some of these are related to personnel and change management, while others are more technological considerations. Until these issues have been resolved, the project has only shown the theoretical benefits that could be obtained.

REFERENCES

Anderberg, M. (1973). *Cluster analysis for applications*. Academic Press.

Athearn, J. L. (1969). *Risk and insurance* (2nd ed.). New York: Appleton-Century-Crafts, Educational Division, Meredith Corporation.

Bigus, J. P. (1996). *Data mining with neural networks: Solving business problems — From application development to decision support*. New York: McGraw-Hill.

Denenberg, H. S. (1974). *Risk and insurance* (2nd ed.). Englewood Cliffs, NJ: Prentice-Hall.

Han, J., & Kamber, M. (2001). *Data mining: Concepts and techniques*. Morgan Kaufmann Publishers.

MacQueen, J. (1967). Some methods for classification and analysis of multivariate observations. In *Proceedings of the 5th Berkeley Symposium on Mathematical Statistics and Probability*.

Markowitz, H. (1952). Portfolio selection. *Journal of Finance, 7*, 77-91.

Smith, K. A. (1999). *Introduction to neural networks and data mining for business applications*. Melbourne: Eruditions Publishing.

van Gelder, H. (1982). Planning and control in insurance. *European Journal of Operational Research, 9*(2), 105-113.

Yeo, A., Smith, K., Willis, R., & Brooks, M. (2002). A mathematical programming approach to optimise insurance premium pricing within a data mining framework. *Journal of the Operational Research Society, 53*, 1197-1203.

ENDNOTE

1 The name of the company and the names of its employees have been changed to protect their anonymity.

Ai Cheo Yeo became a fellow member of The Association of Chartered Certified Accountants in 1990. She earned her Master's of Business Systems in 1998. She has worked as an auditor in the Singapore Auditor-General's Office, a bank and an oil company. She was also a lecturer with the Business Administration Department of Singapore Polytechnic. She is currently a lecturer with the School of Business Systems, Monash University, Australia. She has completed her PhD focusing on data mining in the automobile insurance industry. She has published several refereed journal papers and book chapters on this topic.

Kate A. Smith is an associate professor in the School of Business Systems, Monash University, Australia, where she also fulfills the roles of deputy head, director of research, and director of the Data Mining Research Group. She holds a BSc (Hons) in mathematics and a PhD in electrical engineering, both from the University of Melbourne, Australia. Kate has published two books on neural networks in business, and more than 100 journal and international conference papers in the areas of neural networks, combinatorial optimization, and data mining. She is a member of the organizing committee for several international data mining and neural network conferences, and regularly acts as a consultant to industry in these areas.

This case was previously published in the *Annals of Cases on Information Technology*, Volume 5/2003, pp.63-73, © 2003.

Chapter XII

Long-Term Evolution of a Conceptual Schema at a Life Insurance Company

Lex Wedemeijer, ABP, The Netherlands

EXECUTIVE SUMMARY

Enterprises need data resources that are stable and at the same time flexible to support current and new ways of doing business. However, there is a lack of understanding how flexibility of a Conceptual Schema design is demonstrated in its evolution over time. This case study outlines the evolution of a highly integrated Conceptual Schema in its business environment. A gradual decline in schema quality is observed: size and complexity of the schema increase, understandability and consistency decrease. Contrary to popular belief, it is found that changes aren't driven only by "accepted" causes like new legislation or product innovation. Other change drivers are identified like error correction, changing perceptions of what the information need of the business is and elimination of derived data. The case shows that a real Conceptual Schema is the result of "objective" design practices as well as the product of negotiation and compromise with the user community.

BACKGROUND

Justification

Many large application systems in government, banking, insurance and other industries are centered around a relational database. A central component is its conceptual schema, being the linking pin between information requirements and perceptions of "reality" as seen by users, and the way how the corresponding data are actually stored in the database. As user requirements can and will evolve over time, it must be expected that changes to the conceptual schema (CS) become necessary. Nevertheless, it is often assumed that superior quality of the initial design is sufficient for it to remain stable over the entire information systems lifecycle. Thus, the ability to adapt to later changes in the user requirements is taken for granted, if not blatantly ignored in most design methods.

This case looks at the cumulative effects of a series of changes on the overall quality of a CS, by tracing the actual evolution of one CS in its natural business environment. Although we do describe the separate change step, we don't intend to study or criticize the individual change projects or the realization of strategic targets. Our aim is to develop an overall understanding of successive changes in the CS, and its change drivers. And by taking the viewpoint of sustained system exploitation, we place the importance of initial design quality into its proper long-term perspective. To our knowledge, these kinds of cases aren't available in contemporary computer science literature. Benefits of the case study for teaching purposes are:

- It provides students with an example of a real schema, instead of academic examples which tend to be unrealistic and untried.
- Showing the evolution of a Conceptual Schema in a real business environment puts the importance of "high-quality design practices" as taught in the university curriculum in its proper perspective.

The Company

The enterprise where this case study has been conducted is a European life insurance company, or to be more exact a pension fund. Pensions provide financial coverage for old-age, death and early-retirement of an employers workforce. From now on, we will refer to it as the "Pension" company.

The Pension company manages pension benefits of over a million (former) employees and family members. The net current value of their pension benefits is in excess of US$1 billion, and the monthly paycheck to pensioners is over US$0.5 billion. However interesting these financial aspects, we will concern ourselves with the data management aspect as pensions require meticulous and complicated recordkeeping.

Figure 1. Value chain of primary business functions

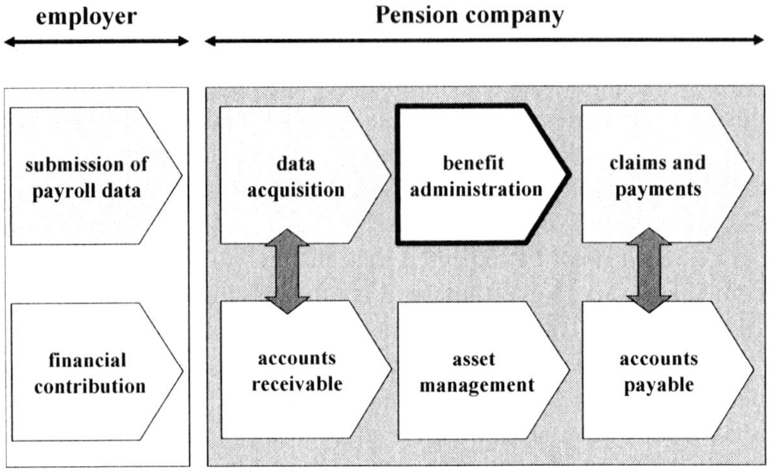

Business Functions

Figure 1 shows the (simplified) chain of primary business functions involved. It shows how employers submit data about their workforce (usually some copy of the payroll) and pay in their financial contributions. These two inflows are carefully checked against each other. The accepted data are then transferred to Benefit Administration for further processing. All claims are processed by the Claims-and-Payments departments. The case study concerns the business function of Benefit Administration only; we will not study the integration of this business function with its neighboring functions.

Management Structure

The Pension company is functionally organized. There is a single Data Acquisition section and Benefit Administration section. The business function of Claims-and-Payments is carried by three "spending" departments: Old-Age Pensions is responsible for payments to old-age pensioners, Dependents-Payments takes care of payments to dependent family members upon decease of the (former) employee, and finally Early-Retirement Payments handles early-retirements. Each department and section employs about 100 full-time workers. An additional 100 workers are employed in several staff sections. Of these, only the Information Management section is of interest as it is their responsibility to safeguard quality of the overall CS layout. Finally, an Information Systems Department of some 300 employees takes care of all hardware and software installation, exploitation and maintenance.

Daily Operations

Responsibilities and activities of the functional departments are broadly as follows:

- Data Acquisition collects data about the participants in the pension scheme (employees and dependant family members) from external sources. The main data source is employers' payrolls. Tape copies of monthly payrolls are received from all employers, and matched with the Accounts Receivable Department collecting the pension contributions. A second data source is the municipal registry offices ("city hall") that is tapped for addresses and family relationships by electronic data interchange. All acquired data are first validated, then reformatted and transferred into various Pension databases.
- Benefit Administration keeps complete records on all pension benefits. This involves recording all job switching, changes in wages, in part-time factor, changes in the type of due benefit, etc. It also involves recording marriages and divorces, because pension benefits is legally a joint property that has to be divided upon divorce. Most, but not all of the data processing is fully automated.
- If a benefit is due, customer data is transferred from the Benefit Administration to the particular Payments department. Their information systems are loosely coupled with the Benefit Administration systems, i.e., claim processing begins by taking out a full copy of all the benefit data.

Information Technology and Modeling Guidelines

Our case study concerns the major information system of the Benefit Administration Department. The information system uses "proven technology," i.e., mainstream graphical user interfaces and relational DBMS, which still dominates today's marketplace. In addition, the Information Management Department formulated guidelines and best-practices on information modeling to direct the design and maintenance efforts of the information systems. The ones that are relevant for the CS are:

- **Single unified view and therefore single point of maintenance** — Benefit Administration demands a single highly integrated database that supports all business functions in all their variants. There is no partitioning in separate modules or local databases that can be maintained independently. It is felt that disintegration would cause problems to coordinate the local changes and their reintegration into a single consistent view. The consequence is that department-wide priority-setting and maintenance deadlines are crucial management decisions that are indispensable but very time-consuming.

- **High level of generalization and therefore low-maintenance** — The CS should rise above the level of ad-hoc, implementation features and focus on persistent properties instead. This guideline steers designers away from quick solutions (that are often not only quick but "dirty" as well) towards the long-term, more stable solutions.
- **Snapshot-Data if possible, Historical-Data where obligatory** — It is typical of life insurance, and pensions in particular, that future benefits are based on past history of the policy holder/employee. It calls for temporal capacities that most of today's databases are yet incapable of delivering. Instead, temporality must be modeled explicitly into the CS which may result in overly large and complex models. The business guideline is to try and convince users not to demand temporal data wherever possible, and keep CS complexity down.
- **Representing derived data in the CS** — Apart from the temporal issue addressed by the previous guideline, an important issue is storage of base data for calculations, the intermediate results, and the final outcomes. These are important modeling decisions to which we will return later on.

Chain of Command in System Development and Maintenance

In practice, the entire system is always under (re)construction, to accommodate the latest set of new laws and legal exception rulings, changes in system and data interfaces with adjacent business functions, etc. Due to size, complexity, broad scope and large number of users, maintenance of the information system has grown to be a well-established but slow managerial process. First, there is a rather informal part where new developments, change requests from users, problem reports, etc. are merely assembled onto what is called the "maintenance stock list." The Information Management section in cooperation with the Information Systems Department analyzes the topics on the stock list and translates them into actual change proposals. All change proposals are submitted to the Pension management team that has the final say on priority-setting, budgeting and resource allocation.

Once a change is committed by upper management, a formal change procedure based on ITIL standards is followed. The procedure cascades through the usual steps of information systems maintenance: design, implementation, testing and operation. The steps are coordinated with other necessary changes, e.g., user training, programming of data conversion routines, and adaptation of standard letters and forms that the system sends out to customers. The Information Management section is responsible to outline all CS changes early in the design phase. These specifications are forward-engineered into technical changes on the operational database (DDL statements) to be implemented by the

Information Systems Department. This is a matter of concern as the technicalities of the actual change on the database level may deviate considerably from the original intentions on the conceptual level.

SETTING THE STAGE

Design vs. Maintenance

Quality of conceptual schema designs has received considerable attention in the literature. See for instance (Lindland, Sindre, & Sølvberg, 1994; Kesh, 1995; Shoval & Shiran, 1997; Moody, 2000). Without attempting to be exhaustive, some of the more prominent CS quality aspects are:

- **Simplicity** — Is the CS easy to understand both for system engineers and the user community?
- **Consistency** — Is the way of modeling consistently applied across all of the CS at all times?
- **Flexibility** — Once the CS is operational, how well are requirements changes accommodated?

Notice that most quality aspects of a CS can be checked at design time; the one exception being its flexibility. A well-designed CS is supposed to be flexible, but this can only be checked in its later evolution. And while many approaches to obtain a high-quality CS design have been proposed, these approaches mostly concentrate on the initial design phase. Much less has been written on maintenance of the CS: what changes does an operational CS accommodate and what is the impact on overall composition and quality of the CS over time?

Flexibility of a Conceptual Schema

This case study is focused around the quality aspect of flexibility. But what is flexibility? In the absence of a well-established and generally accepted definition, we use as a working definition:

> *Flexibility is the potential of the Conceptual Schema to accommodate changes in the information structure of the Universe of Discourse, within an acceptable period of time.*

This definition seems attractive as it is both intuitive and appropriate. It assumes a simple cause-and-effect relation between "structural change" in the UoD (universe of discourse) and changes in the CS. Also, it prevents inappropriate demands of flexibility on the CS by restricting the relevant environment from which changes stem to the UoD only. Based on this working definition, we can investigate CS flexibility according to three dimensions:

- "**Environment**," i.e., what is the driving force of the change, is the CS change justified by a corresponding change in the designated (part of) the Universe of Discourse.
- "**Timeliness**," i.e., do change driver and the corresponding CS change occur in approximately the same period of time. Sometimes a CS change is committed in anticipation, long before it is required by a change materializing in the environment. And some relevant changes may not very urgent, and get postponed.
- "**Adaptability**," i.e., is the CS changed in such a way that its quality aspects (simplicity, consistency etc.) are safeguarded. We will not study this dimension in detail, and judge adaptability by looking only at complexity of the overall CS lattice.

The Case Study Approach

The CS evolution is studied by analyzing documentation collected from the Pension company in the course of time. Every time a new CS version went operational, a full copy of the documentation was obtained and time-stamped for later analysis. The case study approach is to first outline the composition of each consecutive CS, and identify the dominant business changes. Next, we analyze the differences between consecutive CS versions, and finally we assess the level of flexibility in terms of the three dimensions as discussed above.

We decided to leave the CS as "real" as possible, including its modeling errors, overly complex structures, etc. We could certainly have polished up the CS. But we feel that this would severely detract from our purpose: to show an example of "real schema," instead of academic examples which tend to be unrealistic and untried. And polishing up the CS would certainly affect the constructs that we want to see evolve, and thus diminish the value of the case study.

Schema Representation

Our analysis covered all the usual CS constructs, i.e., conceptual entities, relationships, attributes, and constraints. Nevertheless, we only report the evolution of the overall CS structure made up by its entities and relationships. For space reasons, we leave out the ongoing changes in attributes and constraints.

Entities are represented in the diagrams by rectangles. A specialization entity is represented as an enclosed rectangle, so that the "is-a" relationship is immediately obvious. Aggregate "has-a" relationships are drawn as lines connecting the two related rectangles, and cardinality is shown using the customary "crow's foot" notation. An optional relationship, where not all instances of the member entity need to participate in the relationship, is indicated by an "O". These conventions make for compact, yet easy-to-read diagrams. As usual, attributes and constraints are not depicted.

CASE DESCRIPTION

Our case study concerns the "Integrated Benefit Administration" information system. This highly integrated transaction processing system supports most of the daily business processes of the Benefit Administration Department in varying degrees of automation. Our subject for investigation is the CS at the core of this information system. In keeping with its high level of integration, the CS has grown to well over a hundred entities (not counting specializations) and is still growing. Obviously, this is not a comfortable size for our research purpose, and we therefore limit the scope of the case study to the "pension benefit" concept. We trace how this real-world concept is perceived and represented as the Conceptual Schema evolves.

Design and implementation of the system and its CS began in 1994, going operational at the end of 1995. The case study covers the period 1996-1999, but the system is expected to run at least until 2005. The time series of CS versions that we include in the case study is shown in Figure 2. The time intervals between consecutive versions vary between a half and one-and-a-half years. Actually, there were some intermediary versions, but we could eliminate them from our analysis. It was found that those intermediate versions were targeted at other concepts than "pension benefit"; remember that we are dealing here with a highly integrated CS.

In a similar fashion, we excluded CS documentation that was collected for the initial design phase of the CS. These first attempts were considerably improved upon before the "real" CS went operational some months later. In our opinion, these improvements don't reflect flexibility of the CS as a reaction to UoD changes, but rather a progress in understanding and modeling of the UoD by the designers.

This is the CS at the start of the evolution. It has a fairly simple structure. The core concept of the CS is Benefit. It records the exact amount of pension due for a Participation, i.e., what is due to a beneficiary under a particular pension scheme. The Policy entity records the coverage as insured for an employee. All Benefit amounts are computed from Participation Trail data which basically is the historical details of employment and salary, but adjusted (and sometimes readjusted) according to regulations.

The initial production release of the CS provided exactly two types of pension benefit, recorded as the occurrences of Product. "Regular" is the combined old-age and dependents pension that is the default insurance scheme.

Figure 2. Time series of the CS versions

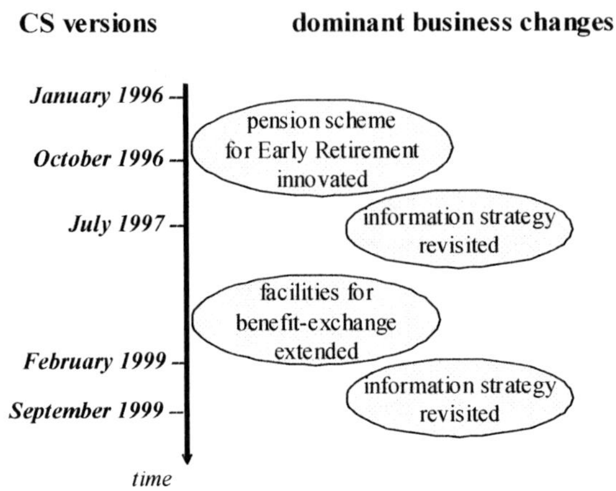

Figure 3. January 1996: Initial production release

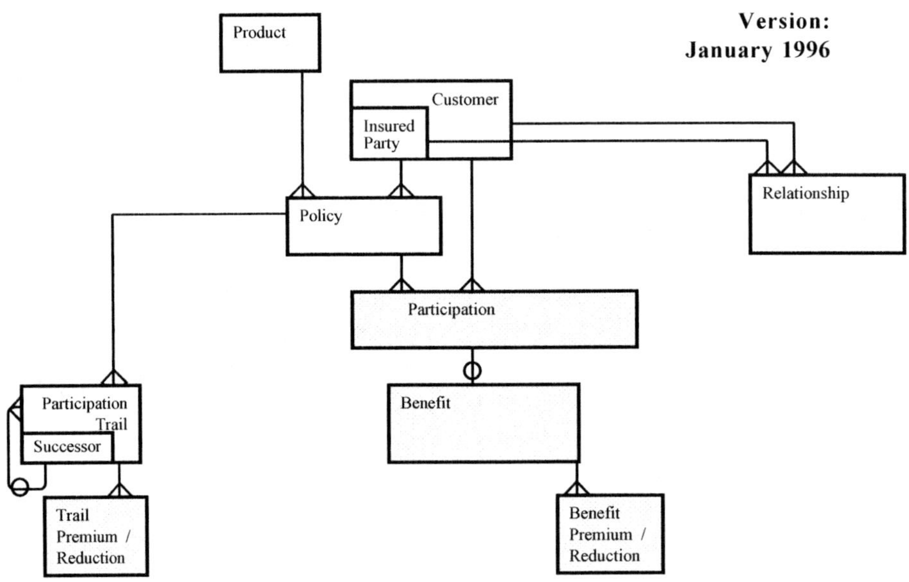

Figure 4. October 1996: Major extension

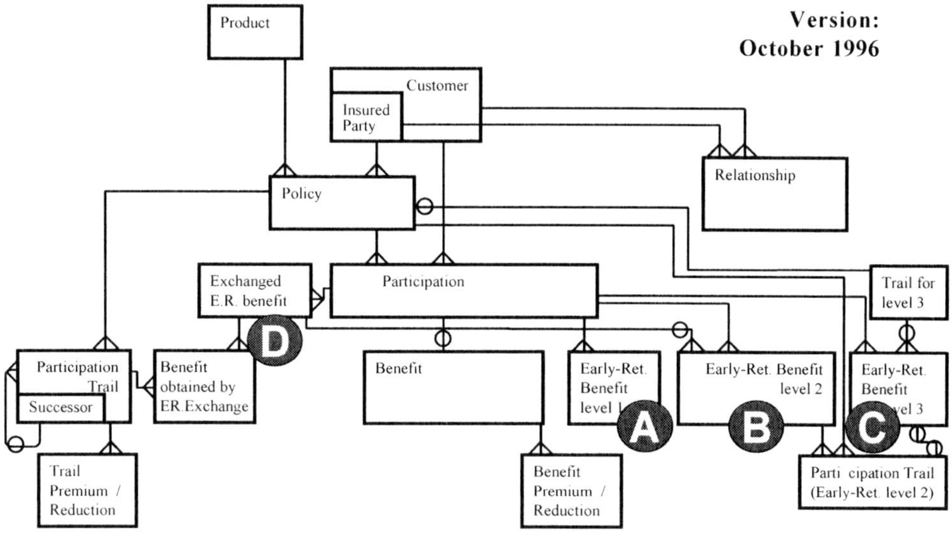

"Separated" is a more peculiar phenomenon where divorce laws have an impact on pensions. Whenever a marriage ends, the accumulated pension benefits are split among ex-partners. The part due to the ex-partner can be partitioned off to become a separate policy for old-age benefit, with the ex as insured party. Of course, benefits due to the other partner are reduced accordingly.

Although the information guidelines advocated a single unified view, the early-retirement pension benefits weren't included in the CS. The reason is that at the time, another information system handled early-retirement pensions and payments reasonably well. It was decided to let that be, and to exclude it from the scope of the new system under design.

The PARTICIPATION TRAIL entity contains base data for the calculation of pension benefits, but the derivation itself is not supported in the CS. The applicable rules and regulations are rather complicated, and in the initial design, they are completely relegated to the applications level.

Change Drivers

A major driving force in the UoD develops nine months later. Completely new facilities and benefits regarding early-retirements are introduced. The old ways of handling early-retirement by the Pension company, and the information system that supported those ways of doing business, become obsolete almost overnight. Two new business processes are pressed into service (other business process improvements are postponed for the time being):

Figure 5. July 1997: Ongoing changes

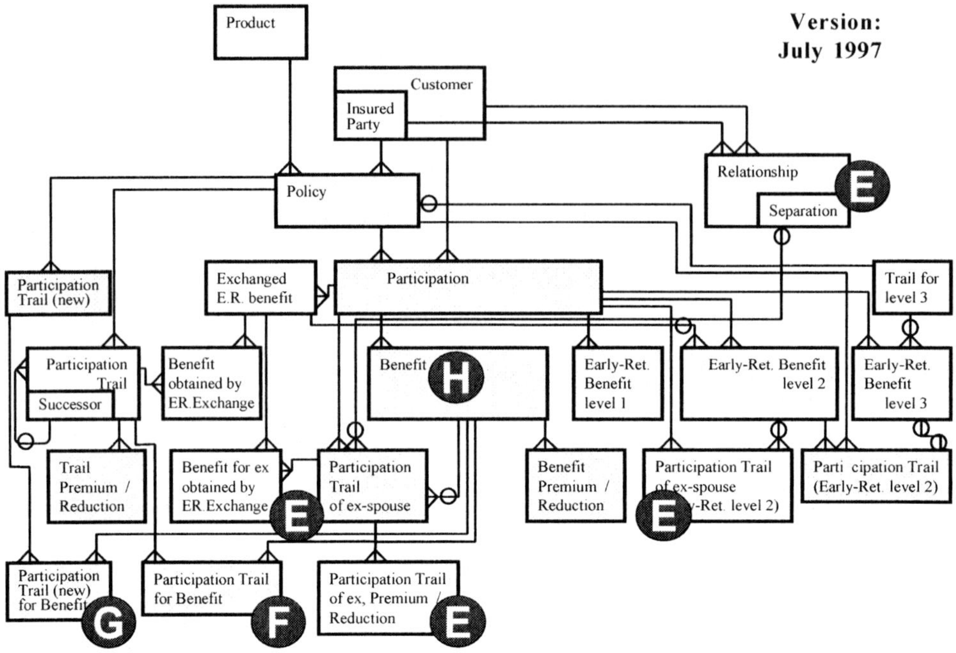

- The administration of early-retirement benefits, and
- The administration of benefit exchange. When an early-retirement benefit hasn't been cashed in (the employee doesn't retire early or dies prematurely) "regular" pension benefits are increased in exchange.

Changes in the CS

The CS is expanded and becomes much more complex. Actually, four coherent groups of additions can be discerned in the CS:

(a) Early-Retirement Benefit level 1. This is a straightforward addition.
(b) Early-Retirement Benefit level 2 and its associated Participation-Trail for level 2.
(c) Early-Retirement Benefit level 3 with an associated entity Trail-for-level-3.
(d) Exchanged Early-Retirement Benefit and Benefit obtained by E.R. exchange.

Flexibility of the CS

As for the "environment" dimension, the CS changes are all justified by the pending changes in early-retirement pensions.

As for "timing," the CS changes precede the real-world changes, and don't coincide with them. While the new early-retirement rules and regulations were contracted in the course of 1996, the new rules only took effect in the spring of 1997. The time lag was necessary to prepare business processes, to train personnel, to inform employers and employees of the innovation in pension benefits etc. And perhaps most importantly: to adjust information systems.

As for "adaptability," notice how the way of modeling has now become inconsistent across the several benefit-like entities, for no apparent reason. And the guideline to go for "high level of integration" in the CS is compromised by the decision not to merge the new entity Early-Retirement Benefit level 2 with the semantically very close entity Benefit. A final observation (not in the schema) concerns the Product entity. The previous version held two instances "regular" and "separated." The new version adds the instance "Early-Retirement." Apparently, the UoD change is accommodated by changes at both the instance and the structural level. This must surely be considered an update anomaly.

Change Drivers

The early-retirement innovation still acts as an important driving force nine months later. The business processes changes that were postponed earlier on, are now being implemented. The CS of our case study is affected by only one of them:

- Having the legalistic peculiarities of benefit division for divorce apply to early-retirement.

There are no other material changes in the UoD. However, there is a changing perception of the UoD:

- The earlier information modeling decision not to represent derivative relationships is reversed.

The reversal has major impact on the CS, and on the application level where existing derivation routines have to be altered and entity update routines added.

Changes in the CS

As before, the CS is expanded and becomes much more complex. Again, we can discern several coherent groups of changes, most of them being additions:

(e) To accommodate "divorce" regulations, SEPARATION and several associated specializations and relationships are intricately woven into the CS, increasing overall complexity.
(f) The complex derivative relationship how BENEFIT is related to PARTICIPATION TRAIL data was absent from the initial CS. It is now modeled by way of the PARTICIPATION-TRAIL-FOR-BENEFIT entity.
(g) The change of strategy even went one step further. Maintenance engineers came to believe that the old way of working with the PARTICIPATION TRAIL entity was "legacy." To prepare a graceful evolution, PARTICIPATION TRAIL (NEW) and PARTICIPATION TRAIL (NEW) FOR BENEFIT are added.

And a final change must be considered a "correction":

(h) Cardinality of the BENEFIT-to-PARTICIPATION relationship is increased from 1:1 to N:1.

Flexibility of the CS

As for the "environment" and "timeliness" dimensions, SEPARATION and its associated CS changes are justified, being a belated consequence of the early-retirement innovation. Not so for the three other changes.

As for "adaptability," the new CS elaborates on the previous CS, making it ever more complex but in a largely consistent way. Only the additions of PARTICIPATION TRAIL (NEW) and PARTICIPATION TRAIL (NEW) FOR BENEFIT are suspect, as these entities create redundancy in the CS.

Change Drivers

(The lower right-hand corner of Figure 6 explains entity names that are abbreviated in the diagram).

For over a year-and-a-half, there are no important changes in our section of the Pension company business. The business isn't at a standstill, rather it means that current ways of doing business in the Benefit Administration Department are satisfactory. The relative quit in the UoD is reflected in the CS: while several intermediate CS versions were implemented, we can ignore them all because they don't concern any features of our CS. Only one change is announced that will become effective as of summer 1999:

- New legislation forces all pension companies to offer their insured parties more freedom of choice for "exchange" of pension benefits.

In the "regular" pension scheme, a dependent's benefits was a fixed proportionality of the corresponding old-age benefit. A customer's freedom to

Figure 6. February 1999: Stabilized

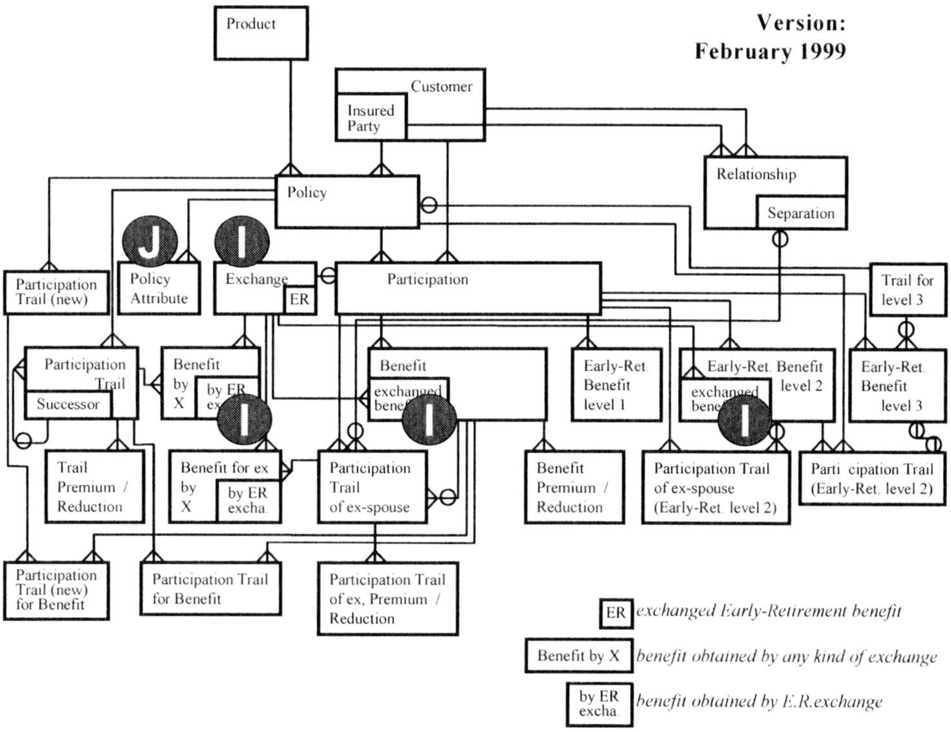

exchange various kinds of pension benefits means that the proportionality now turns into a variable.

Changes in the CS

The CS version of February 1999 is impacted by the upcoming change in the UoD.

(i) In response to the broadened concept of exchange, a generalized EXCHANGE entity is introduced.

It subsumes the former EXCHANGED-EARLY-RETIREMENT-BENEFIT and impacts various other entities and/or specializations. Notice how the EXCHANGE-to-BENEFIT relationship shows a 1-to-1 cardinality whereas the subsumed EXCHANGED-EARLY-RETIREMENT-BENEFIT-to-BENEFIT relationship was N-to-1 cardinality.

Figure 7. September 1999: Simplification

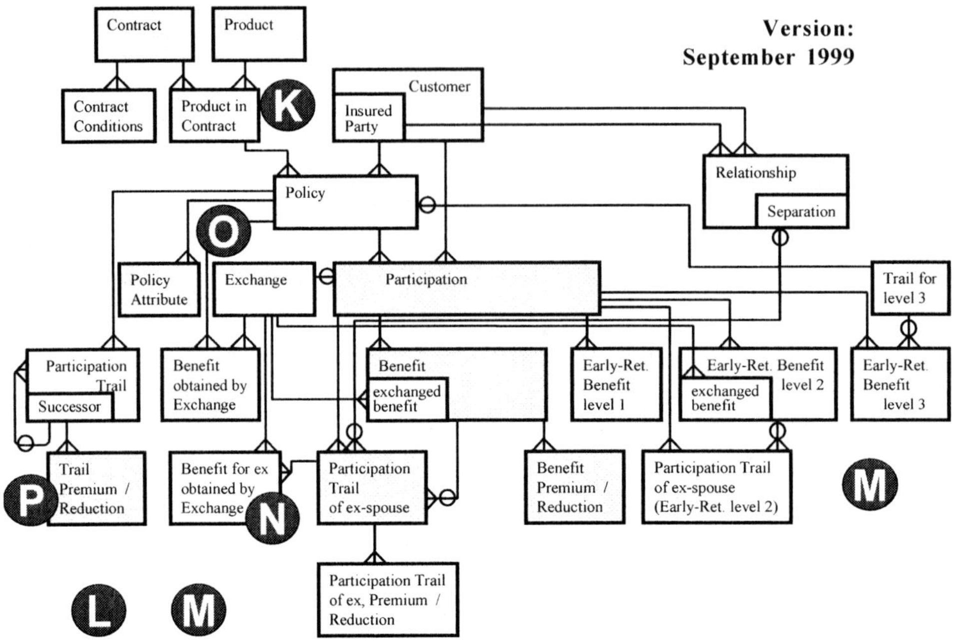

Another minor improvement in the CS is simply motivated as "progressive understanding," without there being a clear need or user requirement that drives the change:

(j) Policy Attribute is added.

Flexibility of the CS

The overall CS structure remains stable. As for "environment" and "timeliness," the upcoming legislation causes advance changes that are gracefully accommodated in the CS. As for "adaptability," quality and complexity aren't much different from the previous CS version.

Change Drivers

Apart from the new legislation, there is only one business change for seven months. Even then, it is internal to the enterprise, a change of perception on the strategic management level where a new philosophy in product engineering is professed:

- Pension products should vary across market segments and employers, instead of being uniform.

But to our surprise, we find that once again the *perception* of the UoD is radically reversed:

- The CS is to record original source data only, while derivative data is to be eliminated from the CS.

Changes in the CS

While the new philosophy in product engineering has little relevance for the current way of recording the benefit data, it drives a change in a "corner" of the CS impacting key integrity of the Policy entity:

(k) The concept of CONTRACT and a dependent entity CONTRACT CONDITIONS are introduced. The relationship POLICY-to-PRODUCT is redirected via an intermediate PRODUCT-IN-CONTRACT entity.

The previous CS versions recorded the intricate deviated relations between BENEFIT and PARTICIPATION TRAIL data, but the new CS version does away with all this. While functionality and complexity now has to be accounted for at the application level, the pay-off at the CS level is a remarkable simplification:

(l) The preparatory entities of PARTICIPATION TRAIL (NEW) and PARTICIPATION TRAIL (NEW) FOR BENEFIT are also eliminated. Notice how these entities were never really used.
(m) PARTICIPATION TRAIL FOR BENEFIT as well as PARTICIPATION TRAIL FOR EARLY-RETIREMENT LEVEL 2 are eliminated.
(n) Three subsumed EXCHANGED-EARLY-RETIREMENT-BENEFIT entities are dropped.
(o) The BENEFIT OBTAINED BY EXCHANGE-to-PARTICIPATION TRAIL relationship is short-circuited into a BENEFIT OBTAINED BY EXCHANGE-to-POLICY relationship.

Finally, one relationship is changed for which we could not ascertain a change driver. The change seems only to pave the way for a simplification in the next CS version:

(p) The TRAIL PREMIUM/REDUCTION-to-PARTICIPATION TRAIL relationship is redirected to SUCCESSOR.

Flexibility of the CS

The "environment" dimension impacts only a small part of the CS. Flexibility in the "adaptability" dimension is evident by the many entity eliminations and the few relationships being redirected. In this case, "timeliness" is less relevant as the change in perception has no significant indication of urgency. But please notice how the shift of TRAIL PREMIUM/REDUCTION-to-PARTICIPATION TRAIL relationship is in anticipation on a change to be made in the next version.

EXPERIENCES

Having described the long-term evolution of this single conceptual schema in considerable detail, we can now look at the overall picture in order to draw conclusions. Apart from the CS as a whole, we also look at how the core constructs are being represented over time.

Stability of the CS

The first and foremost observation is that the CS has successfully adapted to past changes, while its overall composition has remained relatively stable over almost half a decade.

Table 1 quantifies stability by looking at the number of changes in the evolving CS. A fast expansion is seen from January 1996 to July 1997. The period roughly corresponds to the innovation of pension scheme for early-retirement as CS change driver. After that, additions and deletions are more evenly balanced. During this time of relative quiet, major business developments take place but these are accommodated in the CS without expanding very much.

Stability of Concepts

When inspecting each entity of the CS from the viewpoint of users, we find that real-world semantics, once it is modeled into the CS, doesn't evolve that much. Indeed, every entity retains its "structure" or "semantic content" over time, and its relationship to other entities also remains stable as evidenced by their fixed locations in the CS diagrams.

At the same time, most entities change in some way or another, the two exceptions being the CUSTOMER and BENEFIT-REDUCTION/PREMIUM entities. While relationships to higher entities are next to immutable, relationships with lower entities are much more volatile. An entity can aggregate one or two underlying entities at one time, but six or seven at another. This reflects a common practice in maintenance. When adding new entities to a CS, it is easier to create relationships to existing ones than from them. The latter operation has immediate consequences for referential integrity and it is usually avoided.

Table 1. Number of changes in the evolving CS

CS version	entity addition	entity deletion	entity change	count	relationship addition	relationship deletion	relationship change	count
January 1996				9(+ 2)				11(+ 2)
October 1996	7	0	0	16(+ 2)	12	0	0	23(+2)
July 1997	7 (+ 1)	0	0	23(+ 3)	13 (+ 1)	0	1	36(+3)
February 1999	1 (+ 5)	0	3	24(+ 8)	2 (+ 5)	0	6	3 8(+ 8)
September 1999	3	4 (+ 3)	0	23(+ 5)	3	8 (+ 3)	3	33(+ 5)

Numbers in parenthesis in "entity" columns indicate specializations.
Numbers in parenthesis in "relationship" columns indicate corresponding specialization-to-generalization injective relationships.

This points at an important user requirement that is often left unspoken in change requests. It is the demand for compatibility, i.e., to safeguard prior investments in existing CS constructs and applications, and keep these operable in the new design. A more outspoken form of compatibility is extensibility, when existing constructs may not be altered and changes may be implemented as additions only. The latter form is seen in several CS changes, but not all of them. The compatibility demand constitutes a strong drive towards stability, but it also restraints maintenance engineers in their search for problem solutions. They must often produce a design solution with some flaw in it, resulting in loss of quality in the long run.

Contributions of the Modeling Guidelines to CS Stability

We introduced four modeling guidelines that are relevant for engineers working on this case. We now discuss how each has affected overall CS stability.

- **Single unified view and therefore single point of maintenance** — This guideline was well adhered to. Two or three other information systems have been operated in the Benefit Administration section, but their conceptual schemas were in full agreement with the single unified view expressed by our CS. All CS changes could be defined once, and propagation of these changes to the minor systems was almost trivial on all occasions. While the guideline as such doesn't address stability, it has contributed to stability by minimizing schematic discrepancies.
- **High level of generalization and therefore low-maintenance** — This guideline hasn't been adhered to too well. One reason is that business pressures for quick implementations often override long-term intangible goals such as this. But we think there is another reason. Consider the phenomenon of benefit exchange as introduced in 1996. At the time, it is unknown that this facility will be generalized from Early-Retirement benefits to other kinds of benefits as well. The guideline doesn't help to determine what the "best" or "essential" generalization is. As a result, the guideline is impractical for business usage.
- **Snapshot-Data if possible, Historical-Data where obligatory** — This guideline's contribution to stability is uncertain. It has primarily affected various "timestamp" attributes of entities but on the level of the overall CS, no effects of the guideline on entities or relationships were detected.
- **Representing derived data in the CS** — As the guideline itself wasn't stable, it is no surprise that it hasn't contributed to stability at all.

From this brief analysis, we conclude that CS stability can't be achieved by relying on modeling guidelines alone (Schuette and Rotthowe, 1998). Even if the guidelines are based on sound state-of-the-art theoretical arguments, they may still change over time, or be too impractical. Or business developments may take off in a direction that isn't covered by the guidelines.

Dimensions of Flexibility of the CS

We outlined how flexibility can be assessed by considering "environment," "timeliness," and "adaptability." Table 2 summarizes our findings regarding the CS changes for these three dimensions.

As to the environment dimension, approximately half of the 16 changes in the CS could be labeled as "justified." The business changes have clearly been accommodated into the CS by an incremental maintenance approach, taking care that current data and applications aren't disturbed. The other changes were either driven by changes in modeling guidelines, or by maintenance considerations that don't derive from the changing UoD at all such as error correction, or changes in anticipation of future developments.

Table 2. Findings regarding CS changes for three dimensions

change in the CS	environment	timeliness	adaptability
(A) E.R. BENEFIT LEVEL 1 added	by change in UoD	yes, in advance	equal
(B) E.R. BENEFIT LEVEL 2 added	by change in UoD	yes, in advance	increases
(C) E.R. BENEFIT LEVEL 3 added	by change in UoD	yes, in advance	increases
(D) E.R.EXCHANGE added	by change in UoD	yes, in advance	increases
(E) SEPARATION inserted	by change in UoD	yes, but belated	increases
(F) PARTICIPATION TRAIL-FOR-BENEFIT inserted	by change in modelling guidelines	"opportunistic"	increases
(G) PARTICIPATION TRAIL (NEW) inserted	unjustified	N/A (in anticipation)	increases
(H) BENEFIT relation to PARTICIPATION corrected	unjustified	N/A	equal
(I) EXCHANGE generalizes E.R.EXCHANGE	by change in UoD	Yes	equal
(J) POLICY ATTRIBUTE added	unjustified	N/A	equal
(K) CONTRACT etc introduced	by changing perception of the UoD	yes, in advance	equal
(L) PARTICIPATION TRAILS eliminated	by change in modelling guidelines	"opportunistic"	decreases
(M) PARTICIPATION TRAILS (NEW) eliminated	by change in modelling guidelines	"opportunistic"	decreases
(N) subsumed EXCHANGED-E.R.-BENEFIT dropped	by change in modelling guidelines	"opportunistic"	decreases
(O) BENEFIT OBTAINED BY EXCHANGE relation shifted	unjustified	N/A	equal
(P) TRAIL PREMIUM/REDUCTION relation shifted	unjustified	N/A	equal

"Environment" concerns how the CS change was justified.
"Timeliness" expresses whether the CS change was committed in the correct timeframe.
"Opportunistic" indicates that no definite timeframe applies; "N/A" is not applicable.
"Adaptability" indicates overall complexity of the CS.

For timeliness, the UoD and CS display a joint evolution, but the timeframes of their changes don't always coincide. Sometimes there is advance warning of an upcoming UoD change and the CS can be prepared in advance. Strictly speaking, the CS models not only the current UoD but it covers a future UoD as well. That this way of working is not without risk is illustrated by changes (G) and (M), where designers add entities into the CS because of a predicted needs to be eliminated again some time later. Apparently, there is a penalty to be paid when proactive maintenance goes awry. On one occasion (E) the desired change exceeds the capacity for change and had to be postponed. And some kinds of change drivers pose no timeframe at all: the changes in modeling guidelines were accommodated in the CS as opportunity presented itself.

As to adaptability, the case shows how the demand for compatibility has a negative effect on simplicity. Semantically similar structures like BENEFIT ("regular," E.R. LEVEL-1, etc.) are added (changes (A), (B), (C)) and remain in the CS for years. These entities (but not their data content!) could have been generalized but weren't. As a result, maintenance that would apply on the level of the generalization must now be done on each separate specialization, which is a constant source of duplicate maintenance. At the same time, we have learned that the notion of CS simplicity or "understandability" isn't as clear-cut as it may seem. System engineers and the user community grow accustomed to the overall picture, and come to understand its complex constructions. As a result, they will use the existing CS as their yardstick for simplicity. New CS proposals are measured by their difference with the familiar schema, rather than by quality of the new CS by itself.

As they evolve over time, the overall structure of the CS and the semantics of core concepts remain relatively stable. An initial decline in schema quality is observed, when overall size and complexity increase and level of integration, understandability and consistency decrease. Later on, schema quality remains at a constant level.

An important finding is that changes in the CS aren't driven only by dominant changes in the UoD. The actual CS reflects the "objective" user requirements, but also the current modeling guidelines and the subjective perceptions of maintenance engineers.

It is widely recognized that there is no "best possible" CS once and for all. The case study suggests several corollaries. First, the case demonstrates that not only the evolving UoD acts as change driver for changes in the CS, implying that any CS captures more than just UoD features. Second, whenever a CS is being changed, the impact of change is always kept to a minimum, in response to an implicit user demand. The case also brings out the mismatch between changes in CS semantic and the elementary changes that are provided by the (relational of Object-Oriented) data model in use. Some elementary changes, such as simple addition or deletion of an entity, or redirection of a relationship are rarely seen in our case study. Most UoD change drivers cause a series of coherent changes in a whole group of entities. In view of this, we think that a demand that "every aspect of the requirements appears only once in the schema," as formulated by Batini, Ceri, and Navath (1992, p. 140) needs revisiting. Finally, the case shows how suboptimal solutions tend to stick around. There is no drive to make a CS any better if it works well enough.

The combined effect of these corollaries is that the maintenance engineer is kept away from realizing a "best possible" conceptual schema. Of course, a single case study isn't enough to base generally valid conclusions on. But we think that our experiences touch upon several serious problems in conceptual modeling that are in want of further research.

CURRENT CHALLENGES

Our case study has covered the period 1996-1999, and we demonstrated how the CS has successfully accommodated the ongoing changes in the environment so far. Of course, developments haven't come to a standstill since 1999, and the CS still continues to evolve in order to accommodate the changes in its environment. To name a few:

- Increasing differentiation of pension schemes across market segments and employers, instead of being uniform. Some differentiation was expected; it is why CONTRACT and PRODUCT-IN-CONTRACT were introduced in the first place. But the full impact of change hasn't been realized yet. The real challenge is to keep track of historic data, and to do the benefit calculations according to the correct pension scheme while both the pension scheme and the participation in the scheme are changing over time.
- New variants of old-age and early-retirements pension benefits that allow more customer options. Some suggested options are voluntary participation; arbitrary amount of yearly contribution; or a choice of investment funds with different risk and performance profiles. The business function of benefit administration is bound to become more complex as a result.
- Integration of business functions and data usage with Claims-and-Payments departments downstream in the information value chain. The old way of working was to simply transfer all relevant data across an automated interface. While it has clearly been inefficient all along, it was satisfactory. But now the information systems of the Claims-and-Payments departments are approaching the end of their life cycle. The target is to merge the legacy information systems into the "Integrated Benefit Administration" system, expanding its "single global view" ever more.
- Conversion to the new Euro currency. It calls for extensive changes in information systems. All "amount" and "value" attributes in the database must be adjusted: both current and historic data. The impact on applications is even larger: all calculations and derivation rules must be checked for known and unexpected currency-dependencies. For instance, many cut-off values hard-coded into the software are currency-dependent.
- A final challenge facing the Pension company is the drive to "go online," and deliver the benefit data to the customer over the Web, whenever and wherever.

The Pension company considers the overall quality and flexibility of the CS to be high enough for it to remain operative for years to come. The challenges present both the drive and the opportunity for continued CS maintenance, but how this will affect overall composition, schema quality and level of integration is a subject for further research.

ADDITIONAL READING

This case study, describing "real-life" experiences of evolving schema in an existing organization, demonstrates how several areas of conceptual modeling intermingle in practice that current literature often approaches as independent and unrelated.

A general framework for the aspect of CS flexibility is developed in Wedemeijer (2001). For best-practices in design, i.e., how to achieve the required quality level of the CS, one can best turn to textbooks. And it is not necessarily the latest that is best. We find Teorey (1994), Blaha and Premerlani (1998), and Elmasri and Navathe (2000) useful.

Our case study came across the difficulty of recognizing similar concepts and having them merged in the CS. This is the problem of schematic discrepancies, as has been studied by Sheth and Kashyap (1992).

Elementary transformations on the level of the Conceptual Schema have been described in Ewald and Orlowska (1993), and Batini, Di Battista, and Santucci (1993). An investigation how elementary transformations on the schema level propagate to the level of data instances is discussed in Lerner and Habermann (1990).

The first case study of evolving systems to become widely known is Belady and Lehman (1976). A longitudinal study of an evolving Internal Schema has been reported by Sjøberg (1993).

The handling of derived data in business processing has been discussed in Redman(1996). It develops the concept of information chain as can be recognized in our case study. A taxonomy for derived-data at the level of the Conceptual Schema is developed in Wedemeijer (2000).

An important assumption underlying our approach is that the CS documentation is a faithful description of the operational database structure. In other words, we assume that the Internal Schema and the data stored in the DBMS are in full agreement with the Conceptual Schema. This assumption needn't always be true, as has been noticed by several authors engaged in reverse database engineering (Winans & Davis, 1991; Hainaut et al., 1996). The wholesome effect of good user documentation is studied in Gemoets and Mahmood (1990).

REFERENCES

Batini, C. W., Ceri, S., & Navathe, S.B. (1992). *Conceptual database design: An entity-relationship approach*. CA: Benjamin/Cummings Publishing Comp.

Kahn, H. J., & Filer, N. P. (2000). Supporting the maintenance and evolution of information models. In *Proceedings of IRMA-2000 International Conference* (pp. 888-890). Hershey, PA: Idea Group Publishing.

Kesh, S. (1995). Evaluating the quality of entity relationship models. *Information & Software Technology, 37*, 681-689.

Lindland, O. I., Sindre, G., & Sølvberg, A. (1994). Understanding quality in conceptual modeling. *IEEE Software,* 42-49.

Moody, D. L. (2000). Strategies for improving quality of entity relationship models: A 'toolkit' for practitioners. In *Proceedings of IRMA-2000 International Conference* (pp. 1043-1045). Hershey, PA: Idea Group Publishing.

Schuette, R., & Rotthowe, T. (1998). The guidelines of modelling: An approach to enhance the quality in information models. In *Proceedings of the 17th Entity-Relationship Approach Conference*.

Shoval, P., & Shiran, S. (1997). Entity-relationship and object-oriented data modeling: An experimental comparison of design quality. *Data & Knowledge Engineering, 21*, 297-315

FURTHER READING

Batini, C. W., Di Battista, G., & Santucci, G.(1993). Structuring primitives for a dictionary of ER data schemas. *IEEE Transactions on Software Engineering, 19*(4), 344-365.

Belady, L. A., & Lehman, M. M. (1976). A model of large program development. *IBM Systems Journal, 15*(3), 225-252.

Blaha, M., & Premerlani, W. (1998). *Object-oriented modeling and design for database applications*. Upper Saddle River, NJ: Prentice Hall.

Ewald, C. A., & Orlowska, M. E. (1993). A procedural approach to schema evolution. In *International Conference on Advanced Information Systems Engineering CAiSE'93, LNCS 685,* Paris (pp. 22-38). Springer Verlag.

Elmasri, R., & Navathe, S. B. (2000). *Fundamentals of database systems* (3rd ed.). Addison-Wesley Longman.

Gemoets, L. A., & Mahmood, M. A. (1990). Effect of the quality of user documentation on user satisfaction with information systems. *Information & Management, 18*(1), 47-54.

Hainaut, J.-L., Henrard, J., Hick, J.-M., Roland, D., & Englebert, V. (1996). Database design recovery. In *CAiSE '96 Advanced Information Systems Engineering, LNCS 1080* (pp. 272-300). Springer Verlag.

Lerner, B. S., & Habermann, A. N. (1990). Beyond schema evolution to database reorganization. In *Proceedings of the International Conference on OO Programming, Systems, Languages, and Applications, SIGPLAN notices, Vol. 25* (No. 10; pp. 67-76).

Redman, T. C. (1996). *Data quality for the information age*. Boston: Artech House Publishing.

Sheth, A. P., & Kashyap, V. (1992). So far (schematically) yet so near (semantically). In *Proceedings of the IFIP Working Group* 2.6 DS-5 (pp. 272-301).

Sjøberg, D. (1993). Quantifying schema evolution. *Information & Software Technology, 35*(1), 35-44.

Teorey, T. J. (1994). *Database modeling & design: The fundamental principles* (2nd ed.). Morgan Kaufmann.

Wedemeijer, L. (2000). Derived data reduce stability of the conceptual schema. In G. E. Lasker, & W. Gerhardt (Eds.), *Proceedings of 12th International Conference Intersymp2000, International Institute for Advanced Studies in Systems Research and Cybernetics* (pp. 101-108).

Wedemeijer, L. (2001). Defining metrics for conceptual schema evolution. In *Proceedings of International Conference on Data Evolution and Meta Modelling, LNCS.* Springer Verlag.

Winans, J., & Davis, K. H. (1991). Software reverse engineering from a currently existing IMS database to an E-R model. In *ER'91 Entity-Relationship Approach* (pp. 333-348).

Lex Wedemeijer earned an MSc in pure mathematics from the State University of Groningen, The Netherlands. He works as an information architect at ABP Netherlands. Before coming to ABP, he was project manager in systems engineering with the Dutch Royal Mail company. His interests include data administration, database modelling, business process redesign and design methodologies, and quality assurance. He is currently engaged in developing and implementing the unified Corporate Information Model for ABP.

This case was previously published in the *Annals of Cases on Information Technology*, Volume 4/2002, pp. 280-296, © 2002.

Chapter XIII

Designing a First-Iteration Data Warehouse for a Financial Application Service Provider

Nenad Jukic, Loyola University - Chicago, USA

Tania Neild, InfoGrate Incorporated, USA

EXECUTIVE SUMMARY

This case study will describe the efforts behind designing a first iteration of an evolutionary, iterative enterprise-wide data warehouse for AIIA Corp., a financial application service provider. The study demonstrates the importance of the following steps during a data warehousing project: a well-defined mission, effective requirement collection, detailed logical definitions, and an efficient methodology for source systems and infrastructure development. AIIA is a financial distributor that offers separately managed account and investment products with practice management services to financial advisors through a Web-based portal that can also be configured and private-labeled for the advisors to use with their clients. Unlike most companies, AIIA offers the advisors a hybrid of investment information and technology solutions, both designed with an open architecture.

BACKGROUND

AIIA, the company described in this case, is established on the idea of seizing changes in the following three areas of the financial industry:

1. Distribution/Channel
2. Operations (or the Business Model)
3. Manufacture (or Products)

Each will be discussed here as they relate to the opportunity that the company filled.

1. **Distribution/Channel.** In the past 10 years, there has been a substantial migration of brokers away from the institutional brokerage houses (where they turned over large commission to their wire house) to smaller, independent shops that are fee based. There are now over 20,000 registered independent advisors (RIAs), and this new market is growing each year. While some of these advisors are grouped into regional consortiums or independent broker dealers (IBD), the market is still relatively fragmented and distributed. Without the tools, research, and products of their former companies, the advisors have little infrastructure in place to reach and service their clients.
2. **Operations (or the Business Model).** The second main change was the growing acceptance of the application service provider (ASP) business model. Applications could be "leased" for use over the Web on a monthly basis. For the users, this lowers the up-front cost, reduces maintenance costs, and mitigates risk;, allowing new companies to enter a market previously unreachable.
3. **Manufacture (or Products).** As mutual funds became mainstream, new separately managed account products became more palpable to those with $800,000 to $8,000,000 in investable assets (note that the inefficiencies of the mutual fund are not as significant for smaller investments totaling less than $800,000, and for those with more than $8,000,000 there are other advanced products that are available). When an investor owns a mutual fund, they own a slice of a fund in which, while managed according to some style or investment philosophy, the specifics stocks are generally unknown. For clients with multiple investments, transparency of the funds ensures that they are not over-allocated to a particular stock or sector. Additionally, mutual funds have an inherent tax injustice: if one buys a fund today and tomorrow sells a stock with a large capital gain, then he/she would realize the tax consequences of the gain without the appreciation in the asset. For an investor with substantial tax planning issues, the mutual fund is problematic. Separately managed accounts retain the efficiencies of a mutual fund,

allowing the manager to pool assets together, and thereby gaining the same institutional transaction pricing and ability to manage and monitor the collective assets according to a model portfolio style expert. However, separately managed accounts also allow the investor to own, see and tailor their account to handle particular tax and asset allocation nuances of the financial picture.

Together these three trends opened the door to a host of new companies, one of which is AIIA Corp. (see Figure 1).

There are companies that provide technology/applications to the advisors, and there are others that offer separately managed account products. Some companies charge monthly for the technology, some adhere to a transaction-oriented model and others have embraced the fee-based "assets under management" approach. AIIA is designed to offer all of the comforts of the advisors' former brokerage house, both investment products and applications, through a fee-based revenue model. For example, if Investor I places $1,000,000 into a separately managed account with Manager X, via the AIIA platform, and X buys 10 different securities in the portfolio for I, then I would pay based on a fraction of a percentage of the $1,000,000 rather than $Y per manager transaction, as is typically the case with many well-known investment products (such as those provided by Schwab or Fidelity). The unique hybrid of technology and investment products provides "one-stop shopping" for the advisor. An interesting twist on this situation is the pivot point between the old and the new. While the independence of the advisors is new, their core needs are the same. And while the creation of the separately managed accounts is new, traditional investment products are still practical for the average investors. Therefore, the new

Figure 1. AIIA's separately managed account market space

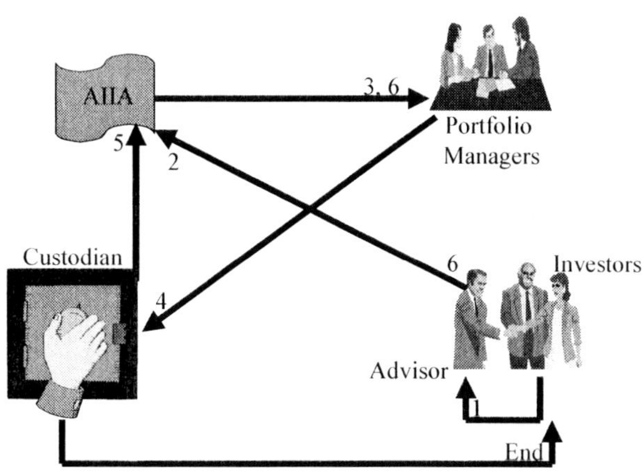

company must back-fill to satisfy the older offering, while embracing the new products and technology. Typically, companies are either converting with the marketplace going from old to new offerings, or they are new and focused predominately on the new solution set. To handle this delicate dynamic, AIIA has formed an operational and technical glue between managers, custodians, and other traditional and relevant investment and technology providers, while building new core value-added offerings.

SETTING THE STAGE

From its beginning nearly two years ago, AIIA's value proposition was its combined offering of business application and investment products to the newly fragmented financial advisor marketplace. Therefore, the CEO and visionary of the company embraced other founders and executive members that were leaders in either marketing/selling to a new advisor's marketplace, crafting leading- edge investment products or delivering robust application solutions. With deep expertise in each area, the company's reach has grown faster than projected. While still privately held and on its C-round of funding, AIIA has already attracted approximately 2,000 RIAs, 50 IBDs, commitments for $1 billion in assets under management (AUM) and holds $9 billion in AIIA's clients' AUM.

Figure 2 shows the organizational structure of the company. While AIIA features a distinct blend of older-world investments and cutting-edge technology, each core area of its business is data-intense. The Sales and Marketing team requires deep analytics to understand this new marketplace. The Investment officers must provide thorough research on the market, managers, and products in order for the advisors or the company itself to make informed recommendations. The Operations and Technology Department must integrate with advisory application offerings and interface with multiple custodians and portfolio ac-

Figure 2. AIIA organization chart

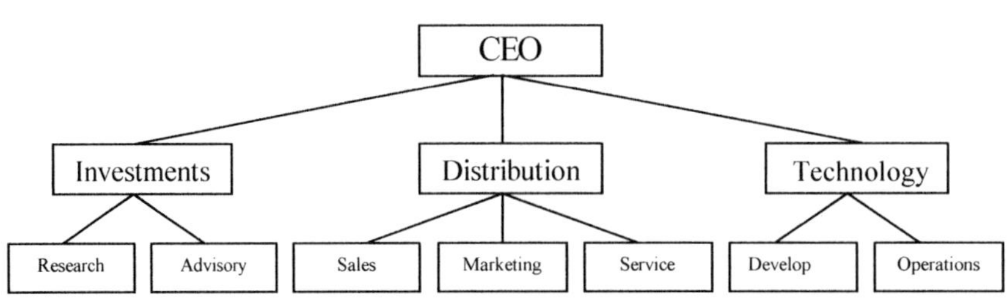

counting platforms, each with formats and methods for handling different types of accounts, transactions and products. Therefore, the mining of their data into knowledge was critical, and even before the data was collected, techniques for processing and leveraging it were considered.

An open architecture was the key to the platform. As each solution was integrated or built, the ability for the solution to permit easy data exchange was at the forefront of the decision. While typically the extract-transform-load (ETL) process presents its own unique challenges for a data warehousing project, AIIA's open architecture eliminated the usual complexities of extraction and load part of the process. Physical integration of the systems was a prerequisite. Flexibility and logical integration became the primary issues, allowing AIIA to concentrate on the mission of the data warehouse rather than on the "how" of the data warehouse.

CASE DESCRIPTION

Introduction

AIIA decided to draw on rich and varied data sources (both internal and external) to build a data warehouse, in order to turn the information into meaningful knowledge and in turn act to convert the knowledge to profit. AIIA's data warehousing project is in compliance with a definition of a data warehouse as a separate physical repository, typically maintained separately from the organization's operational databases, used for consolidating data that has been organized to facilitate analytical processing and strategic decision support (Chaudhuri & Dayal, 1997). Unlike any other information systems initiative, the data warehouse implementation is an iterative process whereby each analytical requirement is built upon the prior system iterations. Therefore, the first iteration of the data warehouse must be both flexible to allow future analytics to be added and structured to minimize future iteration's development ambiguity. This case describes AIIA's efforts of developing its first data warehouse iteration that satisfies those requirements.

Identification of Data Requirements

During the identification of data requirements stage, a series of interviews with AIIA managers and employees from all of the departments shown in Figure 2 (including the CEO) was conducted. The need for the analysis of data capturing customer interactions, as well as the analysis of financial data, was repeatedly expressed by members of each department in the initial interviewing process. Therefore, a subsequent round of interviews focused on fiscal (monetary) and customer interaction management (CIM) data monitoring analytics as the areas for requirement collection for the first iteration of the data warehouse. Consequently, the decision was made that the foundation of the data warehouse should be built upon the need to monitor and analyze fiscal and CIM effectiveness of both AIIA and its advisors. The two main missions of the AIIA data warehouse were defined:

M1. Leveraging the development initiatives by pinpointing effective product and service offerings.
M2. Increasing revenue and profit margins by allowing AIIA and its clients to understand the most promising customer opportunities.

As will be shown, the project continued to refer back to these main two missions (M1, M2) throughout the various stages.

Based on the above-defined missions, conducted interviews and subsequent analysis, AIIA decided to initially monitor its performance through two types of analysis:

- Monitoring and analyzing the fiscal information about AIIA's advisors and their clients'/investors' accounts (herein called Fiscal Analysis or FA). This analysis is intended for AIIA as an organization where all advisors and accounts can be analyzed, and for the individual advisors where an advisor can analyze only their clients' accounts.
- Monitoring and analyzing contacts between AIIA and its advisors, its advisors and their clients/investors (herein called Customer Interaction Management Analysis or CIMA).

In order to perform FA, the transactions, balances, and revenues associated with accounts had to be analyzed. Basic manager, product, and security information was also required. This information represented the dimensions for FA. Given that this information varies over time, the date/time dimension was also considered as another basic building block.

In order to perform CIMA, the information about instances of various contacts (phone, e-mail, Web site, etc.) between AIIA, advisors and investors had to be analyzed. Again, basic money manager, product and security information was required and it represented the dimensions for CIMA. Additionally, specific information about duration and mode of contact was also required. Of course, the number and frequency of contacts varies with time, so the date/time dimension was considered as another critical dimension.

Logical Data Definitions

The pivotal step in any data warehouse project (particularly one built off an open source architecture) is identifying and understanding the appropriate data.

As the size and complexity of the data warehouse iteration can quickly become unmanageable, the goal was to integrate only the necessary data. A logical model was created to aid in the process of understanding the selected data, verifying that all of the required data was available, and disregarding the extraneous data elements. The logical model is the combination of clearly defined logical definitions and conceptual graphical diagrams (which show the relationships within the data captured by logical definitions).

The list of all logical data definitions identified through interviews and the analysis of the existing underlying operational systems as necessary for FA and CIMA is shown in this section. While some of the terms may appear to be common for a particular business unit, they have been described for cross-department clarity. Often terms are used loosely, and these definitions are meant to be the standard within the data warehouse system. Ambiguous or subjective definitions of basic building blocks can lead to miscommunication, erroneous data warehouse implementation and faulty information. Following is the list of the logical data definitions:

- **Advisor:** A financial advisor who is an AIIA client. Advisors can have multiple Clients/Investors for whom they direct Accounts to be handled by a specific Manager according a specific Style.
- **Investor:** An individual or organization that has one or more Accounts overseen by an Advisor.
- **Class:** Refers to a category of investment (e.g., domestic equity, fixed income, global equity, etc.).
- **Style:** Refers to the investment method of the financial Product offered by Managers (e.g., Large-Cap Growth, Large-Cap Value, Small-Cap Growth, etc.).
- **Manager:** A financial expert whose investment Products are featured by AIIA. A Manager can offer more than one Product. Each Product is associated with one Manager. A Manager can have several Classes and within each class a certain Style (or styles).
- **Product:** AIIA Advisors place investment assets in a Product. Each Product is offered by a Manager. Managers can offer more than one Product.
- **Account:** An individual investment account owned by a single Investor. An account is associated with exactly one AIIA Product. However, an Account can have a discrepancy with the associated Product. In other words, the list and percentages of securities in the Product and the Account do not have to match. In addition to the tax and accounting requirements, this Product customization requires that transaction-level details per Account per Security be maintained (as depicted later by the Security Transaction Fact in Figure 4).

- **Custodian:** A financial institution that physically hosts each Account. Each Account has one Custodian and a Custodian can host multiple Accounts.
- **Contact Item:** The item that is the topic of the contact between AIIA and its Advisor or Investor. This item can either be a Manager, Product, Security, Account, or Other (e.g., news story on the Web site, technical question, etc.).
- **Item Type:** A type that every Contact Item is associated with and it indicates if the Contact Item is a Manager, Product, Security, Account, or Other.
- **Item Category:** Used to divide all Item Types (and consequently all Contact Items) into two categories: MPSA (Manager/Product/Security/ Account) or Other.
- **Contact Mode:** Indicates the mode of contact (e-mail, Web, phone, etc.). Each Contact Item can be accessed via various Contact Modes.
- **Department:** Indicates to which Department the AIIA Contact Handler belongs.
- **Sub-Department:** Indicates to which Sub-Department (e.g., Service) and consequently a Department (e.g., Service is a sub-department of Distribution Department) an AIIA Contact Handler belongs.
- **AIIA Contact Handler:** Is an AIIA process which supports contact between AIIA and the Advisors and/or Managers and/or Investors. For example, an AIIA Contact Handler could be a person, a Web site, or automated phone system.
- **Date, Month, Quarter, Year:** All members of the dimension Time/Date. A Time instance belongs to a particular Date, which belongs to a particular Month, which belongs to a particular Quarter, which belongs to a particular Year.

The logical model is illustrated at the highest level in Figures 3 and 4, which use a dimensional modeling notation as given in Kimball et al. (1998). In particular, Figure 3 illustrates dimensions and facts principal for FA, and Figure 4 illustrates dimensions and facts principal for CIMA.

The following is the description of dimensions and facts that were identified as necessary for FA and CIMA and used in the dimensional model shown in Figures 3 and 4:

- **Dimension 1 — ACCOUNTS:** Advisors can have many Investors, who can have many Accounts. In addition, one Account is associated with one Custodian and one Product (Custodians and Products can have many Accounts). An Advisor and Investor can have Accounts across a number of Custodians.

- **Dimension 2 — PRODUCTS:** Managers can offer many Products. A Class of Products can have a number of Styles of Products. Consequently, a Product belongs to one Style and Class. In addition a Manager can offer Products of different Classes and Styles.
- **Dimension 3 — SECURITY:** Financial security (e.g., stock).
- **Dimension 4 — TIME:** Depicts that the Year is composed of Quarters, which are composed of Months, which are composed of individual Dates.
- **Dimension 5 — CONTACT HANDLERS:** Departments can have a number of Sub Departments, which contain AIIA Contact Handlers.
- **Dimension 6 — CONTACT ITEM:** Contact Item Category can have a number of Contact Item Types, which contain a number of Contact Items.
- **Dimension 7 — CONTACT MODE:** Contact Items can be accessed via various Contact Modes (Web, phone, e-mail, etc.).
- **Fact 1 (in Support of M1) — BALANCE/HOLDING:** Refers to the monetary value of a certain Security within a certain Account (associated with a certain Product) at a certain Date.
- **Fact 2 (in Support of M2) — REVENUE:** Refers to the monetary value of revenue generated by a certain Account (associated with a certain Product) at a certain Quarter. The amount of revenue is calculated based on the Account Manager's fee schedule with AIIA and the balance of the account throughout the Quarter.
- **Fact 3 (in Support of M1) — SECURITY TRANSACTION:** Refers to the event of Investor's assets being added or taken out from a balance of a certain Security (including cash) within a certain Account (associated with a certain Product).
- **Fact 4 (in Support of M2 as it relates to expenses) — ADVISOR CONTACT:** Refers to an instance of a recorded contact, which occurred at a certain Time via a certain Mode between an Advisor and an AIIA Contact Handler regarding a certain Contact Item. This fact stores the nature of the contact (e.g., routine, emergency, positive feedback, negative feedback, etc.), the duration of the contact and whether the Advisor or AIIA initiated the contact.
- **Fact 5 (in Support of M2 as it relates to expenses) — INVESTOR CONTACT:** Refers to an instance of a recorded contact, which occurred at a certain Time via a certain Mode between an Investor and an AIIA Contact Handler regarding a certain Contact Item. This fact stores the nature of the contact, the duration of the contact, and whether the Investor or AIIA initiated the contact.

Applications and User Prioritization of Data Needs

As mentioned in the introduction, AIIA's mission for the data warehousing system is:

Figure 3. FA

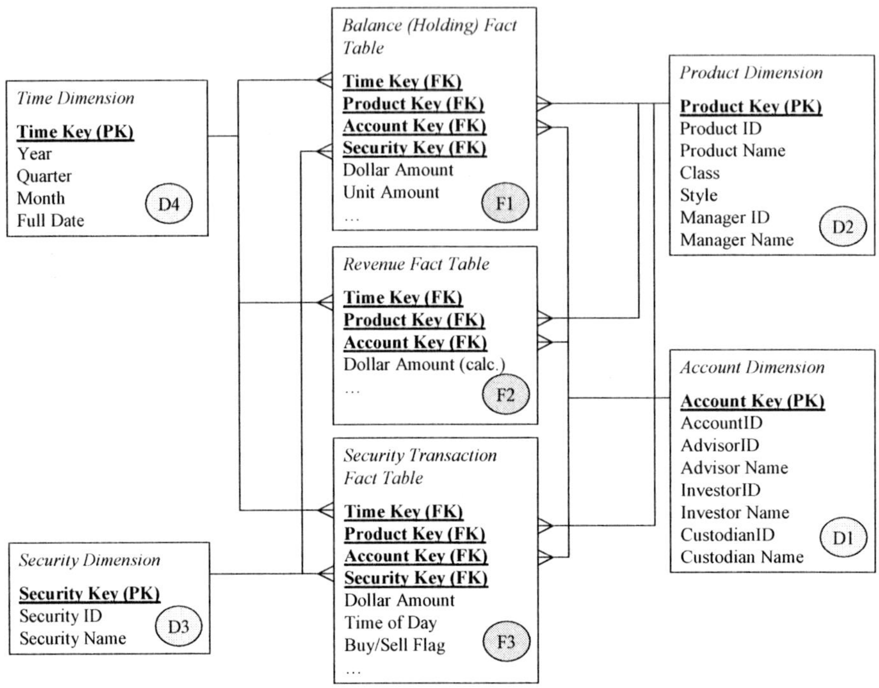

Figure 4. CIMA

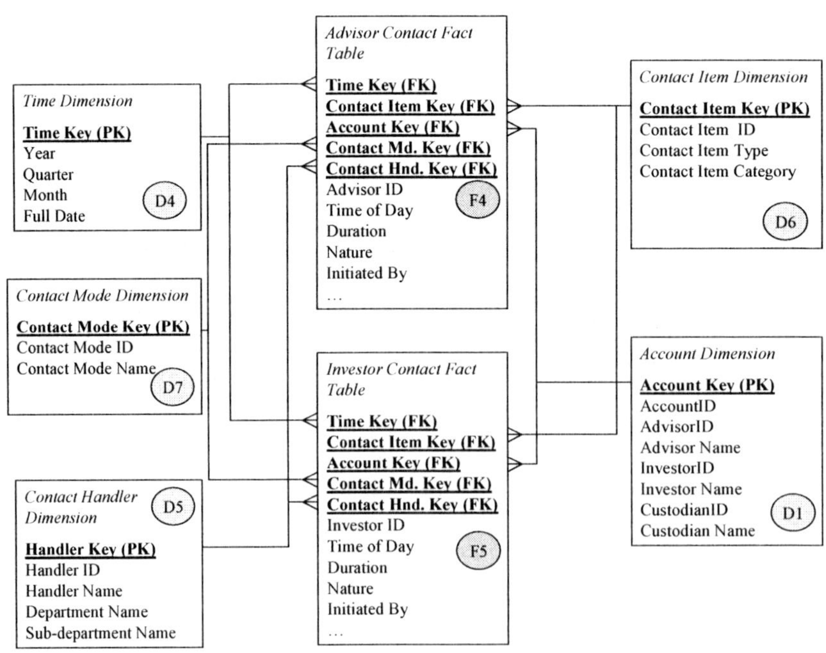

M1. Leveraging the development initiatives by pinpointing effective product and service offerings.
M2. Increasing revenue and profit margins by allowing AIIA and its clients to understand the most promising customer opportunities.

As stated in identification of requirements, FA and CIMA were selected as two types of analysis that the data warehouse will provide. Therefore, in the first iteration of the data warehouse, the applications will support FA and CIMA in the context of the two stated goals (M1, M2). The following is a representative list of reports and queries that focus on this stated mission.

Fiscal Analysis

While the most common queries for FA concern accounts by advisor and balances within one account, examples of other desired FA calculations and roll-ups include:

- List the managers whose products are used by less than 10% of advisors. (M1)
- Find the top/bottom 10 most profitable accounts. (M2)
- Find the top/bottom 10 most profitable advisors. (M2)
- Find the top/bottom 10 securities by the amount of holdings in all accounts. (M1)
- Compare the holdings in all accounts between domestic and international equity for the last four quarters and then roll it up for the whole last year. (M1)
- For each month within the past two years, list the manager whose product attracted most newly created accounts. (M1 & M2)
- Compare revenue generated by advisors from different territories. (M2)
- Compare the list of 10 most profitable advisors with the list of 10 advisors whose accounts have the highest cumulative AIIA transactional cost. (M2)
- List the top 15 securities by the amount of holdings across all accounts. (M1)

In addition to the AIIA internal analysis (as illustrated by the above listed examples), individual advisors will be able to perform FA as well, within their own accounts. Individual advisors will be provided with the possibility to get answers to queries such as:

- For each month within the past two years, list the manager whose product attracted most of my investor's accounts. (M1)

Customer Interaction Management Analysis

While the most common queries for CIMA concern contacts by advisor and by investor, examples of other desired CIMA calculations and roll-ups include:

- Compare the list of 10 advisors who make the most phone calls to AIIA with the list of 10 advisors who make the least phone calls to AIIA. (M1)
- Find the top 10 products that generate most contacts by Advisors. (M2)
- Calculate and compare the ratio of contacts via phone vs. contacts via Web for advisors for each of the past six months. (M2 as expenses relate to profit)
- Find out which day of the month, for each of the last 12 months, had the most phone-call contacts. (M2)

The AIIA data warehouse will allow for combined FA-CIMA calculations and roll-ups, such as:

- Compare the list of 10 advisors with highest cumulative duration of incoming phone contacts with the list of top 10 most profitable advisors for each of the past four quarters. (M2)
- Calculate and compare the ratio of contacts via phone vs. contacts via Web for the top 10 revenue-producing advisors for each of the past six months. (M2)

The examples of analysis listed within this section demonstrate the power of the data warehouse (such analysis would not be available on an on-demand basis without a data warehouse), and build a case project. It is at this stage (once possibilities for analysis are illustrated) that most of the constituencies within the organization realize the value of the data warehousing initiative.

Data Warehouse Project Scope and Implementation

Regardless of the logical data definitions or applications, a data warehouse is only as good as the loaded data. A data warehouse reflects the data loaded into it; if there is complete and clean data loaded into it, the data warehouse will be complete and clean. On the other hand, if not all of the required data is loaded or if incorrect data is loaded, the data warehouse will be incomplete and incorrect. Like with all information systems, the old adage "Garbage-In-Garbage-Out" applies to data warehouses as well. A prerequisite for any data warehouse is complete and correct data.

Potential data sources (shown in Figure 5) were identified. Given that AIIA is only two years old, the systems were designed and implemented to be open. Therefore, the ETL process was reduced to mostly T process where data files where converted from one layout to another. Also, given the fact that data

Figure 5. Data sources

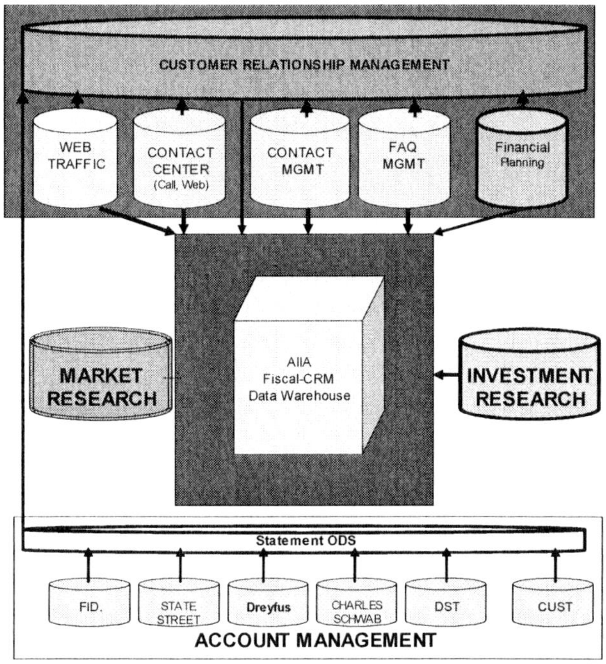

repositories were relatively new, the dedicated database and system monitoring capabilities were in place, and sound database methods with foreign keys, integrity constraints, domain value restrictions were used, the source data was of high quality. In addition, given the nature of the financial market and need for accuracy of the investment data, the Operations Department was made responsible for a daily reconciliation and cleaning of the underlying data sources, eliminating the need for cleaning the data during the ETL process.

The following gives the description of the content of the underlying data sources.

- **Account Management Database:** Contains all necessary account-related fiscal information (e.g., information about accounts, investors, securities, balances, transactions, custodians, generated revenues, etc.).
- **Investment Research Database:** Contains all product-related fiscal information (e.g., information about products, managers, etc.).
- **Customer Interaction Management System:** FAQ MGMT database contains information about FAQs (Frequently Asked Questions) and of the sources for Contact Item class. Web Traffic, Contact Center, and Contact

Management databases are used as sources for each of the three fact tables for CIMA as well as a source for Contact Item and Contact Handler classes. Financial Planning system contains financial planning and asset allocation applications that state investor demographic objectives.

- **Market Research:** Contains news and markets information presented to AIIA's clients via a Web site as a part of the service provided. This is one of the sources for Contact Item class.

Even though some of the underlying data sources were not implemented at the beginning of the data warehouse design process, AIIA felt that this fact was not detrimental to the process of conceptually designing a data warehouse. In fact, synchronized-simultaneous design processes for data warehouse and its underlying operational systems mutually influenced each other into adopting standardized design approaches. Consequently, this resulted in the reduction of the amount of time and effort needed for the implementation phases of the data warehousing project.

While the underlying source data was clean, there was still a need to convert the data from one file format to another. Many of the sources overlap in the content. For example, there are multiple custodial data feeds that all provide account transaction and balance information. After translating a couple of custodial formats into the data warehouse format, others followed a similar logic and were relatively easy to convert. In other cases, some of the sources, like the contact center source, covered unique sets of information and the transformation logic was distinct. Regardless of the breadth or overlap of the source data, ETL tools (provided by Sagent, Informatica and InfoGrate) were used to streamline and hold the meta-data and transformation logic.

The primary key to a successful data warehouse is the ability to use the combination of hardware and multi-tiered servers in any one of a number of ways and to keep the configuration as flexible as possible over time to address the changing profile of the data warehouse. When source data changes, warehouse views need to be maintained so that the two remain consistent (Labio et al., 1999). In addition, as the warehouse continues to expand, both business needs and the requirements relating to the technological infrastructure will continue to change as well. Addressing this change through the implementation of an open-system, multi-tiered format is critical to the success of the data warehouse. For example, one of the standard configurations for a Decision Support System (DSS) application calls for a database server coupled with a "fat" client running a DSS presentation and query tool that may or may not address back to an intermediary query processing server or "engine." However, AIIA opted for a newer standard to create applications based upon browser type technologies to reduce the loads on the client workstations and provide open connectivity to the data warehouse. This type of an application requires a Web server, a query

Figure 6. AIIA's three-tier data warehouse architecture

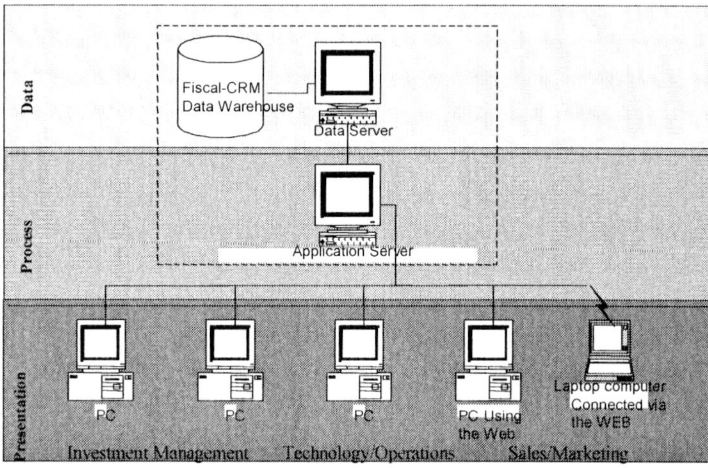

engine and a database server to/from the data warehouse, and it provides the computational component to the client's display device.

A three-tier data warehouse architecture was developed. Figure 6 illustrates the three-tier architecture with the three shades of gray. The dark gray tier contains the presentation services in which users will be able to access the data and these services include the interface to the users. The middle tier contains the processing services in which large user requests and data manipulation are executed. The light gray tier contains the data services in which the data is stored and maintained.

CURRENT CHALLENGES/PROBLEMS FACING THE ORGANIZATION

The scope of this case study was to present AIIA's efforts during the conceptual design phase for the first iteration of the enterprise-wide data warehouse. Successful completion of this phase enabled AIIA to proceed with its data warehousing project with a clear vision of future benefits and efforts required.

The stages subsequent to the design phase involved their own complex and labor-intensive issues, but due to the successful completion of the conceptual phase described in this case study, the potential for "wasted effort and extra expense" scenario (Mattison, 1996) was minimized and the implementation phase was straightforward.

Currently, the AIIA data warehousing system is used by the initial core of users. Most of these initial users were, in some fashion, involved with the creation of the system. Therefore they were quite familiar with the system from the inception, and they did not require formal training. Since the user population is expected to grow significantly and expand outside the self-reliant core, one of the pending tasks for AIIA is developing adequate end-user education and support strategy. Some preliminary steps addressing that issue, such as developing educational-focused documentation, have already been undertaken.

Another challenge facing the organization is maintaining the data warehouse and managing the growth. Due to the fact that AIIA is a relatively new company in which the data warehouse was developed in parallel with the operational systems, the likelihood for changes and additions to the structure of the data warehouse underlying systems is higher than in the typical data warehousing project, where the data warehouse collects the data from mature systems. Consequently, the structural changes in the data warehouse itself are probable. In acknowledgment of this fact, AIIA has delayed the transition from the data warehousing development team to the data warehousing growth and maintenance team. This transition will eventually involve downsizing the number of members devoted to the project, and at this point AIIA feels that this step would be premature.

Finally, AIIA still has to evaluate the accomplishment of the clear missions for the warehouse, set as detecting effective product and offerings and understanding the most promising revenue opportunities, in order to make attaining an appropriate and justifiable ROI apparent. This evaluation will be done gradually, as the system is used for the amount of time significant enough to evaluate its impact (or non-impact).

REFERENCES

Chaudhuri, S., & Dayal, U. (1997). An overview of data warehousing and OLAP technology. *SIGMOD Record*, *26*(1), 65-71.

Kimball, R., Reeves, L., Ross, M., & Thornthwaite, W. (1998). *The data warehouse lifecycle toolkit*. New York: John Wiley & Sons.

Labio, W., Yang, J., Cui, Y., Garcia-Molina, H., & Widom, J. (1999). *Performance issues in incremental warehouse maintenance*. Technical Report, Stanford University.

Mattison, R. (1996). *Data warehousing: Strategies, technologies and techniques*. McGraw Hill

FURTHER READINGS

Adamson, C., & Venerable, M. (1998). *Data warehouse design solutions.* NY: John Wiley & Sons.

Agosta, L. (2000). *The essential guide to data warehousing.* Prentice Hall.

Barquin, R., & Edelstein, H. (1997). *Building, using, and managing the data warehouse.* Prentice Hall.

Bischoff, J., & Alexander, T. (1997). *Data warehouse: Practical advice from the experts.* Prentice Hall.

Inmon, W. H. (1996). *Building the data warehouse.* New York: John Wiley & Sons.

Inmon, W. H., Rudin, K., Buss, C. K., & Sousa, R. (1999). *Data warehouse performance.* New York: John Wiley & Sons.

Inmon, W. H., Welch, J. D., & Glassey, K. L. (1997). *Managing the data warehouse.* New York: John Wiley & Sons.

Mattison R. (1996). *Data warehousing: Strategies, technologies and techniques.* McGraw-Hill.

Nenad Jukic is an assistant professor at the Information Systems and Operations Management Department of the School of Business Administration, Loyola University - Chicago. He earned his BS in electrical engineering and computer science from the University of Zagreb, Croatia. He earned his master's and PhD degrees in computer science from the University of Alabama. His research has focused on the areas of database management, e-business, data warehousing, and systems integration.

Tania Neild is president and director of research and technology at InfoGrate Incorporated, a data integration tools and services provider. With a National Physical Science Consortium 6-Year Full Doctorate Scholarship, she graduated from Northwestern University with a PhD in computer engineering, with a concentration in heterogeneous database integration. She earned her Master's of Computer Sciences from the University of Maryland where she concentrated in software specification, and her BA from Emory University, majoring in mathematics and computer science.

This case was previously published in the *Annals of Cases on Information Technology,* Volume 4/2002, pp. 487-498, © 2002.

Chapter XIV

A Case Study of One IT Regional Library Consortium: VALE — Virtual Academic Library Environment

Virginia A. Taylor, William Paterson University, USA

Caroline M. Coughlin, Consultant, USA

EXECUTIVE SUMMARY

Historic models of library management are being tested and modified in the digital age because of several interrelated factors. First, the importance of place or a home library space changes as electronic opportunities for dispersal of library collections increase with IT innovations and availability. Second, the high cost of IT has made library managers more sensitive to issues of cost in general while the ability of IT systems to provide easy access to managerial data, data previously difficult to capture, has allowed library managers to begin to differentiate costs for services based on use. As a result of these two factors, new, partially cost-focused models for delivering IT systems and information sources to library users are being developed. The new IT library regional models raise many questions about appropriate organizational and funding strategies. In this case, one strategy is examined in depth. Suggestions for alternative managerial strategies and economic models for IT regional library managers to pursue are given, based on the lessons to be gleaned from this experience and an examination of the literature describing other regional IT digital library ventures.

BACKGROUND

Today libraries are being challenged to develop digital library services, utilizing all the best information technology (IT) has to offer. These same institutions are also facing escalating costs for subscriptions to journals and indexes. Over the years, many librarians have chosen to form voluntary associations or consortiums. The majority of these ventures state as their goal the improvement of library services to users of each member library. In the past, the ability of individual libraries to pay the full costs of their use of the service being offered was not the primary issue library managers faced when building the association. It was common practice for wealthier libraries to cover the majority of the costs. Costs were not systematically reviewed, and decisions to subsidize some members were based on sentiments that favored inclusive, egalitarian models of service. This case centers on the work done by IT library professionals in New Jersey to develop a cooperative program for the digital distribution of information resources. VALE is an acronym for the phrase selected to describe the goal of the new New Jersey consortium — Virtual Academic Library Environment (VALE, 2001). As a not-for-profit library regional cooperative venture, VALE exists to provide electronic databases and journals to its members, a large group of academic libraries in New Jersey. It has been in existence for almost five years, and it is an example of a collaborative organizational approach to the provision of information technology-based services in more than one library.

Data Sources for Case Materials

In building this case we reviewed all VALE public records, including minutes of meetings of the 28 member VALE Task Force held since June 1997. An Executive Committee with nine members is responsible for ongoing operation and growth of VALE, including budgetary accountability and planning for future funding. Accordingly, we also examined the minutes of their meetings held between December 1998 and November 2000. Two key members of the VALE leadership team were interviewed at length. The head of the VALE Executive

Committee met with us for two hours. A leading member of the Task Force, one of the individuals responsible for introducing the idea to the state, who is also the person who has been the volunteer manager/business agent for VALE, met with us for over four hours. In addition to participating in the interviews, both of these individuals have regularly responded to requests for additional information or clarification of a source document. Each has also been willing to speak off the record about issues surrounding VALE's future. We have been in regular contact with both individuals since our initial meetings in November 1999 in preparation for a paper on value-added measurement perspectives available to libraries, especially libraries with significant IT investments. The study yielded evidence to show the applicability of three business models to the VALE project. They are Stakeholder Theory, Value-Added Model and Managerial Accounting. That paper was presented at the IRMA Conference in Anchorage in May 2000 (Taylor & Coughlin, 2000).

Issues in Consortium Formation

Agencies like VALE are being formed in many different states at this time, and the issues surrounding the formation, continuation and growth of IT library regional cooperatives are issues of significance to the future of all IT-based library services. IT regional digital library initiatives are often described as significant opportunities for the provision of innovative library services. However, it can be argued that the real significance of many collaborative IT library ventures lies in the transformation of each individual member library's funding structure. If more than one library can share a subscription because its digital nature allows for disparate locations, all the old patterns of funding libraries can be challenged. When economic realities demand that each library in the consortium pay based on its use of the subscription, all the older models of altruistic library cooperation are also challenged. These issues are often bypassed because IT library managers tend to focus their attention on the technical problems of building systems. In many cases, including VALE, the initial challenges for the regional library IT agency are perceived by the founders to be primarily challenges of structure, infrastructure needs for hardware, software, installation and training and funding, especially post-grant funds or matching fund formulation. From the start of a project, decisions about membership status and rights of the individual member institutions are present as issues of selectivity. Decisions must be made about whether participants must all do the same things to the same degree and at the same price. The development of VALE is illustrative of one-way management, and economic issues are handled when the goal is finding a way to offer new digital library services in a constrained funding environment.

When libraries enter the digital library age, there are many changes in the way users receive information. These have been studied by experts such as

Michael Buckland, who calls for using technology to encourage a radical re-centering of libraries towards users (Buckland, 1992). In the past, libraries, like their universities, have focused on inputs. Today the focus is on other stakeholders. The end users perception of value received is often the cornerstone of an outcomes assessment to judge the best resource allocation for available funds. Christine Borgman, another well-known commentator on these issues, views the future for libraries in global rather than local terms and thus appreciates the antiquated nature of most individual library governance and funding systems (Borgman, 2000). Less obvious, but equally important to study, are the ways in which the infrastructure of libraries may change in the digital library environment. The studies of Bruce Reid and William Foster are pioneering in this respect (Reid & Foster, 2000). It is also important to understand why some types of IT library-related changes can be more difficult to implement than others and bring questions of structure (Saunders, 1999) and cost (Kantor, 1995) to the forefront in new ways. As with other important issues in life, if a person seeks answers to why questions, often there is a need to explore the history of the situation. In the case of IT library regional consortia development, including VALE, understanding the historical context of both library IT efforts and consortia developments is vital. Each history significantly influences the decisions of present day leaders in the field as they build new organizations.

SETTING THE STAGE

Because VALE is an information technology (IT) centered library consortium, it operates within the context and value structures of libraries and library consortia. The history of libraries is essentially a history of non-profit, stand-alone organizations that are willing to share their resources with other libraries at little or no charge. Consortia are latecomers in a library history that spans centuries. Over time and at times, individual libraries have been willing to cooperate on the development of supplemental library services but each library accepts as its focus, a primary responsibility to deliver basic services to its own constituency within the parameters of its own budget. When there is cooperation it is generous. The library loaning an item or giving the supplemental service to other libraries often absorbs the cost of the service being delivered. This is a matter of professional ethics. In the world of non-profits, it is believed that it is right and good for institutions to help each other. This belief applies to relationships between institutions at equivalent levels of strength as well as to relationships between stronger libraries and all other libraries and library-related agencies.

Each of the above statements applies to the great majority, if not all, libraries established until the later part of the 20th century. Starting in the mid-19th century, improvements in communication systems and technology made it possible for libraries in the same geographical area, or libraries with similar missions, to develop voluntary associations. The typical association was established to further some forms of cooperation, notably to support interlibrary loan among libraries and to help create union catalogs listing holdings of several libraries. The working plan of these voluntary groups was to facilitate the sharing of resources at little or no additional cost, except the contributed cost of volunteer labor or the absorbed cost of staff time devoted to an association project. Many of these voluntary associations and their attendant practices are still in existence. VALE, the IT library consortia featured in this study, is technically in this category of association. Because of the enormous changes brought about in all library operations with the advent of IT, there have been strains on the typical library cooperative venture trying to service a 21st century library in the midst of a technological revolution with a 19th century model of library association management.

Values in Transition

As with all revolutions there have been both anticipated and unanticipated consequences. The traditional model of stand-along libraries freely offering other libraries supplemental services is being dismantled even as it is still being honored as the norm. The newer models of library service assume linkages among libraries, and expect that there will be fees to pay when libraries rely on others to provide services. Fee structures are not unknown to libraries, thanks to the development of commercial vendors offering libraries services for a price. Although still controversial for some applications, the practice of paying outside agencies to accomplish certain library tasks at a set or variable price is also now accepted as a reasonable managerial approach. This practice, often called outsourcing, has been used to purchase cataloging data and develop book collections, and with it came an acceptance of unit pricing, volume discounts, and other typical pricing structures. Although the practice of paying outsiders to do library work has modestly increased the willingness of libraries to pay each other for work done, there is still a very strong tradition in librarianship that calls for libraries to share freely with each other. It is this tradition that hovers over the current generation of IT library regional systems such as VALE.

In these instances, IT is both the change itself and the facilitator of related changes. IT handles enormous amounts of data efficiently, encourages standardization and yet permits flexibility, and these facts alone significantly change the way in which any library handles its core functions. IT also permits easy linkages among libraries and facilitates accounting for costs among various libraries. This ability to communicate easily changes the picture when it comes to libraries offering supplemental services or developing shared programs. At the time of the creation of any regional IT library program, it is of necessity dependent on the state of IT innovation in general.

Intertwined Foci of National, Local, and Regional IT Library Models

The IT library model developed over the past forty years has three foci: national, local, and regional. From the beginning of IT activity in libraries, the foci have been intertwined in practice. The national IT in libraries focus came first, supported in part by research in national agencies such as the National Science Foundation, the National Library of Medicine, National Library of Agriculture and the Library of Congress. In the national IT arena, the key tasks have been the establishment of standards and the testing and development of computerized systems for processing materials. Developing a standard for entering catalog data into the computer was a task taken on by the Library of Congress in its role as the de facto national library when it created the MARC record format for machine readable cataloging. This notable national achievement is the cornerstone of much other related IT-based database development. It represents the key first-generation national library IT effort.

First-Generation IT in Local Libraries

Shortly after IT experimentation began at the national level, innovative libraries in many different localities also began to try and find library applications for computers. The local focus on IT in the first generation of automated libraries often centered on the development of experimental uses of an available mainframe computer for listing and circulating library materials. In these cases, activity occurs within the parameters of a single library or a library system located in one political district or on one campus. Size was relevant but not the determining factor. Libraries large and small, of all types, were involved in these experiments. The number of library outlets was not important. In addition to the presence of IT interest and talent on the staff, the other key factor in the ability of a library or library system to experiment with IT was the presence of funding from the parent agency. In the wealthier locales support for funding IT efforts occurred when it was well articulated and linked to the library's goals. For the first round of libraries to receive IT funding, it sometimes meant that the parent institution or governing agency was interested in being judged a leader or innovator among their peers. For the late IT local adapters, the funding agency was either finally persuaded by the success stories of the early adapters, or shamed by their locale's delay in implementing IT.

What is essential to remember is that all these first-generation local IT implementation decisions were designed for and funded by a particular constituency. In this sense, the first-generation local IT world is really not very different from the 19th century world of wealthy stand-alone libraries with a sense of noblesse oblige to share their good fortune with poorer libraries. To use economic terminology, one could say this was a situation where stakeholders' expectations created social pressure for IT library development. Examples are: (1) government officials and private citizens sought to democratize information; (2) student and faculty scholars wanted convenient and timely access to information; (3) parent universities sought improved scholarly productivity; and (4) funders such as taxing authorities, universities themselves and benefactors share a desire for efficient resource allocation. This encouraged innovation and investment in order to satisfy stakeholder expectations.

Regional IT Efforts Begin

Soon these two strains of IT effort at the national and local level begin to infect each other, as in the case of a successful mounting of a local system using the emerging national standard of the MARC record. In the library field numerous meetings are held to share information about successes, learn from mistakes and begin to experiment with replication of code or sharing of IT resources, especially mainframe computers, both for the purpose of sharing and to attempt to achieve cost savings. Many of the efforts to share knowledge and computing power become the basis of the first generation of regional IT efforts. In the regional arena the IT players address IT development, education and linkage issues among the local institutions as well as between the local agencies and the national service providers. The regional IT library efforts are a mix of voluntary efforts via association activities and funded efforts based in agencies supported by member fees.

Questions of Cost and Payment Emerge

As national and regional IT library services developed, one key distinction emerged. Services were not necessarily freely offered; instead the cost of providing the service was determined and charged to the participating library. Business economic models became important to library managers because cost behavior analysis requires an understanding of the fixed and variable costs involved as well as allocation methods. (Snyder & Davenport, 1997) Often U.S. agencies funded the creation of IT library services and products as part of a research and demonstration program. In many of these situations, the options for continuation were further government funding or passing the costs along to the service's clients after any introductory, government-sponsored grant period ended. In the same manner, regional entities might also decide to eventually charge for services that they offered freely at the beginning of the service. However, the regional agencies might not, especially if the library region was defined as having the same boundaries as the local taxing and funding authority, either a multi-county government agency or a state. In these cases governmental appropriations could be sought to fund IT services for one public institution in the area or for a group of them. If it were the latter, then the establishment of the group became the equivalent of forming a regional governmental agency. When the group included privately supported libraries as well as public ones, the need for an agency to manage the cooperative effort increased. In either case cost-benefit analysis would be a useful tool in justifying any appropriation of funds.

OCLC'S Impact Defines the Second-Generation IT Library Systems and Regional Efforts

While it is the creation of MARC standard to create electronic bibliographic records that triggered the first-generation IT efforts, it is the availability of MARC records in disparate databases that triggers the start of the second generation of IT work in libraries. In the second generation the barriers and boundaries accepted by libraries since ancient days begin to crumble. The development of OCLC, Inc. dominates the second generation of IT in libraries and in library cooperative ventures. It offers the technological mechanism for cooperation and develops an organizational structure to pay for it.

When OCLC was begun in the late 1960s, the initials stood for the Ohio College Library Cooperative and represented a geographically based effort to harness IT to share the task of cataloging library materials. OCLC was established to allow a select group of Ohio libraries to copy the catalog record made by another member library. The MARC records of the Library of Congress were the main source, in the form of MARC tapes, freely given to OCLC to load onto a mainframe in Columbus, Ohio. Once the tapes were in the OCLC database, they could be viewed on OCLC-dedicated, local terminals and used to develop local cataloging copy. At first OCLC was funded with national and state grants. But, when the audience for the OCLC product reached beyond state borders, it was decided that the use of the file would not be free. Ohio legislators felt no need to pay for Indiana libraries and the leadership of OCLC wanted new funds to go beyond survival funding and pay for new IT. When OCLC sets its fee structures, based on use, a new era was born in libraries.

Over time the initials OCLC have come to mean Online Computer Library Center and OCLC has become a major player in the library world. It is a supplier to libraries of software to manage many disparate library services, and it is the manager of an enormous bibliographic database that is the engine which controls ever-increasing volumes of shared cataloging, collection development collaborations, electronic database provision and interlibrary loan activities among libraries. The economic principle of return on investment (ROI) applies in these activities, whether the libraries call it by this technical term. They may simply celebrate that their collaborative ventures have increased the chances that one book, purchased by one library, will be used by other readers in other libraries. Or they may view the transaction in economic terms and see the above as leading to the growth of more knowledge and greater democratization of information, lower unit cost to deliver particular information packages and a geometric expansion of knowledge if research results are shared or published. Library managers who may be unfamiliar with the ROI term have become knowledgeable about unit costs, volume and time-of-use discounts, as well as learning how to strengthen their bargaining and purchasing power by increasing the use of volume purchases.

From the start, OCLC illustrated the classic "if you build it, they will come" scenario. As more libraries joined OCLC and purchased its cataloging services, more libraries knew what each other had and the knowledge led to an increase in interlibrary loan (ILL) activities. This increase in borrowing and lending has transformed interlibrary loan from a minor activity in libraries to a significant program area, now called resource sharing. Now, more libraries seek to borrow more frequently from each other and then, in some strategic alliances, more libraries seek to share the costs of purchasing more items. OCLC is the national center of these efforts, but it is not a monopoly. In an attempt to share power equally among OCLC members, the decision was made to provide OCLC services via regional networks and to use the networks to help govern OCLC. The reach of OCLC is enormous.

Third Generation of IT Regional Library Efforts

Nowadays, when a new IT effort is envisioned and created in libraries, the work is often intertwined with OCLC and one or more of its regional affiliates. OCLC demonstrates the power of incremental additions to historic practices to change the earlier resource sharing practices of libraries. But third-generation IT regional library planning is not simply a matter of paying OCLC for some service; it is a broader effort, one based on the Internet. While local libraries are still the source of decision making and funding, and national organizations are still the source of much innovative IT work, in this third generation, IT regional library groups are the linchpin of significant change efforts. Their goal is ambitious. IT regional library leaders seek to use both the resources of the library-specific IT agencies such as OCLC and the IT power of the World Wide Web. They want to build new virtual communities for information seekers in many disciplines, as well as create digital libraries and design other yet-to-be imagined library/information services. That vision is fairly clear. Less clear is the source of funds to pay for the digital programs.

Persistence of 19th Century Managerial and Economic Models

The driving force for third-generation IT library services is the dream of digital library service. It is a dream of the one big library in the sky based in the future. With the technological choices now available to libraries, longstanding barriers between libraries and users and libraries can dissolve. A document can reside in many libraries and homes at once. It can be viewed by a number of people at the same time. Individual library IT innovators have resolved the issues of time and space as they offer digital library services to their patrons. They spend their dollars to feature these newer services, viewing the additional costs as worth it, given the greatly increased access offered to users. But it takes enormous amounts of money to do it all and choices must be made. Anyone familiar with the quest for distance education models that are both cost effective and quality centered is familiar with these issues. The two bodies of literature — distance education and regional IT library efforts — do not often overlap, but they are definitely parts of the same picture. Richard Katz calls the IT effort "dancing with the devil" (Katz, 1999) while Trevor Haywood considers the distance teaching effort a search for a balance between richness and reach (Haywood, 2000). The question of change is not only a search for sufficient funding for technology. It is a question of traditional approaches and their values. There is still tacit approval given to the vision of a student studying in a hushed cathedral like library or engaging with fellow students in a spirited dialogue in small classes led by a dynamic and dedicated professor. In both cases there is truth and myth intertwined. There is also the reality of proprietary rights. There are over 2,000 independent colleges and universities in the United States. These facts combine to make it very difficult to abandon the 19th century vision of higher education as a independent enterprise practiced on many unique independent campuses. Technology can change that, but first must come the acceptance of technology as a key player in new campus strategies. Philip Evans may be comfortable calling his vision of the future, Blown to Bits, but others are not so sure they want to be caught in the crossfire (Evans, 2000).

The promise of globally available digital libraries seems to make local library funding a bit of an oxymoron, but free Internet ideologies non-withstanding, the reality is cash is still needed to pay for library resources, digital or print. In 2001 over 98% of all library funding is generated locally; therefore the local library must be the base for any regional digital efforts. At the same time, managers know digital services are by nature capable of wide distribution and therefore should be supported over a wider base than one library. Finding ways to fund digital libraries on a regional basis is the key. As the various players in the library community build new resource sharing models, they deviate from some 19th century funding practices and cling to others. Third-generation models no longer assume charity towards all — all the time — is the preferred budget model. Yet, many of these models assume that subsidies towards less wealthy libraries are valid and that much volunteer work on the part of professionals is the way to accomplish agency goals. Others may still believe in the need for subsidies but think that volunteer approaches are not sufficiently dynamic to handle digital library initiatives. They build new organizations, with new sources of funding, and staff them to provide a distinct set of services to the regional library IT community.

CASE DESCRIPTION

VALE'S Models and Their Founding Rationales

There are a number of experiments in developing consortia for digital library services. One of the earliest is called OhioLINK; it serves the academic libraries of Ohio and began in 1987. In 1988 the Texas State Library began its digitally focused resource sharing effort, and called it TEX SHARE. By 1994-1995 the library community begins hearing about comparable efforts in three other states. In Virginia the effort is called VIVA, or Virtual Library of Virginia (VIVA, 2000), in Louisiana it is called Louisiana Library Network and in Georgia it is called GALILEO, or Georgia Library Learning Online (GALILEO, 2000). Each of these state-based consortia was described in the literature (Potter, 1997) and has been the subject of presentations at one or more professional meetings. The Web sites for VIVA, GALILEO and the other regional library ITs are good sources of detailed and current information about structure, budget and program emphases. The motives of the individuals who begin VALE in 1997 are similar to those who started VIVA and the other IT library regional cooperatives. A few key reasons are cited by many.

Rapidly escalating subscription costs of print journals was a significant motivator for some librarians in the major academic libraries to seek out cooperative ways to share subscription costs and simultaneously experiment with electronic journals (Parang & Saunders, 1994). Other librarians had a strong interest in delivering electronic text to users, either in the library or via the campus network or the Internet (Saunders, 1999). Still others were beginning to explore the advantages of group purchasing for disparately funded libraries. By 1995, most academic libraries had been members of OCLC or the competing network, Research Libraries Information Network (RLIN). Both groups of members had, by then, a decade or so of experience dealing with unit pricing, cooperative purchasing and the cost benefits of shared cataloging. Many librarians understood the nature of vendor-client relationship better after having participated in their institution's negotiations for an online public access library system. The use of the Internet increased rapidly on most U.S. campuses in the mid-1990s after graphical user interfaces such as Netscape were developed and librarians understood the impact this could have on the delivery of library services. By the late 1990s when EDUCAUSE developed guidelines, *The EDUCAUSE Guide to Evaluating Information Technology on Campus*, the premise of it, that access to full texts, not ownership, of library resources is not a disputed issue (Burdick, 2001). What remains a problem for all the libraries and their parent institutions is the development of an equitable funding structure for regional library IT access options. Libraries are not the only agency seeking new financial models for the work that they do. As Gardner says, there is a general need for the valuation of IT in terms of strategy development, valuation and financial planning (Gardner, 2000).

Early Leadership of VALE

The leaders who developed VALE are individuals with these experiences, although not all of them have had the same ones. For some, the 1990s have been a time of battling rising costs and declining budgets; for others it has been a time to focus on selecting their institution's first online public access system. By 1990 most have purchased a few electronic resources in CD-ROM format and established a local network for them. For a few, it has been a time of experimentation with digitizing library collections and putting them on the Web. These are some of their individual experiences.

The individuals who created VALE also have had collective experiences. Many are members of a voluntary association of academic library directors in New Jersey and have been members for several years. Others are members of the New Jersey Library Association as well as national library association and have been active leaders of them. By virtue of residing in a particular location, they have also learned something about the nature of local and state government in their state as well as the strengths of their institutions and their colleagues. There is a reservoir of trust, flexibility and knowledge in the group of creative leaders that come together to shape an idea brought to the table by one of them at a meeting in 1997. By 1998 the group has created an organization named VALE.The mission of VALE is assumed in the document called "Statement of the VALE Project." It is exhibited below.

EXHIBIT ONE

Statement of the VALE Project

The VALE Project calls for the consortium to use matched state bond funds to develop inter-institutional information connectivity and collaborative library application projects among its members. VALE's objective is to help institutions meet the demands of students and faculty for access to scholarly materials. Through cooperation and leveraged purchasing, and through the use of collaboration and cutting-edge technology, VALE seeks to provide a seamless network of access to shared electronic academic information resources throughout the state. This exciting concept has been enthusiastically endorsed by the New Jersey State Library, the New Jersey Library Association and the Council of College and University Library Directors of New Jersey. The VALE Project will provide a level of information access to academic resources that has been unknown in the state.

VALE is a pioneer regional library IT effort. It represents compromise within this particular stakeholder group (consortia members) as well as among competing internal and external stakeholder groups such as scholars, funding agencies, citizens, vendors, authors and other IT professionals. When viewed in the context of innovation in IT library regional efforts, VALE can be seen as a hybrid solution, one that borrows from the technological future while still relying on current managerial and economic models. It represents a compromise. Part of the compromise is necessary given the unresolved national issues of intellectual property rights and author payments. However, there are New Jersey specific issues that call for examination and evaluation with respect to decisions made by VALE leaders.

VALE was established to offer electronic access to library materials to the state's higher education community. VALE is primarily a buying consortium, one that selects electronic databases and mounts them on a network server accessible to all members. What the end user at a given member college sees is a list of periodical indexes mounted on a local library online public access catalog. The user is then able to search the indexes and obtain one of three products: citations, abstracts and/or full-text articles from a range of periodicals. In some cases although full text is desired, it is not available electronically.

Questions of Strategy with Respect to Seeking VALE's Initial Funding

The VALE leaders developed their funding strategy based on currently available sources and amounts of possible funding for IT efforts supported by the state in the higher education community. It was believed that getting a foot in the door would give VALE the opportunity to make a case for greater funding at a later date after the program had enjoyed some successes. Because of New Jersey's IT program guidelines, it was necessary to stress the purchase of equipment. Because of competition from other parts of the higher education community, notably the IT officers of the New Jersey state colleges, it was decided to try and avoid conflict and restrict funding requests to the limited funds perceived to be funds that could be used for a program like VALE.

The rest of the needs as envisioned by the activists creating VALE were needs that would have to be funded locally in the budget parameters of the VALE members. In order to reach this agreement about how to pursue state funding for VALE, it was necessary for a few key library directors in the state to agree to take on VALE tasks within their budgets without an expectation of compensation. One director who agreed to do so did so based on the library's historic role as the leading research library in the state, the library that was already the library of service for interlibrary loans from other state colleges. Another director agreed because the emerging state IT program was a priority of her university's president and she knew she would receive support for the VALE effort from her superiors. In many ways, the VALE funding strategy could be considered a wing and a prayer effort. It relies on obtaining some funds, enjoying much generosity and expecting a well-behaved clientele of noble egalitarians.

Other States, Other Choices: Georgia and Virginia

There are only a few states with active regional library IT efforts and so it is not possible to generalize from these experiences. It is appropriate to review the existing material from other programs for evidence of alternative strategies in the formative stages of regional library IT efforts. The Texas, Ohio and Louisiana sites are good, and could also serve as good sources for alternative foci in developing IT regional library network mission statements (Texas, 2001; Ohio,2001; Louisiana, 2001) Exhibit Two is the statement of the vision for a comparable program in another state, Georgia (GALILEO, 2001).

EXHIBIT TWO

A Vision for One Statewide Library: GALILEO

Goals

- To ensure universal access to a core level of materials and information services for every student and faculty member in the University System of Georgia — regardless of geographic location, size of institution, or mode of instructional delivery: traditional residential, off-campus or distance learning.
- To improve information services and support through increased resource sharing among University System libraries, thus providing a greater return on investment.
- To provide the necessary information infrastructure so that all students in rural or metropolitan settings in the University System can be better prepared to function in an information society.
- To enhance the quality of teaching, research and service by providing worldwide information resources to all faculty.
- To ensure that adequate PeachNet bandwidth and state backbone are available to campuses to support library activities.
- To place the University System in the forefront of library information technology, enhancing its reputation, along with PeachNet and distance education.

GALILEO's vision statement is more ambitious than VALEs and at the same time more direct in indicating value-added outcomes for multiple stakeholder groups and more political. In the opinion of the non-librarian author of this case, it is clearer in its explanation of the goals of the library IT effort. As such, it offers the audience of all non-librarians, be they educators, politicians, students and faculty or citizens, a better opportunity to understand the dimensions of any regional IT library effort , including VALE.

It also addresses subtle but real issues of prestige and fame when it seeks to position Georgia as a leader in the higher education community. This enhances the brand image of the University of Georgia as a premier institution, a strategy that appeals to university leadership. When it calls for infrastructure investments in IT sufficient for the needs of the distance education community among other cohorts, it democratizes information, it reaches out to accommodate disparate groups in rural or poor communities who may be in competition for the same types of state funds. Finally, it is clear about what the academic libraries of the state need with respect to bandwidth and related IT infrastructure issues. While the authors of this case have not had the benefit of interviewing the Georgia leaders of GALILEO directly they have had the opportunity to observe second hand the work of Potter, one of the key organizers of the GALILEO program (Potter, 1997). Potter's position as head of the largest academic library in the system is important, but equally important is his decision to seek substantial amounts of new money for the implementation of a clearly articulated program with many facets. Non-profits and for profits can learn valuable lessons in stakeholder theory from a study of the regionalization of library IT efforts.

Virginia's Version of VALE

A similar analysis can be made of the VIVA program in Virginia. Its goals are equally clear and broad based in terms of reaching various political and academic constituencies. Exhibit Three is the VIVA mission statement and Exhibit Four is the member list. This is followed by a discussion of the budget, benefits, and value-added position. These can all be found on the VIVA Web site (VIVA, 2001).

EXHIBIT THREE

VIVA'S Mission

VIVA'S mission is to provide, in an equitable, cooperative and cost-effective manner, enhanced access to library and information resources for the Commonwealth of Virginia's non-profit academic libraries serving the higher education community.

EXHIBIT FOUR

VIVA's Members

All the libraries of the 39 state-assisted colleges and universities (at 52 campuses) within the Commonwealth of Virginia, including the six doctoral institutions, the nine four-year comprehensive colleges and universities and the 24 community and two-year branch colleges (at 37 campuses). Thirty-two of Virginia's independent (private non-profit) colleges and universities participate as full members where possible.

The Library of Virginia

Discussion of VIVA's Budget, Financial Benefits, and Value-Added Position

The Commonwealth of Virginia's General Assembly provided the first funding for VIVA when it appropriated $5,238,221 as requested in the 1994-96 Biennium Proposal. The approved 2000-2002 biennium budget totals $10,720,619 from all sources. In addition to resources from the General Assembly, individual institutions have supported the VIVA project in a variety of ways, most notably through donations of time by dedicated library staff. VIVA libraries take pride in knowing that significant financial benefits have accrued to members through the group purchases. As of March 31, 2000, VIVA had recorded cost avoidance of more than $32 million. This represents money saved over what would have been spent had each individual institution purchased VIVA resources. In many cases these are resources that the local colleges and universities would not have been able to purchase in an electronic form without the Commonwealth support for VIVA (2001).

The message is clear. Virginia's academic libraries will work together; they will not pick fights among themselves and expect the legislature to solve their problems. It is equally clear that the results of receiving this new state appropriation is a commitment to demonstrating cost savings. Traditionally, libraries have been seen as cost centers for support services. VIVA helped to reposition its members on the value chain. They now are seen as enhancing the raw knowledge materials with selection and distribution functions that add value for stakeholder groups. The record of increased appropriations is a telling affirmation of the success of VIVA in meeting its stated goals. Exhibit Five — the executive summary of a recent VIVA document detailing reduced purchasing costs, cost savings and value added — demonstrates their cost efficiencies (VIVA, 2001).

EXHIBIT FIVE

Executive Summary: Cost Savings and Value Added Survey — 1996-97

The Virginia legislature, working with the State Council of Higher Education in Virginia and the state's academic library community, continued funding for the Virtual Library of Virginia (VIVA) for the 1996-97 fiscal year. By working together, these entities restructured the academic libraries' materials budgets to give VIVA a central budget of $1.8 million for group purchases (collections, software, ILL delivery service and training materials) for fiscal year 1996-97.

The financial benefits to VIVA institutions can be measured in three ways: (1) reduced purchasing costs; (2) cost savings; and (3) value-added benefits.

1. **Reduced purchasing costs:** VIVA calculates financial benefits in terms of reduced purchasing costs for all purchases. During 1996-97, we calculate that VIVA purchased $6.7 million in resources for only $1.8 million. This represents a cost avoidance of approximately $5 million for fiscal year 1996-97.
   In the summer of 1997, for the second year in a row, VIVA institutions were asked to analyze the VIVA resources available to them in fiscal year 1996-97 and to record direct cost savings, indirect cost savings and value-added savings realized during that year. A total of 55 responses were received from 58 VIVA institutions and their branch libraries. Respondents included all 14 of the 15 state-assisted doctoral and comprehensive VIVA institutions, 25 of the 34 public two-year institutions and 16 of the participating 27 independent colleges.
2. **Cost savings:** The survey documented new direct cost savings of $552,188, for the 1996-97 year, a significant increase over the $330,997 recorded for the 1995-96 year. In addition, calculations for continued cost savings with an estimated 10.5% inflation rate for serials equals $274,425 during 1996-97, for a total of $826,613 for the 1996-97 year.
3. **Value added:** This survey documented a financial benefit of $11,443,199 for value-added resources for the 1996-97 year. This is nearly twice the $6,121,031 of value-added benefits documented in 1995-96.

CURRENT CHALLENGES AND PROBLEMS FACING VALE

Impact of Historical Context and Politics on VALE's Initial Funding Choices

While other states requested state funds for the purchase of equipment and subscriptions and services to support a new program of digital library services in a consortium, the VALE leaders chose a different strategy. They sought funds from a state program that focused on increasing the availability of computers and related hardware on the college campuses of the state. This strategy was based on expediency and political realities.

The majority of individuals on the various college campuses in the state who were in charge of IT efforts were more interested in receiving funds for locally based classroom-centered projects on their own campuses. It was not in the interests of most IT campus officials to support a large request for funds from a new, state-based IT library consortia. Key support for the VALE concept came from the IT vice president on one state university campus as he made the VALE case for some funding at the state level. Because of the competition for resources available under the bond issue, it was deemed politically astute to request only hardware for the VALE project. It was believed that this approach better positioned the VALE program as one deserving of bond money support for equipment, in line with the mission of the funding agency. The initial request for state funds was only for the purchase of the servers. Economic constraints on the uses of state funds stem from the nature of the source, bonds. The State of New Jersey insisted the money be used for long-term purchases, such as equipment, that would outlive the terms of the debt. VALE leaders revisit this decision often.

It remains unclear, given the political climate in New Jersey, whether a different strategy would have been wiser in the long run. As the examples from Georgia and Virginia demonstrate, other states have funded digital library initiatives after having been lobbied directly by the state library or the flagship state university for such a program on behalf of the citizens of the state. In these cases the digital library initiative funding supports equipment, software or subscriptions and staffing. Thus, the resulting IT library regional programs for digital library service is understood from the start as a new model of collaborative library service. As a separate innovation, these programs appear to enjoy a visibility that is helpful when additional support is sought from the state legislature for expansion purposes.

Generating Additional Revenue Streams: State Funds and Member Contributions

Ongoing direct costs for VALE include vendor payments, costs associated with servicing the server and program management costs such as negotiations with vendors. Current vendor pricing is based on student population figures. Individual members pay their share, based on subscriptions selected and user population. When participants choose partial participation, vendor negotiations and cost calculations have to be adjusted accordingly. This is an iterative, time-consuming and complex process for the negotiators involved. One of the challenges is establishing cost assessment models based on varying levels of library participation. Models must provide a clear and transparent picture of costs involved, while hedging for contingencies.

Member contributions are viewed in terms of journal payments. This current situation is a matter of practice, not policy. There is nothing in the VALE membership agreement that precludes the group deciding to charge fees to accomplish other program goals such as expanding electronic delivery options, developing vendor-based training programs for faculty and staff, assessing subsequent changes or improvements in use of the system. VALE leadership needs to experiment with several models for outcomes assessment, including cost studies, use studies and benefit studies.

One good byproduct of the current under-funding by the state of New Jersey is that each member library understands how important it will be to make future plans on a sound financial basis if the cooperative digital initiative is to flourish. Cost studies that compare pricing and calculate savings have become more common. There is willingness to explore the principles of activity-based costing and find appropriate opportunities to apply them. At present the leaders recognize the indirect costs relating to the costs of obtaining information from each user library about particular product choices are being absorbed by two institutions. These institutions are swallowing the indirect costs connected to the task of working with vendors to establish pricing schedules for a product as well as the overhead costs of being the host institution for the servers and administrative costs of running a membership organization. None of these costs are currently in the VALE budget.

The two state institutions most affected view the costs as community service contributions that are part of the price they pay to foster a statewide commitment to a digital library initiative. In this age of rampant individualism and competition, generosity and egalitarianism are still very evident in the decisions made by VALE leadership. At times a decision made means that one of the richer libraries carries the cost disproportionately. At other times, the VALE Board continues to provide an earlier generation IT because some members cannot afford to upgrade to the currently recommended IT.

VALE is an example of a 19th century model of library cooperation with some 21st century features. This approach is charitable; but it is also self-limiting for the VALE organization. An organization may be willing and able to give another agency one or two percent of its resources, but even the most willing organization will have difficulty giving more of its resources without clear standards and agreed upon benefits for the monies and in-kind services given. Unless other sources of income can be found, the result appears to threaten stagnation for VALE. In a way this generous gift by two universities in the state to all the other academic libraries allows the entire system of higher education in New Jersey to inappropriately believe that it has fully funded a modern, cutting-edge IT environment for its students and faculty. The present situation does not publicly acknowledge the social benefits of VALE's egalitarian approach with its commitment to improve the quality of education at all colleges as a meaningful value-added approach to domestic welfare and American competitiveness.

The Challenge of Future Funding Strategies

Perhaps the key unresolved issue is how to pay for digital library services that reach beyond the wired environs of one library. Building consortia demands a search for new sources of support beyond the local agency's budget office door. Often the search leads to the state government since most states have a commitment to higher education. Many IT library consortia have strong proponents in the academic communities around the state–constituencies which could be mobilized for a political campaign to address funding issues ranging from incremental additions to disparate base budgets to the creation of a new unified source of new funding.

While the VALE leaderships' early arguments for funding were successful, these same arguments may have built-in pitfalls for the future growth of VALE. Many program management services were donated, limiting the agency's ability to ask for funding. This is the crux of a major VALE problem. When the leaders of VALE examine the program goals of the other IT regional agencies, there are only modest differences. Yet, some of the other agencies have budgets that are more than ten times the VALE budget. Their member libraries have never been expected to bear the brunt of the costs. In return the IT library regional agency is expected to demonstrate cost savings to the state funding agencies and legislature with respect to the new program. VALE lost one important chance to make this economic argument at the time it accepted token funding for equipment; it remains to be seen if it will get the chance again.

Two other decisions have potentially negative impacts on VALE's future growth. First, when individual libraries agreed to join VALE, VALE promised it would not expect the library to change its current IT system to conform to a VALE standard. Instead VALE agreed to work with a multiplicity of systems.

However, it may also be true that a promise of an IT agency to support *all* IT systems is a promise that cannot be kept forever. Secondly, when VALE began, it also agreed that each library was equal when it came to receiving service from the VALE technical support group. However, it may be necessary to develop funding models that include charges for services that go beyond a core group of agreed-upon basic services. There have been conscious efforts to improve funding. One related to lobbying for new monies from a projected state surplus, in concert with the state library agency and the state library association, and with the tacit acceptance of the effort by the state higher education leaders. It netted a modest amount, about one-tenth of what was requested. Another effort is linked to a modest, committee-run public relations campaign designed to demonstrate the satisfactions of library users with VALE. It has generated testimony and glad tidings, and photo opportunities with state officials, but no new monies from either surpluses or budgeted priorities in the state budget.

VALE leaders remain hopeful that the power of the digital library concept will be great enough to move state funding decision makers. At present the explicit VALE goal is the provision of state funds for database expansion. However, a more revolutionary VALE goal might be a modification of the current stand-alone model of library governance and organization into a model that incorporates separately funded IT library regional agencies as the preferred model for the delivery of digital library services to the citizens of New Jersey.

REFERENCES

Borgman, C. (2000). *From Gutenberg to the global information infrastructure: Access to information in the networked world.*

Buckland, M. (1992). *Redesigning library services: A manifesto.* Chicago: American Library Association.

Burdick, B. (2001, March/April). The EDUCAUSE guide to evaluating information technology on campus. *EDUCAUSE Review, 64*. Retrieved from http:// www.educause.edu/consumerguide

Coughlin, C., & Gertzog, A. (1992). *Lyle's administration of the college library.* Metuchen, NJ: Scarecrow.

Evans, P. (2000). *Blown to bits: How the new economics of information transforms strategy*. Boston: Harvard Business School Press.

Gardner, C. (2000). *The valuation of information technology: A guide to strategy development, valuation and financial planning*. New York: Wiley.

Georgia. (2001). Galileo information. Retrieved from http:// www.galileo.peachnet.edu.

Haywood, T. (2000). Defining moments: The tension between richness and reach information. *Communication and Society, 3*(4), 648.

Kantor, P. (1995). *Studying the cost and value of library services: Final report*. New Brunswick, NJ: Rutgers University, School of Communication, Information and Library Studies, Alexandria Project Laboratory.

Katz, R. et al. (1999). *Dancing with the devil: Information technology and the new competition in higher education*. San Francisco: Jossey-Bass.

Louisiana. (2001). Louisiana Library Network (LOUIS) information. Retrieved from http://www.lsu.edu/ocs/louis/

Ohio. (2001). OhioLink network information. Retrieved from http://www.ohiolink.edu/

Parang, E., & Saunders, L. (1994). *Electronic journals in ARL libraries: Issues and trends: A SPEC kit*. Washington, DC: Association of Research Libraries, Office of Management Studies.

Porter, M. (1991). *The competitive advantage of nations*. NY: Free Press.

Potter, W. G. (1997, Winter). Recent trends in statewide academic library consortia. GALILEO in Georgia, the Louisiana Library Network, OhioLINK, TexShare in Texas and VIVA: Virtual Library of Virginia. *Library Trends, 45*, 416-34.

Reid, B. & Foster, W. (Eds.). (2000). *Achieving cultural change in networked libraries*. Brookfield, VT: Gower.

Saunders, L. (Ed.). (1999). T*he evolving virtual library II: Practical and philosophical perspectives*. Medford, NJ: Information Today.

Snyder, H., & Davenport, E. (1997). C*osting and pricing in the digital age*. NY: Neal-Schuman.

Taylor, V. A., & Coughlin, C. M. (1999) Activity based costing. In *Proceedings of the Information Resources Management Association Conference,* Hershey, PA.

Taylor, V. A., & Coughlin, C. M. (2000) Value-added measurement: A business perspective on budgeting and resource allocation applied to the non-profit world of libraries. In *Proceedings of the Information Resources Management Association Conference,* Anchorage, AK.

Texas network information. (n.d.). TexShare information. Retrieved from http://texshare.edu/

VALE. (n.d.). VALE network information. Retrieved from http://www.valenj.org

VIVA. (n.d.). VIVA information. Retrieved from http://www.gmu.edu/library/fen/viva/about.html/

Virginia A. Taylor, PhD, is an associate professor at the Department of Marketing and Management, College of Business, William Paterson University. Her doctorate in international business administration is from the Fox School of Business and Management, Temple University. She passed the CPA exam in NJ, has served as founding director for an MBA program, as national university accreditation site evaluator, and as costing consultant to three major university libraries. Her publications focus on the design of multinational control systems, global strategy and transfer pricing, international business ethics, government and business perceptions of value, location determinants for value-added activities, decision support paradigms, the impact of information technology in the workplace and education, and active learning pedagogy.

Caroline M. Coughlin, PhD, is a library consultant who specializes in library planning and staffing issues. She is co-author (with A. Gertzog) of a standard text on academic librarianship. She served as director of the university library at Drew University during the 1980s and 1990s, and was part of the founding information technology team at the university. Her experience as a professor of library science includes over a decade of full-time teaching at Emory University and Simmons College as well as many years of serving as a visiting lecturer at Rutgers University, University of Washington, and University of Alabama as well as some overseas assignments in Wales, Finland and Estonia. Her MLn degree is from Emory University and her PhD is from Rutgers University.

This case was previously published in the *Annals of Cases on Information Technology,* Volume 4/2002, pp. 345-359, © 2002.

Chapter XV

Prudential Chamberlain Stiehl: The Evolution of an IT Architecture for a Residential Real Estate Firm, 1996-2001

Andy Borchers, Kettering University, USA

Bob Mills, Prudential Chamberlain Stiehl Realtors, USA

EXECUTIVE SUMMARY

This case describes the evolution of an IT architecture for Prudential Chamberlain Stiehl Realtors (PCSR), a 14-office, 250-sales-agent real estate firm located in Southeast Michigan. Initially, the CIO of the firm concentrated on providing basic connectivity to sales agents and a simple World Wide Web (WWW) presence. Although this was accepted by users and moved the firm forward technically, management questioned the value of this technology. In the next phase of development, PCSR worked to build a "rich" set of applications that enhance the firm's relationships with clients and agents. At the end of the case, the CIO ponders future moves in technology and their impact on the firm's strategy.

BACKGROUND

Prudential Chamberlain Stiehl Realtors (PCSR) is a residential real estate brokerage operating in the upscale northern suburbs of Detroit and Flint, Michigan. The firm's roots go back to 1948, but their current organization came about through a series of mergers between several area realtors in the 1990s. In 2001 the firm has two owners that believe that control of the residential real estate market will belong to a set of very large firms and small niche players. The owners have worked aggressively to stake out a significant share of the area's real estate market and survive in an era of escalating competition and declining profit margins.

Current Operation

In 2001 the firm's operation includes 14 sales offices. The organization's employs about 300 employees, including 250 sales representatives and 50 support personnel. The offices are spread across a 70-mile span from north of Flint to Royal Oak, a Detroit suburb. This area comprises one of the richest markets in the state of Michigan. Oakland County, the heart of PCSR's market, had a median income of nearly $60,000 in 1997. The area is home to over 1,000,000 people. PCSR's annual real estate sales in 2000 were approximately $600 million. Broker commissions on these sales were about $18 million per year. The firm is the largest Prudential franchisee in the state of Michigan and one of the largest in the United States. PCSR has a sizeable market share. In the Flint area, for example, nearly 40% of all home sales are through PCSR.

The belief that the company needs to grow to survive is largely created by market conditions. The Southeast Michigan real estate brokerage business is highly fractured with small market share per broker. The sales associates who actually deal with clients (both sellers and buyers) are independent contractors paid on a commission basis. Typically, associates receive commission on a sliding scale. Associates can only be compensated by one broker. However, associates can easily move from one broker to another.

Industry Composition

Although there are a number of national real estate firms, including Century 21, ReMax, Prudential and others, all of these firms franchise local operations. The national firms provide marketing and advertising support. Operation of the local business, however, is strongly controlled by local brokers and their agents.

The industry has seen a reduction in the number of associates, coupled with a sharp increase in sales volumes per associate. For example, during the five years ending in early 2001, nearly half of all sales associates left the Southeast Michigan market. In all likelihood this trend will continue for the foreseeable future. The cost of participating as a sales associate, nearly $4,000 per year to maintain memberships and licenses, plus fierce competition leads weaker associates to leave the field. Strong associates, however, have much to gain by selling more and more homes given the sliding commission scales used to compensate them.

This environment has created intense competition among brokers to recruit effective sales associates. High selling associates can easily change brokers if they see the potential for higher return or better support. This has forced brokers to pay higher commissions to associates and has hurt their profit margins. The competition for sales associates has had other effects besides increased commissions. Brokers are under pressure to provide sales associates with more support. Services such as office facilities, marketing and technology have become points of comparison that sales associates now use to compare brokers.

As a class of goods, homes have several unique characteristics. First, home purchases are typically the single largest purchase made by a consumer. Unlike other major purchases, such as automobiles, each home is unique and the "market" for a home is made through a bid and counter bid process. While comparable properties may be known in the community, putting a home on the market and seeing what a buyer will pay for it is the only true way to determine value.

Purchase Process

The process of buying a home can be viewed as a series of steps taken by buyer and seller. In most cases sellers are simultaneously in the process of buying as well.

1. **Education** — In this phase the buyer asks, "What can I afford?" "What features do I want in a house?" and "What is available in the market?" The seller asks, "What is my house worth?"
2. **Listing** — In this phase the seller arranges to list his property with a broker.
3. **Matching** — In this phase one or more sales associates works to match buyers and sellers. Associates arrange open houses and visits by prospective purchasers.
4. **Negotiation** — In this phase buyers make offers and sellers accept, counter or reject these offer.
5. **Financing** — In this phase the buyer obtains financing for the home.
6. **Closing** — In this final phase the deal is legally executed.

This list is comparable to Crowston's (2000, p. 4-6) analysis.

There are several opportunities for technology to speed up or alter this process.

Crowston (2000) identifies real estate as having strong potential for e-markets as it is "information-intensive and information-driven industry; transaction-based, with high value and asset-specificity; with many market-intermediaries (agents and brokers who connect buyers and sellers rather than buying or selling themselves); and experiencing on-going information technology (IT) related changes." He suggests that Web technology could damage the information monopoly that real estate agents have enjoyed and lead to disintermediation. Indeed, real estate brokers are pure intermediaries (Crowston, 2001). They rarely own the properties that they sell. Their position is at risk if sellers can find lower cost alternatives to market their homes. Further, he warns that such disintermediation could undermine profit margins and ultimately end the broker's business.

PCSR's Strategy

PCSR, however, is operating in strong opposition to this analysis. Instead of letting new Internet sites neutralize their market presence, PCSR is using technology to enhance their position. PCSR's approach focuses on using technology to build a "rich" mix of services to buyers, sellers and sales associates that justifies the cost of a broker in a home sale. The firm believes that "service sells" and that their strategy will succeed in the face of efforts to disintermediate and commoditize their industry. This case outlines the evolution of technology at PCSR and the impact of technology on the firm's competitive position.

SETTING THE STAGE

Historically, technology was not a competitive issue within the real estate market. All brokers belonged to a local association called the Multiple Listing Service (MLS). Computer systems within the office were limited to a few dumb terminals that associates shared. The type, performance, contents and number of terminals was controlled by the MLS, not the broker. This resulted in all brokers having essentially the same technology.

The introduction of the PC and the evolution of the World Wide Web in the late 1990s changed this environment dramatically. The introduction of PCs allowed sales associates and customers to automate and speed up the home buying process. Several vendors introduced low cost tools for sales associates, brokers and related firms. A review of available real estate software shows several categories of software:

- **Appraisal** — Software that automates the appraisal process.
- **Closing** — This category allows for automation of the closing process.
- **Mortgage** — Software that helps identify mortgage options for buyers.
- **Investment analysis** — This category of software helps in valuing real estate.

- **Multiple listing** — MLS (Multiple Listing Services) provide realtors with information about available properties.
- **Property management** — Software to automate the management of rental properties.
- **Relocation** — Cost tracking and reporting software for customers who are relocating.

With the WWW came two well-established Web sites that continue to list large numbers of properties: Homeadvisor.com and Realtor.com. These sites help consumers quickly identify properties of interest in a given locale. However, these sites rarely list the address of actual properties. Customers are given the name of the listing agent and must contact them to view the home. Of further concern, the information listed at these two sites is often out of date.

Acceptance of computer technology has varied significantly among real estate agents, however. In 2001 the average PCSR sales associate, for example, is in his or her early 50s. Although some have embraced computer technology, others have not. Further, they are serving home purchasers that have an average age of just 38. Increasingly PCSR's younger customers have PCs at home and are capable WWW users.

Two other changes also impacted the situation. The first occurred when the MLS dropped the limitations on the number of PCs or terminals in a sales office. This seemingly small change brought competition to the technology area because now a broker could make access to the MLS available to all of his associates. The second change was the MLS allowing agents to have access through their home PCs. This changed the atmosphere of the real estate offices by changing the sales associate's perception that access to the MLS was granted by the broker. The amount of time sales associates spent in the office dropped dramatically. The dependence sales associates had on their brokers also dropped and with it their commitment to a single broker.

These changes challenged two beliefs in the industry among sales associates. First, it was considered normal for 30 sales associates to share two or three PCs. Unlike many other industries where each individual has his own computer, sales associates were used to shared PCs. Second, the sales associates expected the broker to deliver new technology. Computer systems were viewed as the responsibility of the broker, and most sales associates expected that relationship to carry forward.

CASE DESCRIPTION

Bob Mills, VP of Finance and CIO for Prudential Chamberlain Stiehl Realtors, has been responsible for the technology focus of the company from the mid-1990s through the present. In meeting with the case writer in early 2001, he reflected back on the firm's early efforts to build an infrastructure for basic connectivity.

Initial Implementation

"It was early 1996, right after the merger of our two owners, Dan and Jerry, that we really started getting serious about technology," Bob explains. "At that time I was really working in a vacuum. Dan and Jerry are not technically proficient, and never will be. It's not their focus in the business. However, we were getting a lot of pressure from the sales associates to give them the most current tools. Dan and Jerry did believe this was an important area to compete on, and one we could make a difference on."

"I have always struggled to get good input," Bob continues. "It is a very unique industry, often with material differences from market to market. I find people outside the industry don't understand the structure. For example, my customer is really the real estate sales associate, not the person buying a house. An experienced sales associate can go to work for any broker in town. They are in very high demand. Because they are independent contractors, we do not tell them what to do. Each one is an independent business. The only way I can increase the brokers' revenue is to attract more sales associates."

There were several other important issues to deal with in early 1996. The company did not employ any IT staff and with pressure on profit margins, the owners wanted to avoid staff additions if possible. Each office had three or four PCs. All were standalone with modem dial up to the MLS system. Top producing, as well as younger sales associates, bought their own PCs to use at home. Individual agent PCs within the office were still rare.

"I knew that I had to get more input from the customer — our sales associates," Bob explains. "So we created a technology advisory council made up of two associates from each office. I also invited the branch managers to attend to get some management involvement. Response to the council was very enthusiastic. We meet once a month for two hours and attendance has always been excellent. The feedback we get from this group has been invaluable."

"We had these great ideas coming out of the advisory council but we needed some way of testing them," Bob continues. "So we set up a test branch, and started trying out several new ideas. We learned a lot of valuable lessons in a very short period of time. We tested the concept of sales associate rental machines, server-based applications, automating several key processes, and digital circuit connections to the MLS and Internet. We also learned several important lessons on what not to do. I quickly realized that having a server in each sales branch and having a lot of applications loaded on each desktop was not going to be compatible with our goal of minimizing internal IT staff."

Using these lessons learned during 1996, Bob Mills began to put together a long-range IT plan to make PCSR a technology leader in its marketplace. "The goals I focused on were quite simple," explains Bob. "We wanted to offer the best services to our associates, create a dependence by the sales associates on our IT services, keep maintenance and staff requirements to a minimum, and position ourselves to automate some processes that would make us a leader. We also knew that we would have to get the sales associates to participate in the cost, which had proven very difficult in past projects."

"By the end of 1996, I was selling a three-year plan to management," says Bob. "It is very difficult when you are working with such a long-range perspective because you have to stay away from specific details. However, I felt we had so far to go we had to take a long-range approach. Actually, you have to sell your plan to everyone: users, suppliers and management. They are all critical to making it work."

"My approach was to explain the vision which included a WAN (wide area network) connecting all offices, applications delivered from a centralized location, all connections to be reliable digital circuits (no modems), full sharing of data between offices, and centralized administration. Then I would explain some benefits like lower cost, location independence, concentration and specialization of some process that people could relate to. The general game plan was to build the infrastructure in year one, gain sales associate participation in year two, and automate several key processes and integrate with suppliers in year three."

"The hardest part of selling the plan to management was the lack of deliverables in the first year," explains Bob. "Our schedule had us installing a lot of wire, NICs (network interface cards), routers and infrastructure type equipment. Everyone would keep asking "and what do we get for this?" I would have to keep explaining that it was a foundation and that nothing else could be done without it. We got through it, but it took a lot of patience from everyone."

The owners of Prudential Chamberlain Stiehl Realtors did accept the three-year plan and work began in early 1997. The early work of installing local area networks in the sales branches went smoothly. A joint project was started with the largest MLS to install a frame relay network between the company's sales offices, the MLS and the Internet. It was fortuitous as the MLS was installing a new system at this time that was plagued with modem problems. While Prudential's competitors struggled to make the new dial-up system work, Prudential's associates enjoyed fast, trouble-free access to the MLS system.

"It was kind of humorous," recalls Bob Mills. "I was worried about not having a deliverable of any significance in the first year of the plan and suddenly we had a big one. In fact, it created problems that management did not feel we were moving fast enough with the frame relay rollout."

The success of frame relay connections also created a new dilemma. The sales associates were used to having the same MLS service from home and the office. Now they had a faster and more reliable connection at the office.

Requests started coming in from the associates to hook up their own computers to the PCSR network or to rent desktops for their personal use in the office.

This type of participation was a goal of Bob's IT plans and supported the owner's goals for recruitment and retention of associates. However, it was decided to hold to the plan of rolling out the company-wide WAN before adding the associates on a large scale. The decision created some conflict during 1997, but by year-end all of the offices were installed on the WAN.

The goal for 1998 was to gain agent participation. Management decided to offer two options: sales associates could either pay to hook up their own computer to the network, or the firm would provide a turn-key rental unit.

"The first option was easy to provide," explains Bob Mills. "We are just providing a connection method to the MLS or the Internet that's better than a modem connection." This approach was made available first in the sales offices and immediately became popular with the sales associates who had their own portable computers.

The second option proved much more challenging to fulfill. "I really wanted to avoid having to install the half-dozen Windows-based application on each desktop we put out there" explained Bob. "You have to understand we are talking about offices that are an hour-and-a-half drive apart, and users who are not very sophisticated. I knew we had to find a different approach to keep our administrative costs down." The approach that Bob settled on was a product by

Figure 1. Network configuration — 1998 Winframe Solution

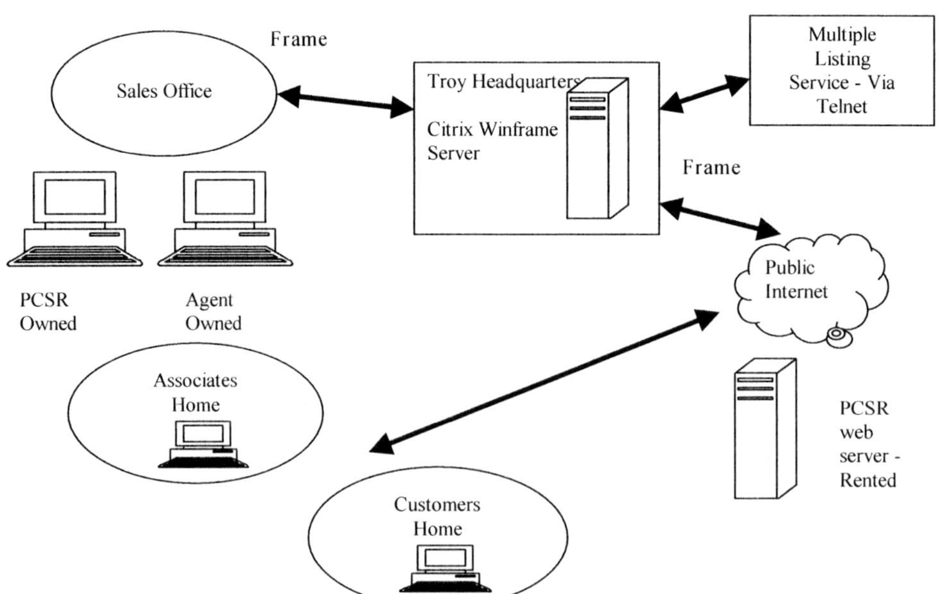

Figure 2. MLS listing — Via Telnet

Address: 875 N ADAMS
City/Township: Waterford
County: Oak
Post Office: Waterford
Zip Code: 48320
Price: $149,900
Total Finish Area: 1290
Status: Active
MLS #: 21175450
Style: Ranch
Aprx. Yr Blt: 1965
Bedrooms: 3
Baths Total: 2
Basement: Y
Garage: 2 Car, Detached
Acreage: 0
Lot Size: 70X126
Paved Road:Y
Water Front:
Design: 1 Story
Basement: Part. Finished, Yes
Exterior: Brick
Fireplace: Y
HVAC: Steam, 2+window Ac
Fuel: Gas
Waste: Sewer Sanitary
Water: Mun. Water
Other Bldgs:
Homestead: Y
Winter Taxes: $3,909.00
Remarks: Ranch Home With Character And Charm. Newer Kitchen, Neutral Decor,natural Fireplace In Living Room, Hardwood Floors Throughout, Partially Finished Basement. 12x9 Sunroom Off 2ndbedroom. Covered Porch Off
Dining Room. Newer Sewer Line Into House. Home Warranty.
Rooms Location Size
Kitchen: 1 12X12
Dining: 1 13X12
Living Room: 1 20X12
Family Room:
Bedroom #1: 12X12
Bedroom #2: 15X09
Bedroom #3: 14X09
Bedroom #4:
Special Rooms:
Misc. Exterior: Porch, Fenced, Outside Lights
Misc. Interior: Stove, Refrigerator, Dishwasher,
Disposal, Cable Tv
For more information call:
Information herein deemed reliable but not guaranteed and may be incomplete.

Citrix called Winframe. It allows for the delivery of Windows-based programs over a dial up or WAN connection, treating the desktop like a dumb terminal. This technology allowed Bob to centrally control software applications and data resources, and minimize the need to visit client PCs in the field.

The Winframe solution provided associates with a number of tools. With this solution agents could:

1. Connect into the MLS using Telnet to view listings.
2. Use Bressers and PACE, two CD ROM databases on property data.
3. Perform file transfer — To circumvent file protection problems, the Winframe solution allowed users to run Word 97 or Excel to open up a file. Users could then save a file to a shared directory.
4. Online forms (purchase agreement, listing agreement, etc.) — These online forms became a common way for sales associates to process transactions.
5. Communicate via e-mail with customers and fellow sales associates.

The new server was installed during the first quarter of 1998, but a large acquisition put everything on hold. "Just as we were ready to start converting the windows applications to the new server, we bought four new offices," Bob explained. "We had to go back and do infrastructure work on the new locations before we could roll out the new system. The acquisition put us into the third

Figure 3. Winframe menu

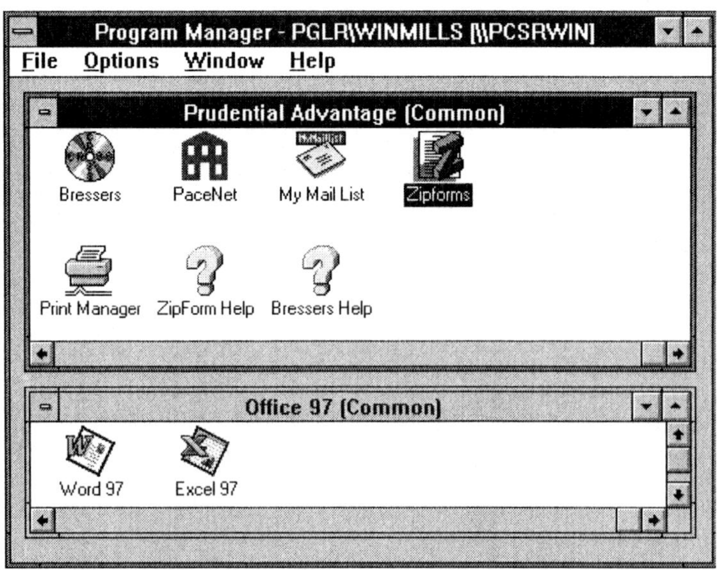

Figure 4. Pace CD display

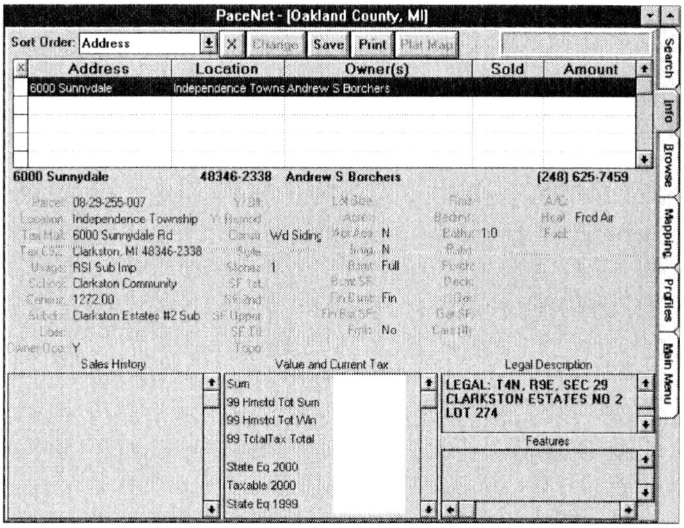

quarter before we could continue with the rollout." The Winframe system was successful in meeting the objectives of providing firm-wide connectivity, access to shared data and a platform for process automation. New desktops could be configured with a minimum of administration and maintenance, and the system was opened up to the agent hookups and rentals in the fourth quarter of 1998. "We spent the last three months adding sales associates to the network," states Bob. "I am really happy with the response, but it has been a zoo. We now have over 50 of our 250 sales associates paying to use our network, and the number is climbing fast. We have even figured out how to give these associates access from home through the Internet, creating our own VPN." A VPN is a Virtual Private Network. VPNs give the appearance of a private network while using the public Internet to keep costs low.

Evaluating the Initial Implementation

In early 2001 Bob Mills took stock of his network configuration and future business plans. Over the prior three years, PC equipment, the Winframe Citrix server and the Internet had become an integrated part of his firm. Bob's IT staff remains limited to his part-time efforts and two part-time college students. This is essential to meet the firm's need for "lean" administration. Indeed, IT costs are viewed as overhead and a drag on bottom-line profits.

The interplay of IT strategy and business strategy at PCSR is an interesting example. At first, IT was hardly a driver for the firm's strategy. Mergers fueled growth and survival for the firm in an increasingly hostile market. The owners viewed IT as providing two key advantages, support of operating processes (such as sales agreements, closing documents, etc.) and as a recruiting tool to draw sales agents from competing brokers. As the IT infrastructure matured and competition increased, the owners increasingly looked to IT for rich information content and as a differentiator for the firm. These areas proved much more challenging to provide than the initial efforts at achieving connectivity.

A Second Implementation

A new effort began in early 2001 to build custom applications that increase PCSR's service to associates, sellers and customers. It was not enough to merely present information to agents, as real estate information is increasingly available for little or no cost. Instead, PCSR had to increase the value of its information to all stakeholders. With respect to agents, Bob wanted them so involved in using the technology that they could not think of working without it. This dependence was important if PCSR was to retain agents, and hence sales revenue.

With this effort Bob installed a new hardware configuration.

At the center of this configuration is an Oracle database server that receives 70,000 records daily from the multiple listing services that support PCSR's service area. PCSR is developing customized applications that process this data into useful information for agents. Bob also has acquired a LINUX-based Web server that presents information to users from the database server. The Citrix Winframe server remains in use to support sales associates. With this data, Bob staked out the following functionality:

- For buyers, Bob wants to provide a "rich" set of information about PCSR listings, including a virtual tour of PCSR properties. Further, he wants to offer customers who are willing to sign a customer agreement the ability to search the MLS by themselves on the WWW, including the ability to see property addresses, without having to contact a PCSR agent.
- For sellers, Bob wants to provide information about what PCSR has done to sell their properties. Given the size of commissions (typically $20,000 on a $400,000 home), sellers need to know that PCSR is actively working to sell their home.
- For PCSR agents, Bob wants to project the image that they have the most up-to-date technology. This is essential to retain them. Tools include CMA (Comparable Market Analysis) that allows the agent to do a market analysis online, access to online property data and MLS, the existing Winframe applications and attractions for buyers, such as the virtual tour.

Figure 5. 2001 configuration

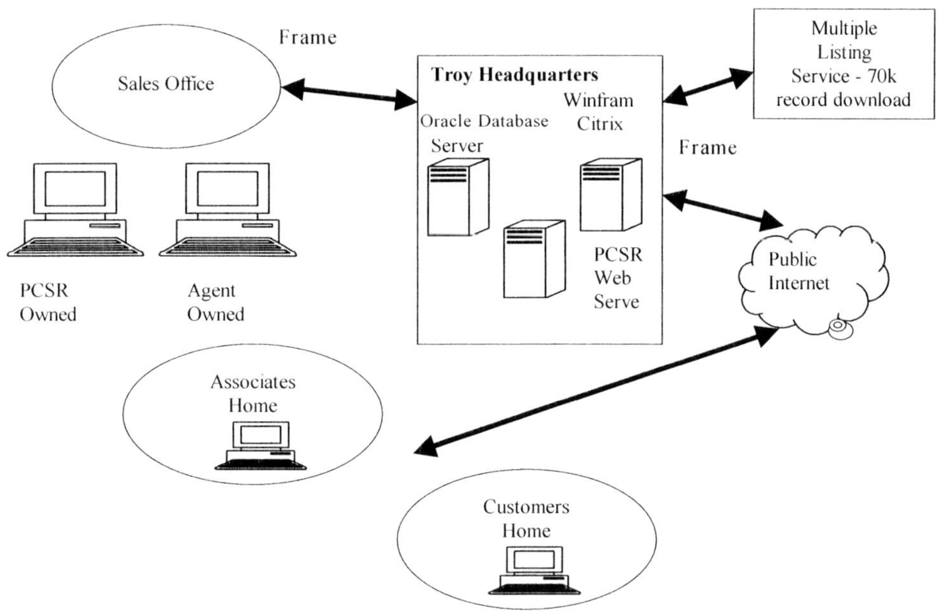

With all of the new applications, agent's work habits will be tied to technology. Virtually all of their activities, from looking for a property to reporting on sales activities to closing, involve the use of PCSR's technology.

- For non-PCSR agents, Bob want to communicate with them in a hope of interesting them in PCSR. After a house showing by a PCSR agent of a non-PCSR-listed property, it is typical to provide feedback to the listing agent. PCSR wants to use this opportunity to e-mail non-PCSR agents.

Evolving Markets

As Bob is introducing this new functionality, competition in the real estate market remains fierce. In 2001 PCSR has approximately the same number of agents as three years ago, but has only been able to maintain this number by acquiring new offices. A number of weaker competitors have dropped out of the market, but the remaining firms are challenging to compete with.

Meanwhile, the growth of the Internet had been nothing less than spectacular. The stock prices of Internet start-up firms such as Amazon.com soared on unrealistic expectations up until mid-2000 and then crashed in early 2001 when reality set in. Expectations continue to run high that virtually all products will be

Figure 6. Home owner's activity report — MLS # 21000774, Randy Goodie Tuesday, January 30, 2001

HOME OWNER'S ACTIVITY REPORT
ACTIVE 29753 Main, Clarkston, MI 48346 $339,900
Activity Date Agent Name Feedback Information
39387 W. Thirteen Mile, Suite 100
Farmington Hill, MI 48331
Phone: (248)999-9999
Email: rgoodie@pcsr.com
Page 1
01/29/01 Progress Report e-mailed activity update to Beth
01/29/01 Showing Home showing from 4:30 pm to 5:30 pm
01/29/01 Reverse Prospect reverse prospect match and brochure follow up completed Match
01/29/01 Showing Nice home. One of the cleanest that they've seen. Priced too high for the sq footage. They are looking for something bigger.
01/28/01 Showing Home showing from 2:00 pm to 4:00 pm
01/28/01 Showing Home showing from 2:00 pm to 4:00 pm
01/28/01 Advertised - Ad # 1 was published in the Detroit News & Free Press Section: DS using format: Detroit News & Fr DS number of lines: 9 Price published: 339,900
01/27/01 Showing purchased another home in same square mile for about the same price -
01/27/01 Showing buyers thought home was priced too high and was not large enouph for them / basement only being partial was a large deterant
01/26/01 Showing Home showing from 1:00 pm to 2:30 pm
01/25/01 Showing Unable to contact agent for comment.
01/24/01 Progress Report written status mailed to home
01/23/01 Showing customer had no interest
01/22/01 Reverse Prospect reverse prospect match and brochure follow up completed Match

bought and sold on the Internet. With the growth of e-commerce comes the commonly accepted wisdom that customers are "king" and all firms seemingly face commoditization of their markets and declining prices.

The reality of the Internet revolution, however, is far more complex than this. As Wilder (1998) identifies, there are numerous myths and realities. Moving from traditional business relationships to Web-enabled commerce is neither easy nor cheap. Not everyone is making the move nor does the Web inevitably to disintermediation. In real estate, for example, early Web implementation by many players focused on only limited aspects of the business such as financing and display of information on properties. To truly upset the traditional sales channel, Web infomediaries need to provide "integrated, single source, highly personalized experience" (Hagel, 1999, p. 61). Such integration is not evident in any current Web presence.

Figure 7. PCSR main Web page

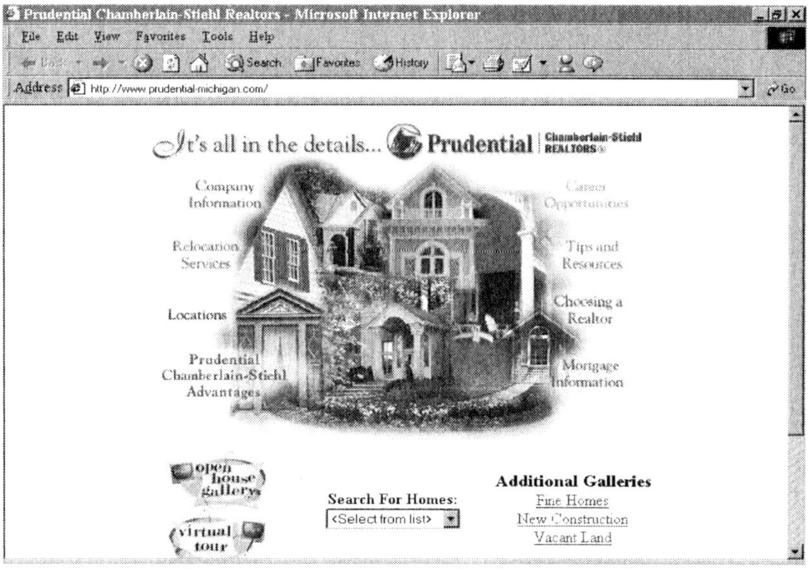

Figure 8. Agent's home page

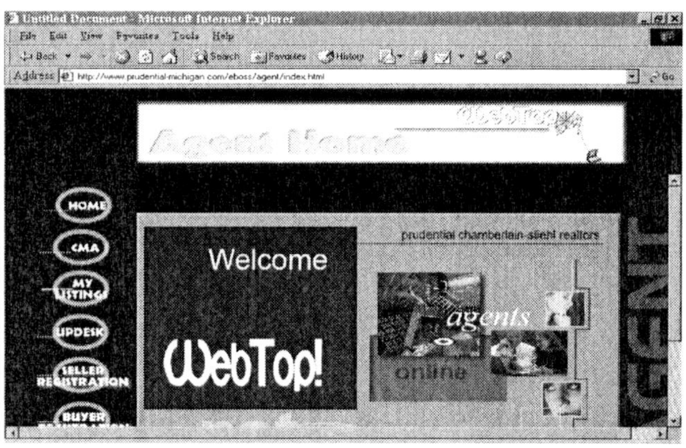

Figure 9. PCSR Listing

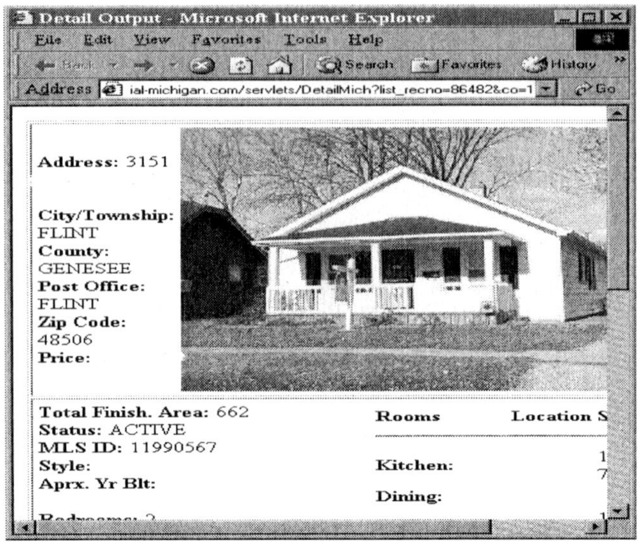

Figure 10. Virtual tour

Bob's strategy can be viewed in the context of Evans and Wurster's (2000) classic richness versus reach analysis. According to Evans (p. 24), firms typically face a tradeoff of "richness" and "reach." For example, a firm can employ a "rich" strategy of using commissioned sales representatives. However, such a strategy is normally restricted by the ability of representatives to make sales calls. Firms, alternatively, can employ high "reach" strategies with lower "reach." For example firms can choose to advertise on TV or radio.

The growth of information technology, and in particular, the Web challenges this tradeoff. With the WWW the tradeoff line can shift upward and to the right, due to the "explosion of connectivity" and "dissemination of standards" (Evans, p. 31). Bob's strategy is to work to the upper left of the tradeoff line with "rich" technology support and the firm's traditional strong personal sales support. Other competitors have used the Web to focus on increasing "reach," primarily in obtaining sales leads. They are working on the lower right part of the tradeoff line.

CURRENT CHALLENGES/PROBLEMS FACING THE ORGANIZATION

As Bob reflected on the state of the firm's IT infrastructure in early 2001, he turned back to the situation at the end of 1998. At that point Dan and Jerry, the owners, were pleased that their sales associates considered themselves technical leaders, but felt there should be more value for their IT spending. Bob's bosses wanted to know then if this IT spending would lead to hiring more sales associates and improved business processes. These questions continue to haunt Bob in 2001. As quickly as PCSR implements technology and improves business operations, management senses a renewed level of competition that has to be responded to. Can PCSR ever achieve and maintain a competitive advantage in the real estate market through IT?

Bob is amazed at the progress the company had made in achieving connectivity throughout the organization and how they had begun to build

Figure 11. Richness/Reach tradeoff

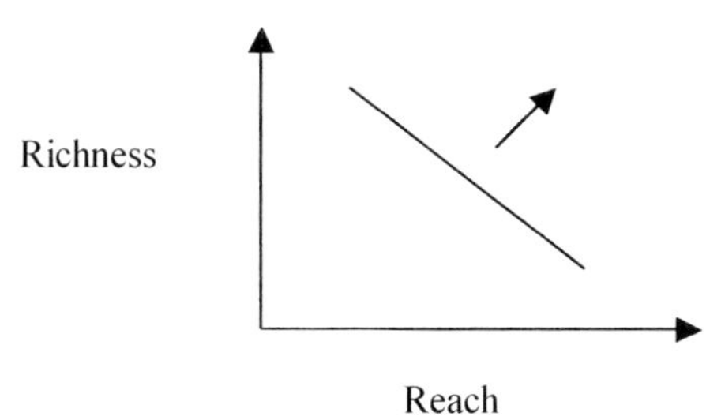

Figure 12. Web usage report — Usage statistics for prudential-michigan.com

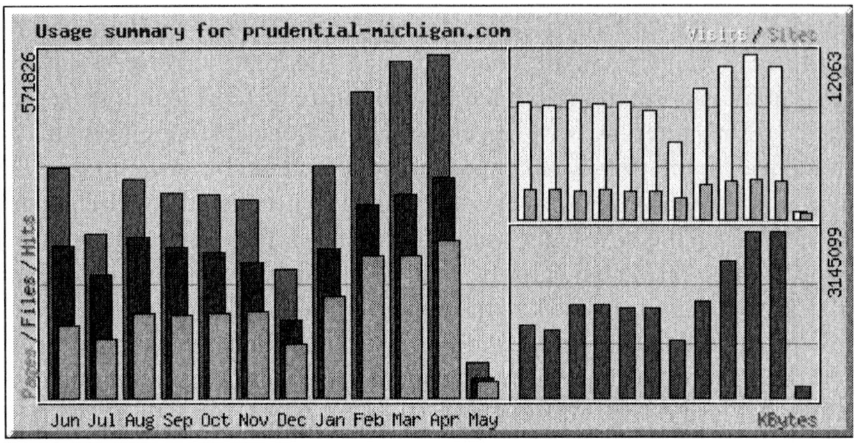

Summary by Month										
Month	Daily Avg				Monthly Totals					
	Hits	Files	Pages	Visits	Sites	KBytes	Visits	Pages	Files	Hits
May 2001	28786	16388	12899	296	451	198793	593	25798	32777	57572
Apr 2001	19060	12138	8696	372	2750	3145099	11177	260888	364166	571826
Mar 2001	18017	10890	7626	389	2936	3134009	12063	236422	337618	558533
Feb 2001	18140	11445	8364	398	2774	2585424	11150	234212	320475	507929
Jan 2001	12367	7962	5402	308	2510	1823284	9555	167475	246829	383394
Dec 2000	6825	4168	2845	181	1587	1069249	5633	88209	129236	211589
Nov 2000	10975	7442	4726	266	2045	1689554	7984	141786	223288	329254
Oct 2000	10874	7798	4506	277	2074	1688964	8594	139694	241738	337101
Sep 2000	11294	8277	4537	280	2105	1748531	8427	136133	248314	338842
Aug 2000	11688	8558	4473	281	2074	1753287	8728	138672	265313	362341
Jul 2000	8807	6627	3093	268	2116	1256423	8310	95887	205437	273044
Jun 2000	12731	8435	3986	286	2143	1356680	8598	119582	253074	381931
Totals						**21449298**	**100812**	**1784758**	**2868265**	**4313356**

Summary Period: Last 12 Months

applications. Even with the acquisitions of new offices, the game plan is basically on track. But as he looked back over the past several years, there is a sinking feeling, however, that this was the easy part. Bob knew that he needed to add new applications to leverage his infrastructure and fully use and share information throughout the firm.

In 2001 Bob also has several management issues to attend to. First, his efforts to build applications based on Oracle and Web technology had proven very difficult to manage. Given the fact that he has no full-time development staff, all development work is outsourced to contract programmers. At this point, Bob is budgeting programming effort and cost, but he has little idea how to manage development of any given project to a completion date. Should Bob continue custom development? Or should he search for third-party software? If he simply buys third-party software, what advantage will he have over his competitors?

Second, Bob wants to combine voice and data to get the most out of his communication dollars. But who should Bob turn to, to provide integrated voice and data? Many of his potential suppliers focused on one or the other. Third, Bob's IT staff is limited to a couple of part-time employees that configure PCs and the network, but as the firm's infrastructure grows, the maintenance and support gets harder to handle. Should Bob consider outsourcing of his network support needs? If so, what type of firm should he look at — a local vendor VAR or systems support firm? Or a support organization out of a national computer firm?

Bob also has to consider how to relate to his peers on the management team. He had delivered the best technology in the industry, but they do not know how to use it to recruit new agents, the single biggest selling point of the technology to management. Bob is confident his implementation offers the best services to the sales associates in the marketplace, but it does not seem to be helping to recruit sales associates. What, Bob wondered, should he say to his peers?

Bob has more tactical matters to consider. Web usage statistics show a respectable hit rate. But Bob wants to double the hit rate on the site. At the same time, Bob wonders, "What is the value of a hit?" "How much does the Web help me reach buyers versus how much does the Web help me satisfy sellers and sales associates?"

Finally, at a more strategic level Bob has to consider the future of the real estate market in Southeast Michigan. First, who will master the Web-enabled real estate market? Will strong regional operators like his firm continue to largely control the business? Or will national firms develop Web strategies and reduce the power of brokers? Or will "pure play" Internet firms invade the industry? Having read of the impact of the Web on other industries, such as travel, Bob is concerned. Echoing Evans and Wurster (2000): "How vulnerable is the "venerable" PCSR in this market?"

Bob wonders how his IT infrastructure will support the firm in coming years. The real estate industry was sure to undergo change. Continued consolidation of brokers was highly likely. Could his infrastructure help the firm adapt to market changes? What new technologies, such as wireless, should he adapt to support the firm's strategic needs?

REFERENCES

Crowston, K., Sawyer, S., & Wigand, R. (2001). Investigating the interplay between structure and information and communications technology in the real estate industry. *Information, Technology and People, 15*(2).

Crowston, K., & Wigand, R. (n.d.). *Real estate war in cyberspace: An emerging electronic market?* Retrieved January 13, 2001, from http://www.isworld.org

Wilder, C. (1998, December 7). Myths and realities. *Information Week.*

FURTHER READING

Afuah, A., & Tucci, C. (2000). *Internet business models and strategies: Text and cases.* New York: McGraw Hill.

Crowston, K., Sawyer, S., & Wigand, R. (2001). Investigating the interplay between structure and information and communications technology in the real estate industry. *Information, Technology and People, 15*(2).

Crowston, K., & Wigand, R. (n.d.). *Real estate war in cyberspace: An emerging electronic market?* Retrieved January 13, 2001, from http://www.isworld.org

D'Aveni, R. A., & Gunther, R. (1994) *Hypercompetition: Managing the dynamics of strategic maneuvering.* New York: Free Press.

Evans, P., & Wurster, T. (1997). The new economics of information. *Harvard Business Review.*

Evans, P., & Wurster, T. (2000). *Blown to bits: How the new economics of information transforms strategy.* Boston: Harvard Business School Press.

Hagel, J., & Singer, M. (1999). *Net worth.* Boston: Harvard Business School Press.

Stanfill, J. (2000). How brokers can counter the risks of disintermediation by embracing leveraging technology trends. *Real Estate Issues, 24*(4).

Turban, E., Lee, J., King, D., & Chung, H. M. (2000). *Electronic commerce: A managerial perspective.* Upper Saddle, NJ: Prentice Hall.

Wilder, C. (1998, December 7). Myths and realities. *Information Week.*

Andy Borchers, DBA, is an associate professor of information systems at Kettering University. He spent 21 years working for General Motors and Electronic Data Systems before turning to full-time teaching in 1997. His teaching and research interests are varied and include database management, electronic commerce and management of information systems organizations. Andy earned a Bachelors of Industrial Administration from Kettering University, an MBA from Vanderbilt University and a DBA from Nova Southeastern University.

Robert Mills is CFO and CIO of Prudential Chamberlin Stiehl Realtors. He holds an MSIS from Lawrence Technological University.

This case was previously published in the *Annals of Cases on Information Technology*, Volume 4/2002, pp. 360-375, © 2002.

About the Editor

Mehdi Khosrow-Pour, DBA, is executive director of the Information Resources Management Association (IRMA) and senior academic technology editor for Idea Group Inc. Previously, he served on the faculty of the Pennsylvania State University as a professor of information systems for 20 years. He has written or edited more than 30 books in information technology management. Dr. Khosrow-Pour is also editor-in-chief of the *Information Resources Management Journal*, *Journal of Electronic Commerce in Organizations*, *Journal of Cases on Information Technology,* and *International Journal of Cases on Electronic Commerce*.

Index

A

account management database 239
ACORN (see Administrative Conversion: Operational Redesign and Innovation)
active server pages (ASP) 155
adaptability 214
administration 113
administrative computing 104
Administrative Conversion: Operational Redesign and Innovation (ACORN) 107
administrative information system (AIS) 105, 122
administrative services 82
agents 271
AIIA Corp. 227
Algos Center 47
alliance 3
alumni development system 110
application service provider (ASP) 132, 228
archiving 184

B

Blackboard™ 155

C

Cabrillo College 105, 106, 111
CAMS© (see Community/course Action/interaction Management System)
CASE (see computer-aided software engineering)
case management subsystem 86
Charlotte-Mecklenburg Police Department (CMPD) 82
CIM (see customer interaction management)
class 233
classification system 127
clustering 196
collaboration 160
Community/course Action/interaction Management System (CAMS©) 154
computer-aided software engineering (CASE) 89
conceptual schema (CS) 203
constraints 68
consulting 72

contract 217
conversion process 110
conversion strategy 107
corporate law reform program (CLERP) 190
cost recovery process 149
cost savings 64, 260
customer interaction management (CIM) 231
customer interaction management system 239
customer quality information system 137

D

data definitions 149
data integrity 113
data maintenance 109
data mining 191, 199
data warehouse (DW) 27, 238
data warehouse design and development 27
data warehouse project 27
data warehousing 135
data warehousing administration 141
decision making 148
decision support 137
decision support system 29
dependent entity contract 217
developing economy 125
dimensional modeling (DM) 36

E

economic models 252
EDI (see electronic data interchange)
EDM (see electronic document management)
EIS (see executive information system)
electronic access 256
electronic data interchange (EDI) 29, 128
electronic document management (EDM) 172
enquiry equivalents (EEs) 9
enterprise resource planning (ERP) 44
environment 214
ERP (see enterprise resource planning)
Euclidean distance 196
executive information system (EIS) 27

F

fiber-optic media 88
financial advisor 233
flow replenishment system 30

G

geographic information system (GIS) 64, 70
global positioning systems (GPS) 70
globalization of business operations 135
graphical user interface (GUI) 191

H

harmonized system 126
human resources 111
human resources analyst 114

I

IS projects 27
implementing 64
import/export unit 127
incident reporting subsystem 84
incremental development 159
information modeling 205
information resource management model 105
information systems (IS) 31, 64, 83
information technology (IT) 42
insurance companies 190
integer programming 196
inter-organizational systems (IOSs) 5
international operating systems (IOS) 72
International Standards Organization (ISO) 137
Internet service provider 131
investment research database 239
investor 233
IS (see information systems)
ISO 9002 171
ISO (see International Standards Organization)
IT (see information technology)
IT projects 27

J

JeansWear 26

K

Knowledge-Based Community Oriented Policing System (KBCOPS) 81

L

LAN (see local area network)
LIBNET 1
library management 244
library systems 3
Life Care Program (LCP) 47
local area network (LAN) 88
logistics 66

M

Malcolm Baldrige Award 137
management 285
management initiative 95
managerial models 252
manufacturing 64
map data 71
market research 240
market response system 29
Melbourne Automobile Insurers (MAI) 190
method of operation (MO) 86
micro-marketing 31
Monash University 191
monolithic software model 106

N

near infrared (NIR) light 78
network interface cards (NICs) 273
neural networks 196
neurons 197
NICs (see network interface cards)
nonrivalous consumption 2

O

OCMS (see online course management systems)
OLAP and data mining 30
online analytical processing (OLAP) 190
online course management systems (OCMS) 154
operations 64

P

PC Trade 127
planogramming 31
point-of-sale (POS) 29
policy holders 190
policy-to-product 217
POS (see point-of-sale)
power plant 172
private sector 3
process improvement 171
product-in-contract 217
Prudential Chamberlain Stiehl Realtors (PCSR) 268
public good 2
public information 127
public sector 3
pull strategy 29
push strategy 29

Q

quality improvement 135
quality systems 171

R

redesign of business processes 135
registered independent advisors (RIAs) 228
registrar 114
relational database management system (RDBMS) 64
relational database system 119
Research Libraries Information Network (RLIN) 254
retail floor space management (RFSM) 31
retailers 36
risk groups 192
routers 273

S

sales associates 271

sales planning 31
scope creep 89
SDLC (see systems development life cycle)
security 143
shareholding structure 17
SONET (see synchronous optimal network) 88
South African Machine Readable Cataloguing (SAMARC) 8
SQL (see structured query language)
startup company 65
strategic alliance 3
strategic vision 108
structured query language (SQL) 143
supply chain management 135
synchronous optimal network (SONET)
system implementation 112
systems development life cycle (SDLC) 88

T

target organization 175
tariff structure 22
technology services 82
timeliness 214

U

ultraviolet light (UV) 78
universe of discourse (UoD) 207
University of Redlands 105
user interface tool 143

V

VALE Project 255
value oriented systems planning (VOSP) 138
VF Corporation 27
Virtual Academic Library Environment (VALE) 245

W

WAN (see wide area network)
Web course support 157
Web-based technologies 185
Whirlpool Corporation 136
wide area network (WAN) 273
work processes 186

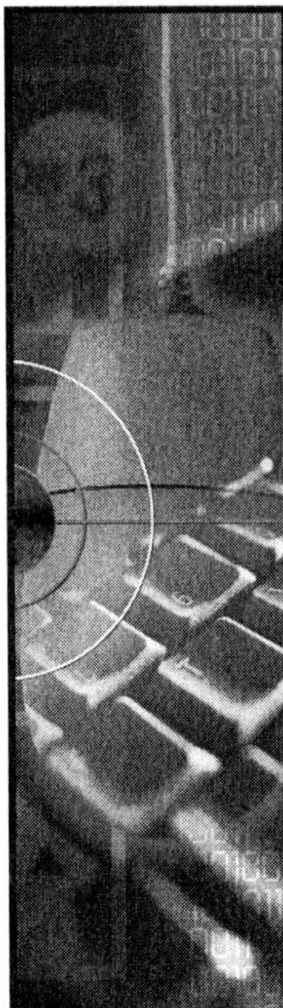